Access
Handbook

Achieving Optimal Database Application Performance and Scalability

The Data Access Handbook

Achieving Optimal Database
Application Performance and
Scalability

John Goodson and Robert A. Steward

PRENTICE
HALL

Upper Saddle River, NJ • Boston • Indianapolis • San Francisco
New York • Toronto • Montreal • London • Munich • Paris • Madrid
Cape Town • Sydney • Tokyo • Singapore • Mexico City

The publisher offers excellent discounts on this book when ordered in quantity for bulk purchases or special sales, which may include electronic versions and/or custom covers and content particular to your business, training goals, marketing focus, and branding interests. For more information, please contact:

U.S. Corporate and Government Sales
(800) 382-3419
corpsales@pearsontechgroup.com

For sales outside the United States, please contact:

International Sales
international@pearsoned.com

Library of Congress Cataloging-in-Publication Data
Goodson, John, 1964-
  The data access handbook : achieving optimal database application performance and scalability /
John Goodson and Robert A. Steward. — 1st ed.
    p. cm.
  ISBN 978-0-13-714393-1 (pbk. : alk. paper) 1. Database design—Handbooks, manuals, etc. 2.
Application software—Development—Handbooks, manuals, etc. 3. Computer networks—
Handbooks, manuals, etc. 4. Middleware—Handbooks, manuals, etc. I. Steward, Robert A.
(Robert Allan) II. Title.
  QA76.9.D26G665 2009
  005.3—dc22
                                    2008054864

Pearson Education, Inc.
Rights and Contracts Department
75 Arlington Street, Suite 300
Boston, MA 02116
Fax: (617) 848-7047

ISBN-13: 978-0-137-14393-1
ISBN-10: 0-137-14393-1
Text printed in the United States on recycled paper at RR Donnelley, Crawfordsville, Indiana.
First printing March 2009

Associate Publisher
Mark Taub

Acquisitions Editor
Bernard Goodwin

Managing Editor
Patrick Kanouse

Senior Project Editor
Tonya Simpson

Copy Editor
Karen A. Gill

Indexer
Ken Johnson

Proofreader
Sheri Cain

Technical Reviewers
Phil Gunning
Howard Fosdick
Mike Pizzo

Publishing Coordinator
Michelle Housley

Book Designer
Louisa Adair

Composition
Bronkella Publishing, LLC

Contents

CHAPTER 7   .NET APPLICATIONS: WRITING GOOD CODE   193

CHAPTER 11 DATA ACCESS IN SERVICE-ORIENTED ARCHITECTURE (SOA) ENVIRONMENTS 299

Preface

The world is flat. For thousands of years, all the mathematicians, explorers, and philosophers of the world knew this to be true. In the sixth century, several Greek philosophers presented evidence that the world was round. Yet, the experts shunned their ideas for hundreds of years more.

All database application performance and scalability problems can be solved by tuning the database. Ask the database experts—they'll tell you this. They'll even convince you to spend thousands to millions of dollars a year to tune the database software to solve performance issues. When tuning doesn't resolve the problem, they'll tell you that the database software or hardware, or both, is simply at capacity. But, if only 5% to 25% of the time it takes to process a database request is actually spent in well-tuned database software, does it make sense that performance bottlenecks occur because of these "at capacity" systems? If a business analyst waits 10 seconds for a query to process and only half a second of this time is spent in the database, does it make sense to spend time and money figuring out how to improve that half second? Or, does it make more sense to try to figure out how to improve the other 9.5 seconds? Hundreds of books, consultants, and Web sites are dedicated to solving database tuning problems, but relatively no information is available on how to design data-centric applications, tune data access application code, select and tune database drivers, and understand and tune the flow of data to and from database applications and, eventually, the database. We wrote this book to provide information that will help you focus on reducing those 9.5 seconds of time and show that all database application performance and scalability problems cannot be solved by simply tuning the database.

The journey of writing this book started in different ways for John and Rob but ended up in the same place.

John Goodson: Several years ago, I was at an IBM conference making a presentation on how to improve the performance of JDBC applications. After my presentation, an IT director approached me and said, "Where do I get more information on this? This type of information is impossible to find." I thought about it for a moment, and I told him there really was no one place you can obtain this type of information—it was stuck in the heads of a few people scattered throughout the world. This incident was followed by many others involving IT director after IT director telling me, "I never knew a database driver could make such a big difference" or, "I always thought that database application performance was a database problem." Every technical paper we wrote on the subject was in great demand, and every presentation we gave on the subject was to a full audience. We wrote this book because it was time to dispel the myths about performance and scalability being exclusively a database problem. The guidelines, tips, and techniques for improving performance that are presented in this book should be available to everyone.

Rob Steward: Writing a book is something I thought I would never do. I once asked an author friend of mine who writes software books whether it was really worth it to write one. He told me emphatically that there is only one reason that I should ever write a book about software. He said "Only write a book if there is something you strongly feel compelled to say." Having been in the database middleware business for 15 years now, I have seen a lot of badly written data access code, and consequently, a lot of applications that ran way too slowly and had to be fixed. I have literally spent years of my life helping people fix the problems they have created due to their lack of knowledge about what really happens on the client side when they make a call to the database. John and I have talked on the subject at many conferences and written a number of articles and white papers in an effort to help as many developers as possible understand the intricacies of data access code. When John approached me about coauthoring this book, I immediately agreed. I instantly felt compelled to share on a much broader scale that knowledge that we have been sharing in bits and pieces in various forums over the years. It's my hope that every reader will find something in this book that makes the difference between "too slow" and "blazing fast" in all their future applications.

The authors hope that this book will be used by software architects, IT staff, DBAs, and developers in their daily work to predict, diagnose, and solve performance issues in their database applications. Tuning the database is essential to good performance and scalability. We know that to be true. However, in an environment with a well-tuned database system, most performance problems are caused by the following:

- Poorly designed data access architecture
- Poorly optimized data access source code
- Inefficient or poorly tuned database drivers
- Lack of understanding about the environment in which database applications are deployed

This book addresses all these issues—the world is round.

This book contains the following chapters:

Chapter 1, "Performance Isn't What It Used to Be," describes the evolution of database middleware and identifies where performance bottlenecks can appear.

Chapter 2, "Designing for Performance: What's Your Strategy?," provides guidelines for designing your database application and tuning the database middleware that connects your application to the database server for optimal performance.

Chapter 3, "Database Middleware: Why It's Important," explains what database middleware is, what it does, and how it affects performance. It also describes what you should look for in a database driver, one of the most important components of database middleware.

Chapter 4, "The Environment: Tuning for Performance," describes the different environment layers that data requests and responses flow through, explains how they affect performance, and provides guidelines for making sure the environment does not become a performance bottleneck.

Chapter 5, "ODBC Applications: Writing Good Code," describes some good coding practices that can provide optimal performance for your ODBC applications.

Chapter 6, "JDBC Applications: Writing Good Code," describes some good coding practices that can provide optimal performance for your JDBC applications.

Chapter 7, ".NET Applications: Writing Good Code," describes some good coding practices that can provide optimal performance for .NET applications.

Chapter 8, "Connection Pooling and Statement Pooling," provides details about different connection pool models, describes how reauthentication works with connection pooling, and tells how using statement pooling with connection pooling might consume more memory on the database server than you realize.

Chapter 9, "Developing Good Benchmarks," provides some basic guidelines for writing benchmarks that many developers don't follow but absolutely should.

Chapter 10, "Troubleshooting Performance Issues," walks you through how to troubleshoot performance issues and provides case studies to help you think through some varied performance issues and figure out how to resolve them.

Chapter 11, "Data Access in Service-Oriented Architecture (SOA) Environments," provides some general guidelines to make sure that your database applications perform well in SOA environments.

The Glossary defines terms used in this book.

Acknowledgments

This book has been a two-year project based on the contributions, knowledge, and support of many people. John Goodson and Rob Steward have lived, breathed, and dreamed about database middleware since graduating from college. Cheryl Conrad and Susan King did a wonderful job of materializing our thoughts into words. Progress Software Corporation allowed us the opportunity to write this book.

Many people supplied extremely detailed information that we have used throughout the book and, for this, we are very grateful. In particular, special thanks go to Scott Bradley, John Hobson, Jeff Leinbach, Connie Childrey, Steve Veum, Mike Spinak, Matt Domencic, Jesse Davis, and Marc Van Cappellen for very time-consuming contributions. No book would be complete without extremely thorough reviewers and other contributors. These include Lance Anderson, Ed Long, Howard Fosdick, Allen Dooley, Terry Mason, Mark Biamonte, Mike Johnson, Charles Gold, Royce Willmschen, April Harned, John Thompson, Charlie Leagra, Sue Purkis, Katherine Spinak, Dipak Patel, John De Longa, Greg Stasko, Phil Prudich, Jayakhanna Pasimuthu, Brian Henning, Sven Cuypers, Filip Filliaert, Hans De Smet, Gregg Willhoit, Bill Fahey, Chris Walker, Betsy Kent, and Ed Crabtree.

We also would like to provide special thanks to our family members and friends who supported us through this adventure.

We would be grateful to readers who want to alert us to errors or comments by sending e-mail to Performance-book@datadirect.com.

About the Authors

John Goodson: As the executive leader of DataDirect Technologies, John is responsible for daily operations, business development, product direction, and long-term corporate strategy.

John was a principal engineer at Data General for seven years, working on their relational database product, DG/SQL. Since joining DataDirect Technologies in 1992, he has held positions of increasing responsibility in research and development, technical support, and marketing. John is a well-known and respected industry luminary and data connectivity expert. For more than 15 years, he has worked closely with Sun Microsystems and Microsoft on the development and evolution of database connectivity standards including J2EE, JDBC, .NET, ODBC, and ADO. John has been involved with the ANSI NCITS H2 Committee, which is responsible for building the SQL standard, and the X/Open (Open Group) SQL Access Group, which is responsible for building call-level interfaces into relational databases. He is actively involved in Java standards committees, including the JDBC Expert Group. In addition, John has published numerous articles and spoken publicly on topics related to data management. John is also a patent holder in the area of distributed transactions for Microsoft SQL Server Java middleware.

John holds a Bachelor of Science in computer science from Virginia Polytechnic Institute and State University in Blacksburg, Virginia.

Rob Steward: As vice president of research and development for DataDirect Technologies, Rob is responsible for the development, strategy, and oversight of the company's data connectivity products, including the Shadow mainframe integration suite client software and the industry-leading DataDirect Connect family of database drivers and data providers: Connect for ODBC, Connect for JDBC, and Connect for ADO.NET. Additional product development responsibilities include DataDirect Sequelink and DataDirect XQuery, as well as the management of DataDirect's Custom Engineering Development group.

Rob has spent more than 15 years developing database access middleware, including .NET data providers, ODBC drivers, JDBC drivers, and OLE DB data providers. He has held a number of management and technical positions at DataDirect Technologies and serves on various standards committees. Earlier in his career, he worked as lead software engineer at Marconi Commerce Systems Inc.

Rob holds a Bachelor of Science in computer science from North Carolina State University, Raleigh.

CHAPTER ONE

Performance Isn't What It Used to Be

Odds are very good that one or more of your company's database applications is suffering from performance issues. This should hardly come as a surprise to those who deal with application design, development, or deployment. What may be surprising is that the root cause of many of these issues is the database middleware, the software that connects applications to databases.

When we say performance issues, we mean your application is suffering from unacceptable response time, throughput, or scalability. **Response time** is the elapsed time between a data request and when the data is returned. From users' points of view, it is the time between when they ask for some data and when they receive it. **Throughput** is the amount of data that is transferred from sender to receiver over a period of time. **Scalability** is the ability of an application to maintain acceptable response time and throughput when the number of simultaneous users increases.

Before we get into why database middleware is so important to the optimal performance of your database applications, let's look at how the performance landscape has changed over the past decade.

Ten to 15 years ago, if you were having performance issues with your database application, 95% of the time the issues were caused by your database management software. At that time, tuning the database was considered magic to everyone except for a select group of engineers and database experts, who most likely worked for the database vendors. They kept details about their databases a secret; it was proprietary.

The performance landscape started to change when these experts began sharing their knowledge by writing books about database tuning and giving seminars for the public. Today, because of the volumes of database tuning information available through any bookstore or the Internet, years of experience, and vastly improved database monitoring tools, the task of tuning databases has become less painful.

Other changes were taking place during these years, such as hardware costs decreasing and computing power increasing. Along with faster and less expensive hardware came the move from monolithic to networked environments and client/server computing (two- and three-tier environments). Today, most database applications communicate with databases over a network instead of communicating directly through interprocess communication on a single computer, as shown in Figure 1-1.

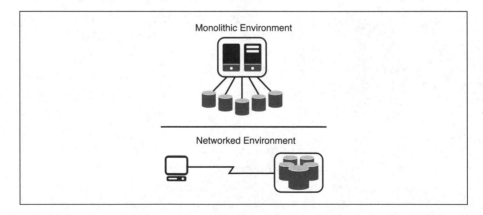

Figure 1-1   Database environment

With the shift to networked environments, software was needed to provide connectivity between the application and database that now were located on different computers. The database vendors were the first to provide this software as proprietary database middleware components for their databases, which added a new factor to the performance puzzle.

Database middleware consists of all components that handle the application's data request until that request is handed to the database management software, as shown in Figure 1-2.

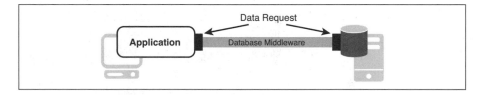

Figure 1-2   Database middleware

With the introduction of the networked environment, the database middleware layer included components such as these:

- The network
- Database client software such as Oracle Net8
- Libraries loaded into the application's address space when it connects to a database such as SSL libraries for data encryption across the network

Soon, the industry began to see a need for database connectivity standards, which would provide a common application programming interface (API) to access multiple databases. Without a common API, the industry was faced with multiple database connectivity solutions; each database vendor provided its own proprietary API. For example, to develop an application that could access Microsoft SQL Server, Oracle, and IBM DB2, a developer would have to know three very different database APIs: Microsoft Database Library (DBLIB), Oracle Call Interface (OCI), and IBM Client Application Enabler (CAE), as shown in Figure 1-3. The advent of database connectivity standards, such as ODBC, solved this problem.

With the introduction of database connectivity standards, *database drivers* were added to the database middleware layer. Among many other things, a database driver processes the standards-based API function calls, submits SQL requests to the database, and returns results to the application. Read Chapter 3, "Database Middleware: Why It's Important," for detailed information about what database drivers do and how your choice of drivers can affect the performance of your database applications.

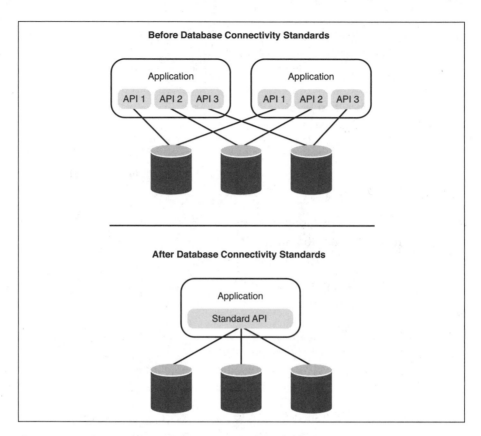

Figure 1-3   Emergence of database connectivity standards

Where Are We Today?

Today, even when the database is tuned well, we know that database applications don't always perform as well as we would like. Where does that leave us? Where do we find the performance issues today? For the majority of database applications, the performance issues are now found in the database middleware. For most applications, 75% to 95% of the time it takes to process a data request is spent in the database middleware compared to 10 to 15 years ago, when the majority of the time was spent in the database management software.

In most cases, performance issues seen in database applications are caused by the following:

- The network
- Database drivers

- The environment
- Poorly coded database applications

This book goes into detail about database middleware and database application performance issues. For now, let's look at a few examples.

The Network

One of the most common performance issues of the network is the number of round trips required to complete an operation. The size of network packets contributes to how many round trips are needed. Network packets carry an application's messages via the database middleware to the database and vice versa. The size of the packets makes a difference in the performance of your database application. The main concept to remember is that fewer packets sent between the application and the database equates to better performance; fewer packets mean fewer trips to and from the database.

Think of it this way: Jim's manager asks him to move five cases of diet soda from a second-floor office to the first-floor kitchen. If Jim's packet size is a 6-pack rather than a case, he has to make 20 trips to the kitchen instead of five, which means he is taking longer to move the soda to the kitchen.

We discuss more about networks, how they affect performance, and what you can do to optimize the performance of a network in Chapter 4, "The Environment: Tuning for Performance."

The Database Driver

All database drivers are not created equal. The choice of which driver to use in database application deployments can largely impact performance. The following real-world scenario explains how one company solved its performance issues by changing only the database driver.

DataBank serves the informational needs of both large and small companies through the retrieval, storage, and delivery of data. DataBank's reputation and financial security depend on response time and system availability. It has contracts with its customers that require specific response times and system availability. If these requirements are not met, DataBank must pay its customers a fine.

After a mandated upgrade to a new version of its database system and its accompanying middleware, DataBank began having serious performance issues. It was routinely paying more than $250,000 a month in fines due to missed contractual obligations.

The situation was unacceptable; the company had to find the performance issues in its database application deployment. DataBank started by making sure that its database was optimally tuned. Even with the database performing well, the company was still missing its contractual service-level requirements.

The system architect made a phone call to a database consultant, and the consultant asked, "Have you considered trying a different database driver?" The architect responded, "I didn't even know that was an option." The consultant recommended a database driver that he had used with success.

Losing no time, the architect had the recommended database driver installed in a test environment. Within two days, the QA department reported a threefold improvement in average response time between the new and the currently deployed database drivers, as well as the elimination of stability problems.

Based on the results of its performance testing, DataBank moved forward to purchase the new database driver. After the new database driver had been deployed for a couple of months, DataBank analyzed the revenue it was saving.

DataBank was paying $250,000 in fines in September and reduced that to $25,000 by November. That is a savings of 90% in two months by simply changing the database driver. The new driver handled connection pooling and memory management more effectively than the old driver.

DataBank solved several issues by deploying a new database driver: loss of revenue, dissatisfied customers, and overworked IT personnel, to name a few.

Chapter 3 details the many ways that database drivers can affect performance and what you can do about it.

The Environment

To learn how the environment can affect performance, see Figure 1-4 for an example of how different Java Virtual Machines (JVMs) can cause varied performance results for a JDBC-enabled database application. In this example, the same benchmark application was run three times using the same JDBC driver, database server, hardware, and operating system. The only variable was the JVM. The JVMs tested were from different vendors but were the same version and had comparable configurations. The benchmark measured the throughput and scalability of a database application.

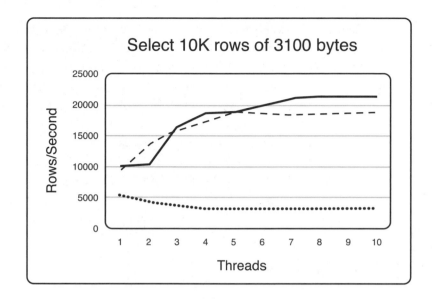

Figure 1-4   Comparing Different JVMs

As you can see in Figure 1-4, the throughput and scalability of the application using the JVM represented by the bottom line is dramatically less than the other two JVMs.

In Chapter 4, we discuss how your environment, both software and hardware (such as the operating system, memory, and CPU), can affect performance.

Your Database Application

Another important performance-related component is your database application. If your application is not coded efficiently, data requests that your application passes along to the database middleware can negatively affect performance. One common example is transaction management. With most standards-based applications, the default transaction mode requires the database driver to process expensive Commit operations after every API request. This default auto-commit mode can impose severe performance constraints on applications.

Consider the following real-world example. ASoft Corporation coded a standards-based database application and experienced poor performance in testing. Its performance analysis showed that the problem resided in the bulk five million Insert statements sent to the database. With auto-commit mode on, this

meant an additional five million `Commit` statements were being issued across the
network, and every inserted row was written to disk immediately following the
execution of the insert. When auto-commit mode was turned off in the application, the number of statements issued by the driver and executed on the database
server was reduced from ten million (five million `Inserts` + five million
`Commits`) to five million and one (five million `Inserts` + one `Commit`). As a consequence, application processing was reduced from eight hours to ten minutes.
Why such a dramatic difference in time? Significantly less disk input/output
(I/O) was required by the database server, and 50% fewer network round trips
were needed.

In general, your database application should be written to do the following:

- Reduce network traffic
- Limit disk I/O
- Optimize application-to-driver interaction
- Simplify queries

See the following chapters to learn about some general guidelines for good
coding practices that improve database application performance:

- For ODBC users, see Chapter 5, "ODBC Applications: Writing Good Code."
- For JDBC users, see Chapter 6, "JDBC Applications: Writing Good Code."
- For ADO.NET users, see Chapter 7, ".NET Applications: Writing Good
  Code."

Our Goal for This Book

The goal of this book is to equip you, as software architects and developers, with
techniques and knowledge to predict, diagnose, and solve performance issues in
your database applications. Specifically, this book provides information that will
help you achieve the following tasks:

- Understand the different components of database middleware that can cause
  performance issues.
- Design for optimal performance.
- Write good application code.
- Develop good benchmarks, tests that measure the performance of a database
  application on a well-defined task or set of tasks.
- Troubleshoot performance issues.
- Set realistic performance expectations.

CHAPTER TWO

Designing for Performance: What's Your Strategy?

Designing your database application and the configuration of the database middleware that connects your application to the database server for optimal performance isn't easy. We refer to all these components as your database application deployment. There is no one-size-fits-all design. You must think about every component to get the best performance possible.

Often you are not in control of every component that affects performance. For example, your company may dictate that all applications run on an application server. Also, your database administrator most likely controls the database server machine's configuration. In these cases, you need to consider the configurations that are dictated when designing your database application deployment. For example, if you know that the applications will reside on an application server, you probably want to spend ample time planning for connection and statement pooling, which are both discussed in this chapter.

Your Applications

Many software architects and developers don't think that the design of their database applications impacts the performance of those applications. This is not true; application design is a key factor. An application is often coded to establish a new connection to gather information about the database, such as supported data types or database version. Avoid establishing additional connections for this purpose because connections are performance-expensive, as we explain in this chapter.

This section explores several key functional areas of applications that you need to consider to achieve maximum performance:

- Database connections
- Transactions
- SQL statements
- Data retrieval

Some functional areas of applications, such as data encryption, affect performance, but you can do little about the performance impact. We discuss these areas and provide information about the performance impact you can expect.

When you make good application design decisions, you can improve performance by doing the following:

- Reducing network traffic
- Limiting disk I/O
- Optimizing application-to-driver interaction
- Simplifying queries

For API-specific code examples and discussions, you should also read the chapter for the standards-based API that you work with:

- For ODBC users, see Chapter 5, "ODBC Applications: Writing Good Code."
- For JDBC users, see Chapter 6, "JDBC Applications: Writing Good Code."
- For ADO.NET users, see Chapter 7, ".NET Applications: Writing Good Code."

Database Connections

The way you implement database connections may be the most important design decision you make for your application.

Your choices for implementing connections are as follows:

• Obtain a connection from a connection pool. Read the section, "Using Connection Pooling," page 12.
• Create a new connection one at a time as needed. Read the section, "Creating a New Connection One at a Time as Needed," page 16.

The right choice mainly depends on the CPU and memory conditions on the database server, as we explain throughout this section.

Facts About Connections

Before we discuss how to make this decision, here are some important facts about connections:

- Creating a connection is performance-expensive compared to all other tasks a database application can perform.
- Open connections use a substantial amount of memory on both the database server and database client machines.
- Establishing a connection takes multiple network round trips to and from the database server.
- Opening numerous connections can contribute to out-of-memory conditions, which might cause paging of memory to disk and, thus, overall performance degradation.
- In today's architectures, many applications are deployed in connection pooled environments, which are intended to improve performance. However, many times poorly tuned connection pooling can result in performance degradation. Connection pools can be difficult to design, tune, and monitor.

Why Connections Are Performance-Expensive

Developers often assume that establishing a connection is a simple request that results in the driver making a single network round trip to the database server to initialize a user. In reality, a connection typically involves many network round trips between the driver and the database server. For example, when a driver connects to Oracle or Sybase, that connection may take anywhere from seven to ten network round trips to perform the following actions:

- Validate the user's credentials.
- Negotiate code page settings between what the database driver expects and what the database has available, if necessary.

- Get database version information.
- Establish the optimal database protocol packet size to be used for communication.
- Set session settings.

In addition, the database management system establishes resources on behalf of the connection, which involves performance-expensive disk I/O and memory allocation.

You might be thinking that you can eliminate network round trips if you place your applications on the same machine as the database system. This is, in most cases, not realistic because of the complexity of real-world enterprises—many, many applications accessing many database systems with applications running on several application servers. In addition, the server on which the database system runs must be well tuned for the database system, not for many different applications. Even if one machine would fit the bill, would you really want a single point of failure?

Using Connection Pooling

A **connection pool** is a cache of physical database connections that one or more applications can reuse. Connection pooling can provide significant performance gains because reusing a connection reduces the overhead associated with establishing a physical connection. The caveat here is that your database server must have enough memory to manage all the connections in the pool.

In this book, we discuss client-side connection pooling (connection pooling provided by database drivers and application servers), not database-side connection pooling (connection pooling provided by database management systems). Some database management systems provide connection pooling, and those implementations work in conjunction with client-side connection pooling. Although specific characteristics of database-side connection pooling vary, the overall goal is to eliminate the overhead on the database server of establishing and removing connections. Unlike client-side connection pooling, database-side connection pooling does not optimize network round trips to the application. As we stated previously, connecting to a database is performance-expensive because of the resource allocation in the database driver (network round trips between the driver and the database), and the resource allocation on the database server. Client-side connection pooling helps solve the issue of expensive resource allocation for both the database driver and database server. Database-side connection pooling only helps solve the issue on the database server.

How Connection Pooling Works

In a pooled environment, once the initial physical connection is established, it will likely not be closed for the life of the environment. That is, when an application disconnects, the physical connection is not closed; instead, it is placed in the pool for reuse. Therefore, re-establishing the connection becomes one of the fastest operations instead of one of the slowest.

Here is a basic overview of how connection pooling works (as shown in Figure 2-1):

1. When the application or application server is started, the connection pool is typically populated with connections.
2. An application makes a connection request.
3. Either the driver or the Connection Pool Manager (depending on your architecture) assigns one of the pooled connections to the application instead of requesting that a new connection be established. This means that no network round trips occur between the driver and the database server for connection requests because a connection is available in the pool. The result: Your connection request is *fast*.
4. The application is connected to the database.
5. When the connection is closed, it is placed back into the pool.

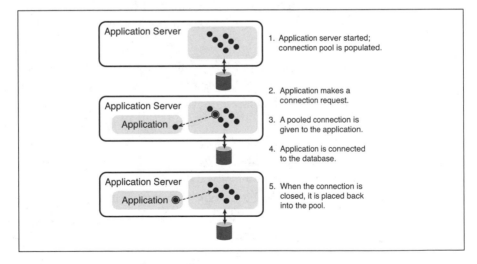

Figure 2-1   Connection pooling

Guidelines for Connection Pooling

Here are some general guidelines for using connection pooling. For details about different connection pooling models, see Chapter 8, "Connection Pooling and Statement Pooling."

- A perfect scenario for using connection pooling is when your applications reside on an application server, which implies multiple users using the applications.

- Consider using connection pooling if your application has multiple users and your database server has enough memory to manage the maximum number of connections that will be in the pool at any given time. In most connection pooling models, it is easy to calculate the maximum number of connections that will be in a pool because the connection pool implementation allows you to configure the maximum. If the implementation you are using does not support configuring the maximum number of connections in a pool, you must calculate how many connections will be in the pool during peak times to determine if your database server can handle the load.

- Determine whether the number of database licenses you have accommodates a connection pool. If you have limited licenses, answer the following questions to determine if you have enough licenses to support a connection pool:

  a. Will other applications use database licenses? If yes, take this into account when calculating how many licenses you need for your connection pool.

  b. Are you using a database that uses a streaming protocol, such as Sybase, Microsoft SQL Server, or MySQL? If yes, you may be using more database connections than you think. In streaming protocol databases, only one request can be processed at a time over a single connection; the other requests on the same connection must wait for the preceding request to complete before a subsequent request can be processed. Therefore, some database driver implementations duplicate connections (establish another connection) when multiple requests are sent over a single connection so that all requests can be processed in a timely manner.

- When you develop your application to use connection pooling, open connections just before the application needs them. Opening them earlier than necessary decreases the number of connections available to other users and can increase the demand for resources. Don't forget to close them when the database work is complete so that the connection can return to the pool for reuse.

When Not to Use Connection Pooling

Some applications are not good candidates for using connection pooling. If your applications have any of the following characteristics, you probably don't want to use connection pooling. In fact, for these types of applications, connection pooling may degrade performance.

- **Applications that restart numerous times daily**—This typically applies only to architectures that are not using an application server. Depending on the configuration of the connection pool, it may be populated with connections each time the application is started, which causes a performance penalty up front.
- **Single-user applications, such as report writers**—If your application only needs to establish a connection for a single user who runs reports two to three times daily, the memory usage on the database server associated with a connection pool degrades performance more than establishing the connection two or three times daily.
- **Applications that run single-user batch jobs, such as end-of-day/week/month reporting**—Connection pooling provides no advantage for batch jobs that access only one database server, which typically equates to only one connection. Furthermore, batch jobs are usually run during off hours when performance is not as much of a concern.

Performance Tip

When your application does not use connection pooling, avoid connecting and disconnecting multiple times throughout your application to execute SQL statements, because each connection might use five to ten times as many network requests as the SQL statement.

Creating a New Connection One at a Time as Needed

When you create a new connection one at a time as needed, you can design your application to create either of the following:

- One connection for each statement to be executed
- One connection for multiple statements, which is often referred to as using multiple threads

Figure 2-2 compares these two connection models.

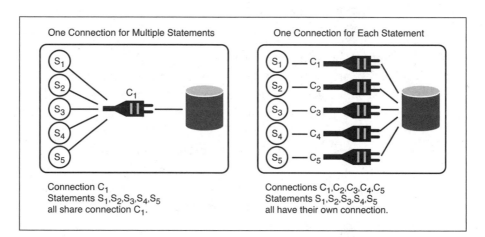

Figure 2-2   Comparing two connection models

The advantage of using one connection for each statement is that each statement can access the database at the same time. The disadvantage is the overhead of establishing multiple connections.

The advantages and disadvantages of using one connection for multiple statements are explained later in this section.

One Connection for Multiple Statements

Before we can explain the details of one connection for multiple statements, we need to define **statement**. Some people equate "statement" to "SQL statement." We like the definition of "statement" that is found in the *Microsoft ODBC 3.0 Programmer's Reference*:

A statement is most easily thought of as an SQL statement, such as SELECT * FROM Employee. *However, a statement is more than just an SQL statement— it consists of all of the information associated with that SQL statement, such as any result sets created by the statement and parameters used in the execution of the statement. A statement does not even need to have an application-defined SQL statement. For example, when a catalog function such as* SQLTables *is executed on a statement, it executes a predefined SQL statement that returns a list of table names.*[1]

To summarize, a statement is not only the request sent to the database but the result of the request.

How One Connection for Multiple Statements Works

Note

Because of the architecture of the ADO.NET API, this connection model typically does not apply.

When you develop your application to use one connection for multiple statements, an application may have to wait for a connection. To understand why, you must understand how one connection for multiple statements works; this depends on the protocol of the database system you are using: streaming or cursor based. Sybase, Microsoft SQL Server, and MySQL are examples of streaming protocol databases. Oracle and DB2 are examples of cursor-based protocol databases.

Streaming protocol database systems process the query and send results until there are no more results to send; the database is uninterruptable. Therefore, the network connection is "busy" until all results are returned (fetched) to the application.

Cursor-based protocol database systems assign a database server-side "name" (cursor) to a SQL statement. The server operates on that cursor in incremental time segments. The driver tells the database server when to work and how much information to return. Several cursors can use the network connection, each working in small slices of time.

---

[1] *Microsoft ODBC 3.0 Programmer's Reference and SDK Guide,* Volume I. Redmond: Microsoft Press, 1997

Example A: Streaming Protocol Result Sets

Let's look at the case where your SQL statement creates result sets and your application is accessing a streaming protocol database. In this case, the connection is unavailable to process another SQL statement until the first statement is executed and all results are returned to the application. The time this takes depends on the size of the result set. Figure 2-3 shows an example.

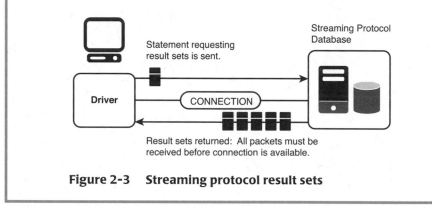

Figure 2-3   Streaming protocol result sets

Example B: Streaming Protocol Updates

Let's look at the case where the SQL statement updates the database and your application is accessing a streaming protocol database, as shown in Figure 2-4. The connection is available as soon as the statement is executed and the row count is returned to the application.

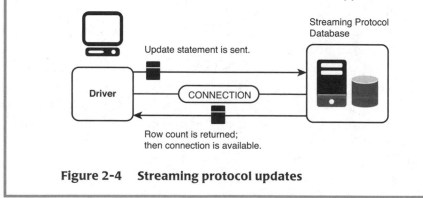

Figure 2-4   Streaming protocol updates

Example C: Cursor-Based Protocol/Result Sets

Last, let's look at the case where your SQL statement creates result sets and your application is accessing a cursor-based protocol database. Unlike Example A, which is a streaming protocol example, the connection is available before all the results are returned to the application. When using cursor-based protocol databases, the result sets are returned as the driver asks for them. Figure 2-5 shows an example.

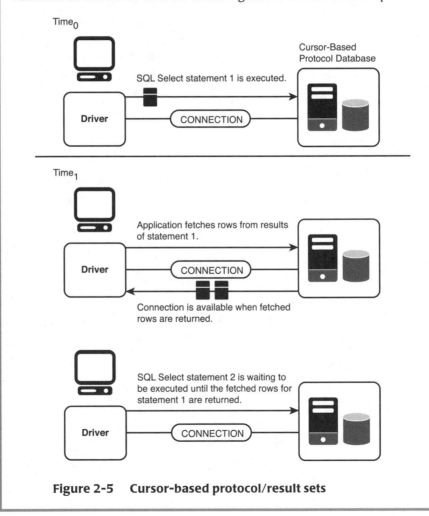

Figure 2-5   Cursor-based protocol/result sets

Advantages and Disadvantages

The advantage of using one connection for multiple statements is that it reduces the overhead of establishing multiple connections, while allowing multiple statements to access the database. The overhead is reduced on both the database server and client machines.

The disadvantage of using this method of connection management is that the application may have to wait to execute a statement until the single connection is available. We explained why in "How One Connection for Multiple Statements Works," page 17.

Guidelines for One Connection for Multiple Statements

Here are some guidelines for when to use one connection for multiple statements:

- Consider using this connection model when your database server has hardware constraints such as limited memory and one or more of the following conditions are true:
  a. You are using a cursor-based protocol database.
  b. The statements in your application return small result sets or no result sets.
  c. Waiting for a connection is acceptable. The amount of time that is acceptable for the connection to be unavailable depends on the requirements of your application. For example, 5 seconds may be acceptable for an internal application that logs an employee's time but may not be acceptable for an online transaction processing (OLTP) application such as an ATM application. What is an acceptable response time for your application?
- This connection model should not be used when your application uses transactions.

Case Study: Designing Connections

Let's look at one case study to help you understand how to design database connections. The environment details are as follows:

- The environment includes a middle tier that must support 20 to 100 concurrent database users, and performance is key.

- CPU and memory are plentiful on both the middle tier and database server.
- The database is Oracle, Microsoft SQL Server, Sybase, or DB2.
- The API that the application uses is ODBC, JDBC, or ADO.NET.
- There are 25 licenses for connections to the database server.

Here are some possible solutions:

- Solution 1: Use a connection pool with a maximum of 20 connections, each with a single statement.
- Solution 2: Use a connection pool with a maximum of 5 connections, each with 5 statements.
- Solution 3: Use a single connection with 5 to 25 statements.

The key information in this case study is the ample CPU and memory on both the middle tier and database server and the ample number of licenses to the database server. The other information is really irrelevant to the design of the database connections.

Solution 1 is the best solution because it performs better than the other two solutions. Why? Processing one statement per connection provides faster results for users because all the statements can access the database at the same time.

The architecture for Solutions 2 and 3 is one connection for multiple statements. In these solutions, the single connection can become a bottleneck, which means slower results for users. Therefore, these solutions do not meet the requirement of "performance is key."

Transaction Management

A **transaction** is one or more SQL statements that make up a unit of work performed against the database, and either all the statements in a transaction are committed as a unit or all the statements are rolled back as a unit. This unit of work typically satisfies a user request and ensures data integrity. For example, when you use a computer to transfer money from one bank account to another, the request involves a transaction: updating values stored in the database for both accounts. For a transaction to be completed and database changes to be made permanent, a transaction must be completed in its entirety.

What is the correct transaction commit mode to use in your application? What is the right transaction model for your database application: local or distributed? Use the guidelines in this section to help you manage transactions more efficiently.

You should also read the chapter for the standards-based API that you work with; these chapters provide specific examples for each API:

- For ODBC users, see Chapter 5.
- For JDBC users, see Chapter 6.
- For ADO.NET users, see Chapter 7.

Managing Commits in Transactions

Committing (and rolling back) transactions is slow because of the disk I/O and potentially the number of network round trips required. What does a commit actually involve? The database must write to disk every modification made by a transaction to the database. This is usually a sequential write to a journal file (or log); nevertheless, it involves expensive disk I/O.

In most standards-based APIs, the default transaction commit mode is auto-commit. In auto-commit mode, a commit is performed for every SQL statement that requires a request to the database, such as Insert, Update, Delete, and Select statements. When auto-commit mode is used, the application does not control when database work is committed. In fact, commits commonly occur when there's actually no real work to commit.

Some database systems, such as DB2, do not support auto-commit mode. For these databases, the database driver, by default, sends a commit request to the database after every successful operation (SQL statement). This request equates to a network round trip between the driver and the database. The round trip to the database occurs even though the application did not request the commit and even if the operation made no changes to the database. For example, the driver makes a network round trip even when a Select statement is executed.

Because of the significant amount of disk I/O required to commit every operation on the database server and because of the extra network round trips that occur between the driver and the database, in most cases you will want to turn off auto-commit mode in your application. By doing this, your application can control when the database work is committed, which provides dramatically better performance.

Consider the following real-world example. ASoft Corporation coded a standards-based database application and experienced poor performance in testing. Its performance analysis showed that the problem resided in the bulk five million Insert statements sent to the database. With auto-commit mode on, this meant an additional five million Commit statements were being issued across the network and that every inserted row was written to disk immediately following the execution of the `Insert`. When auto-commit mode was turned off in the application, the number of statements issued by the driver and executed on the database server was reduced from ten million (five million `Inserts` + five million `Commits`) to five million and one (five million `Inserts` + one `Commit`). As a consequence, application processing was reduced from eight hours to ten minutes. Why such a dramatic difference in time? There was significantly less disk I/O required by the database server, and there were 50% fewer network round trips.

Performance Tip

Although turning off auto-commit mode can help application performance, do not take this tip too far. Leaving transactions active can reduce throughput by holding locks on rows for longer than necessary, preventing other users from accessing the rows. Typically, committing transactions in intervals provides the best performance as well as acceptable concurrency.

If you have turned off auto-commit mode and are using manual commits, when does it make sense to commit work? It depends on the following factors:

- The type of transactions your application performs. For example, does your application perform transactions that modify or read data? If your application modifies data, does it update large amounts of data?
- How often your application performs transactions.

For most applications, it's best to commit a transaction after every logical unit of work. For example, consider a banking application that allows users to transfer money from one account to another. To protect the data integrity of that work, it makes sense to commit the transaction after both accounts are updated with the new amounts.

However, what if an application allows users to generate reports of account balances for each day over a period of months? The unit of work is a series of `Select` statements, one executed after the other to return a column of balances. In most cases, for every `Select` statement executed against the database, a lock is placed on rows to prevent another user from updating that data. By holding locks on rows for longer than necessary, active transactions can prevent other users from updating data, which ultimately can reduce throughput and cause concurrency issues. In this case, you may want to commit the `Select` statements in intervals (after every five `Select` statements, for example) so that locks are released in a timely manner.

In addition, be aware that leaving transactions active consumes database memory. Remember that the database must write every modification made by a transaction to a log that is stored in database memory. Committing a transaction flushes the contents of the log and releases database memory. If your application uses transactions that update large amounts of data (1,000 rows, for example) without committing modifications, the application can consume a substantial amount of database memory. In this case, you may want to commit after every statement that updates a large amount of data.

How often your application performs transactions also determines when you should commit them. For example, if your application performs only three transactions over the course of a day, commit after every transaction. In contrast, if your application constantly performs transactions that are composed of `Select` statements, you may want to commit after every five `Select` statements.

Isolation Levels

We will not go into the details of isolation levels in this book, but architects should know the default transaction isolation level of the database system they are using. A **transaction isolation level** represents a particular locking strategy used in the database system to improve data integrity.

Most database systems support several isolation levels, and the standards-based APIs provide ways for you to set isolation levels. However, if the database driver you are using does not support the isolation level you set in your application, the setting has no effect. Make sure you choose a driver that gives you the level of data integrity that you need.

Local Transactions Versus Distributed Transactions

A **local transaction** is a transaction that accesses and updates data on only one database. Local transactions are significantly faster than distributed transactions because local transactions do not require communication between multiple databases, which means less logging and fewer network round trips are required to perform local transactions.

Use local transactions when your application does *not* have to access or update data on multiple networked databases.

A **distributed transaction** is a transaction that accesses and updates data on multiple networked databases or systems and must be coordinated among those databases or systems. These databases may be of several types located on a single server, such as Oracle, Microsoft SQL Server, and Sybase; or they may include several instances of a single type of database residing on numerous servers.

The main reason to use distributed transactions is when you need to make sure that databases stay consistent with one another. For example, suppose a catalog company has a central database that stores inventory for all its distribution centers. In addition, the company has a database for its east coast distribution center and one for the west coast. When a catalog order is placed, an application updates the central database and updates either the east or west coast database. The application performs both operations in one distributed transaction to ensure that the information in the central database remains consistent with the information in the appropriate distribution center's database. If the network connection fails before the application updates both databases, the entire transaction is rolled back; neither database is updated.

Distributed transactions are substantially slower than local transactions because of the logging and network round trips needed to communicate between all the components involved in the distributed transaction.

For example, Figure 2-6 shows what happens during a local transaction.

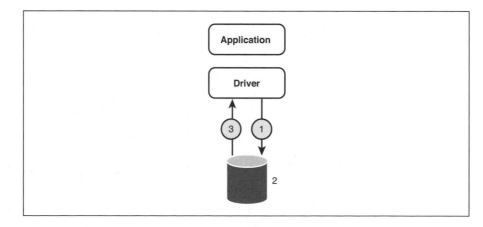

Figure 2-6   Local transaction

The following occurs when the application requests a transaction:

1. The driver issues a commit request.
2. If the database can commit the transaction, it does, and writes an entry to its log. If it cannot, it rolls back the transaction.
3. The database replies with a status to the driver indicating if the commit succeeded or failed.

Figure 2-7 shows what happens during a distributed transaction, in which all databases involved in the transaction must either commit or roll back the transaction.

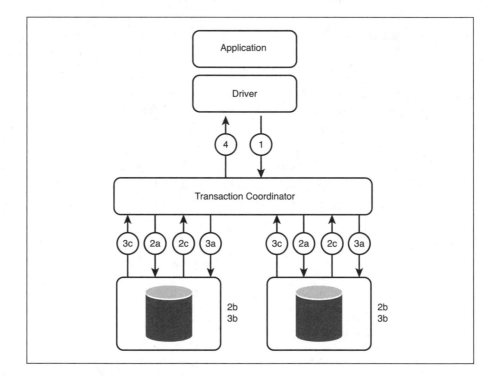

Figure 2-7   Distributed transaction

The following occurs when the application requests a transaction:

1. The driver issues a commit request.
2. The transaction coordinator sends a precommit request to all databases involved in the transaction.

    a. The transaction coordinator sends a commit request command to all databases.

    b. Each database executes the transaction up to the point where the database is asked to commit, and each writes recovery information to its logs.

    c. Each database replies with a status message to the transaction coordinator indicating whether the transaction up to this point succeeded or failed.

3. The transaction coordinator waits until it has received a status message from each database. If the transaction coordinator received a status message from all databases indicating success, the following occurs:

    a. The transaction coordinator sends a commit message to all the databases.

    b. Each database completes the commit operation and releases all the locks and resources held during the transaction.

    c. Each database replies with a status to the transaction coordinator indicating whether the operation succeeded or failed.

4. The transaction coordinator completes the transaction when all acknowledgments have been received and replies with a status to the driver indicating if the commit succeeded or failed.

Note for Java Users

The default transaction behavior of many Java application servers uses distributed transactions, so changing that default transaction behavior to local transactions, if distributed transactions are not required, can improve performance.

SQL Statements

Will your application have a defined set of SQL statements that are executed multiple times? If your answer is yes, you will most likely want to use prepared statements and statement pooling if your environment supports it.

Using Statements Versus Prepared Statements

A **prepared statement** is a SQL statement that has been compiled, or prepared, into an access or query plan for efficiency. A prepared statement is available for reuse by the application without the overhead in the database of re-creating the query plan. A prepared statement is associated with one connection and is available until it is explicitly closed or the owning connection is closed.

Most applications have a set of SQL statements that are executed multiple times and a few SQL statements that are executed only once or twice during the life of an application. Although the overhead for the initial execution of a prepared statement is high, the advantage is realized with subsequent executions of the SQL statement. To understand why, let's examine how a database processes a SQL statement.

The following occurs when a database receives a SQL statement:

1. The database parses the statement and looks for syntax errors.
2. The database validates the user to make sure the user has privileges to execute the statement.
3. The database validates the semantics of the statement.
4. The database figures out the most efficient way to execute the statement and prepares a query plan. Once the query plan is created, the database can execute the statement.

When a prepared query is sent to the database, the database saves the query plan until the driver closes it. This allows the query to be executed time and time again without repeating the steps described previously. For example, if you send the following SQL statement to the database as a prepared statement, the database saves the query plan:

```
SELECT * FROM Employees WHERE SSID = ?
```

Note that this SQL statement uses a parameter marker, which allows the value in the WHERE clause to change for each execution of the statement. Do not use a literal in a prepared statement unless the statement will be executed with the same value(s) every time. This scenario would be rare.

Using a prepared statement typically results in at least two network round trips to the database server:

- One network round trip to parse and optimize the query
- One or more network round trips to execute the query and retrieve the results

---

Performance Tip

If your application makes a request only once during its life span, it is better to use a statement than a prepared statement because it results in only a single network round trip. Remember, reducing network communication typically provides the most performance gain. For example, if you have an application that runs an end-of-day sales report, the query that generates the data for that report should be sent to the database server as a statement, not as a prepared statement.

Note that not all database systems support prepared statements; Oracle, DB2, and MySQL do, and Sybase and Microsoft SQL Server do not. If your application sends prepared statements to either Sybase or Microsoft SQL Server, these database systems create stored procedures. Therefore, the performance of using prepared statements with these two database systems is slower.

Some database systems, such as Oracle and DB2, let you perform a prepare and execute together. This functionality provides two benefits. First, it eliminates a round trip to the database server. Second, when designing your application, you don't need to know whether you plan to execute the statement again, which allows you to optimize the next execution of the statement automatically.

Read the next section about statement pooling to see how prepared statements and statement pooling go hand in hand.

Statement Pooling

If you have an application that repeatedly executes the same SQL statements, statement pooling can improve performance because it prevents the overhead of repeatedly parsing and creating cursors (server-side resource to manage the SQL request) for the same statement, along with the associated network round trips.

A **statement pool** is a group of prepared statements that an application can reuse. Statement pooling is not a feature of a database system; it is a feature of database drivers and application servers. A statement pool is owned by a physical connection, and prepared statements are placed in the pool after their initial execution. For details about statement pooling, see Chapter 8, "Connection Pooling and Statement Pooling."

How does using statement pooling affect whether you use a statement or a prepared statement?

- If you are using statement pooling and a SQL statement will only be executed once, use a statement, which is not placed in the statement pool. This avoids the overhead associated with finding that statement in the pool.
- If a SQL statement will be executed infrequently but may be executed multiple times during the life of a statement pool, use a prepared statement. Under similar circumstances without statement pooling, use a statement. For example, if you have some statements that are executed every 30 minutes or so (infrequently), the statement pool is configured for a maximum of 200 statements, and the pool never gets full, use a prepared statement.

Data Retrieval

To retrieve data efficiently, do the following:

- Return only the data you need. Read "Retrieving Long Data," page 31.
- Choose the most efficient way to return the data. Read "Limiting the Amount of Data Returned," page 34, and "Choosing the Right Data Type," page 34.
- Avoid scrolling through the data. Read "Using Scrollable Cursors," page 36.
- Tune your database middleware to reduce the amount of information that is communicated between the database driver and the database. Read "The Network," page 44.

For specific API code examples, read the chapter for the standards-based API that you work with:

- For ODBC users, see Chapter 5.
- For JDBC users, see Chapter 6.
- For ADO.NET users, see Chapter 7.

Understanding When the Driver Retrieves Data

You might think that if your application executes a query and then fetches one row of the results, the database driver only retrieves that one row. However, in most cases, that is not true; the driver retrieves many rows of data (a block of data) but returns only one row to the application. This is why the first fetch your application performs may take longer than subsequent fetches. Subsequent fetches are faster because they do not require network round trips; the rows of data are already in memory on the client.

Some database drivers allow you to configure connection options that specify how much data to retrieve at a time. Retrieving more data at one time increases throughput by reducing the number of times the driver fetches data across the network when retrieving multiple rows. Retrieving less data at one time increases response time, because there is less of a delay waiting for the server to transmit data. For example, if your application normally fetches 200 rows, it is more efficient for the driver to fetch 200 rows at one time over the network than to fetch 50 rows at a time during four round trips over the network.

Retrieving Long Data

Retrieving long data—such as large XML data, long varchar/text, long varbinary, Clobs, and Blobs—across a network is slow and resource intensive. Do your application users really need to have the long data available to them? If yes, carefully think about the most optimal design. For example, consider the user interface of an employee directory application that allows the user to look up an employee's phone extension and department, and optionally, view an employee's photograph by clicking the name of the employee.

Employee	Phone	Dept
Harding	X4568	Manager
Hoover	X4324	Sales
Lincoln	X4329	Tech
Taft	X4569	Sales

Returning each employee's photograph would slow performance unnecessarily just to look up the phone extension. If users do want to see the photograph, they can click on the employee's name and the application can query the database again, specifying only the long columns in the Select list. This method allows users to return result sets without having to pay a high performance penalty for network traffic.

Having said this, many applications are designed to send a query such as SELECT * FROM employees and then request only the three columns they want to see. In this case, the driver must still retrieve all the data across the network, including the employee photographs, even though the application never requests the photograph data.

Some database systems have optimized the expensive interaction between the database middleware and the database server when retrieving long data by providing an optimized database data type called LOBs (CLOB, BLOB, and so on). If your database system supports these data types and long data is created using those types, then the processing of queries such as SELECT * FROM employees is less expensive. Here's why. When a result row is retrieved, the driver retrieves only a placeholder for the long data (LOB) value. That placeholder is usually the size of an integer—very small. The actual long data (picture, document, scanned image, and so on) is retrieved only when the application specifically retrieves the value of the result column.

For example, if an employees table was created with the columns FirstName, LastName, EmpId, Picture, OfficeLocation, and PhoneNumber, and the Picture column is a long varbinary type, the following interaction would occur between the application, the driver, and the database server:

1. **Execute a statement**—The application sends a SQL statement (for example, SELECT * FROM table WHERE ...) to the database server via the driver.

2. **Fetch rows**—The driver retrieves all the values of all the result columns from the database server because the driver doesn't know which values the application will request. All values must be available when needed, which means that the entire image of the employee must be retrieved from the database server regardless of whether the application eventually processes it.

3. **Retrieve result values into the application**—When the application requests data, it is moved from the driver into the application buffers on a column-by-column basis. Even if result columns were prebound by the application, the application can still request result columns ad hoc.

Now suppose the employees table is created with the same columns except that the Picture field is a BLOB type. Now the following interaction would occur between the application, the driver, and the database server:

1. **Execute a statement**—The application sends a SQL statement (for example, SELECT * FROM table WHERE ...) to the database server via the driver.

2. **Fetch rows**—The driver retrieves all the values of all the result columns from the database server, as it did in the previous example. However, in this case, the entire employee image is not retrieved from the database server; instead, a placeholder integer value is retrieved.

3. **Retrieve result values into the application**—When the application requests data, it is moved from the driver into the application buffers on a column-by-column basis. If the application requests the contents of the Picture column, the driver initiates a request to the database server to retrieve the image of the employee that is identified by the placeholder value it retrieved. In this scenario, the performance hit associated with retrieving the image is deferred until the application actually requests that data.

In general, LOB data types are useful and preferred because they allow efficient use of long data on an as-needed basis. When the intent is to process large amounts of long data, using LOBs results in extra round trips between the driver and the database server. For example, in the previous example, the driver had to initiate an extra request to retrieve the LOB value when it was requested. These extra round trips usually are somewhat insignificant in the overall performance of the application because the number of overall round trips needed between the driver and the database server to return the entire contents of the long data is the expensive part of the execution.

Although you might prefer to use LOB types, doing so is not always possible because much of the data used in an enterprise today was not created yesterday. The majority of data you process was created long before LOB types existed, so the schema of the tables you use may not include LOB types even if they are supported by the version of the database system you are using. The coding techniques presented in this section are preferred regardless of the data types defined in the schema of your tables.

Performance Tip

Design your application to exclude long data from the Select list.

Limiting the Amount of Data Returned

One of the easiest ways to improve performance is to limit the amount of net-work traffic between the database driver and the database server—one way is to write SQL queries that instruct the driver to retrieve from the database and return to the application only the data that the application requires. However, some applications need to use SQL queries that generate a lot of traffic. For example, consider an application that needs to display information from support case histories, which each contain a 10MB log file. But, does the user really need to see the entire contents of the file? If not, performance would improve if the application displayed only the first 1MB of the log file.

Performance Tip

When you cannot avoid returning data that generates a lot of network traffic, control the amount of data being sent from the database to the driver by doing the following:

- Limiting the number of rows sent across the network
- Reducing the size of each row sent across the network

You can do this by using the methods or functions of the API you work with. For example, in JDBC, use setMaxRows() to limit the number of rows a query returns. In ODBC, call SQLSetStmtAttr() with the SQL_ATTR_MAX_LENGTH option to limit the number of bytes of data returned for a column value.

Choosing the Right Data Type

Advances in processor technology have brought significant improvements to the way that operations, such as floating-point math, are handled. However, when the active portion of your application does not fit into on-chip cache, retrieving and returning certain data types is expensive. When you are working with data on a large scale, select the data type that can be processed most efficiently. Retrieving and returning certain data types across the network can increase or decrease network traffic. Table 2-1 lists the fastest to the slowest data types to process and explains why.

Table 2-1   Fastest to Slowest Processing of Data Types

Data Type	Processing
binary	Transfer of raw bytes from database to application buffers.
int, smallint, float	Transfer of fixed formats from database to application buffers.
decimal	Transfer of proprietary data from database to database driver. Driver must decode, which uses CPU, and then typically has to convert to a string. (Note: All Oracle numeric types are actually decimals.)
timestamp	Transfer of proprietary data from database to database driver. Driver must decode, which uses CPU, and then typically has to convert to a multipart structure or to a string. The difference between timestamp processing and decimal is that this conversion requires conversion into multiple parts (year, month, day, second, and so on).
char	Typically, transfer of larger amounts of data that must be converted from one code page to another, which is CPU intensive, not because of the difficulty, but because of the amount of data that must be converted.

Figure 2-8 shows a comparison of how many rows per second are returned when a column is defined as a 64-bit integer data type versus a decimal(20) data type. The same values are returned in each case. As you can see in this figure, many more rows per second are returned when the data is returned as an integer.

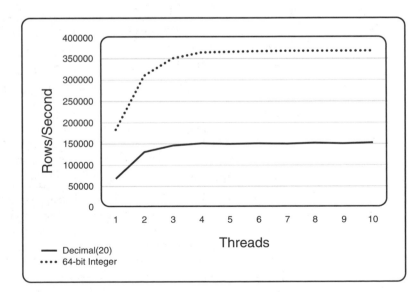

Figure 2-8   Comparison of different data types

> **Performance Tip**
>
> For multiuser, multivolume applications, it's possible that billions, or even trillions, of network packets move between the driver and the database server over the course of a day. Choosing data types that are processed efficiently can incrementally boost performance.

Using Scrollable Cursors

Scrollable cursors allow an application to go both forward and backward through a result set. However, because of limited support for server-side scrollable cursors in many database systems, drivers often emulate scrollable cursors, storing rows from a scrollable result set in a cache on the machine where the driver resides (client or application server). Table 2-2 lists five major database systems and explains their support of server-side scrollable cursors.

Table 2-2   Database Systems Support of Server-Side Scrollable Cursors

Database System	Explanation
Oracle	No native support of database server-side scrollable cursors. Drivers expose scrollable cursors to applications by emulating the functionality on the client.
MySQL	No native support of database server-side scrollable cursors. Drivers expose scrollable cursors to applications by emulating the functionality on the client.
Microsoft SQL Server	Server-side scrollable cursors are supported through stored procedures. Most drivers expose server-side cursors to applications.
DB2	Native support of some server-side scrollable cursor models. Some drivers support server-side scrollable cursors for the most recent DB2 versions. However, most drivers expose scrollable cursors to applications by emulating the functionality on the client.
Sybase ASE	Native support for server-side scrollable cursors was introduced in Sybase ASE 15. Versions prior to 15 do not natively support server-side scrollable cursors. Drivers expose scrollable cursors to applications by emulating the functionality on the client.

One application design flaw that we have seen many times is that an application uses a scrollable cursor to determine how many rows a result set contains even if server-side scrollable cursors are not supported in the database system. Here is an ODBC example; the same concept holds true for JDBC. Unless you are certain that the database natively supports using a scrollable result set, do not call SQLExtendedFetch() to find out how many rows the result set contains. For drivers that emulate scrollable cursors, calling SQLExtendedFetch() results in the driver returning all results across the network to reach the last row.

This emulated model of scrollable cursors provides flexibility for the developer but comes with a performance penalty until the client cache of rows is fully populated. Instead of using a scrollable cursor to determine the number of rows, count the rows by iterating through the result set or get the number of rows by submitting a Select statement with the Count function. For example:

```
SELECT COUNT(*) FROM employees WHERE ...
```

Extended Security

It is no secret that performance penalties are a side effect of extended security. If you've ever developed an application that required security, we're sure that you've discovered this hard truth. We include this section in the book simply to point out the penalties that go along with security and to provide suggestions for limiting these penalties if possible.

In this section, we discuss two types of security: network authentication and data encryption across the network (as opposed to data encrypted in the database).

If your database driver of choice does not support network authentication or data encryption, you cannot use this functionality in your database application.

Network Authentication

On most computer systems, an encrypted password is used to prove a user's identity. If the system is a distributed network system, this password is transmitted over the network and can possibly be intercepted and decrypted by malicious hackers. Because this password is the one secret piece of information that identifies a user, anyone knowing a user's password can effectively *be* that user.

In your enterprise, the use of passwords may not be secure enough. You might need network authentication.

Kerberos, a network authentication protocol, provides a way to identify users. Any time users request a network service, such as a database connection, they must prove their identity.

Kerberos was originally developed at MIT as a solution to the security issues of open network computing environments. Kerberos is a trusted third-party authentication service that verifies users' identities.

Kerberos keeps a database (the Kerberos server) of its clients and their private keys. The **private key** is a complex formula-driven value known only to Kerberos and the client to which it belongs. If the client is a user, the private key is an encrypted password.

Both network services that require authentication and clients who want to use these services must register with Kerberos. Because Kerberos knows the private keys of all clients, it creates messages that validate the client to the server and vice versa.

In a nutshell, here is how Kerberos works:

1. **The user obtains credentials that are used to request access to network services**. These credentials are obtained from the Kerberos server and are in the form of a Ticket-Granting Ticket (TGT). This TGT authorizes the Kerberos server to grant the user a service ticket, which authorizes his access to network services.

2. **The user requests authentication for a specific network service**. The Kerberos server verifies the user's credentials and sends a service ticket to him.

3. **The user presents the service ticket to the end server.** If the end server validates the user, the service is granted.

Figure 2-9 shows an example of requesting a database connection (a network service) when using Kerberos.

An application user requests a database connection after a TGT has been obtained:

1. The application sends a request for a database connection to the Kerberos server.

2. The Kerberos server sends back a service ticket.

3. The application sends the service ticket to the database server.

4. The database server validates the client and grants the connection.

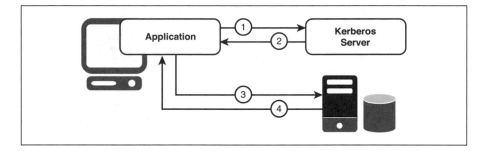

Figure 2-9   Kerberos

Even when you don't use Kerberos, database connections are performance-expensive; they can require seven to ten network round trips (see the section, "Why Connections Are Performance-Expensive," page 11, for more details). Using Kerberos comes with the price of adding more network round trips to establish a database connection.

Performance Tip

To get the best performance possible when using Kerberos, place the Kerberos server on a dedicated machine, reduce the networking services run on this machine to the absolute minimum, and make sure you have a fast, reliable network connection to the machine.

Data Encryption Across the Network

If your database connection is not configured to use data encryption, data is sent across the network in a "native" format; for example, a 4-byte integer is sent across the network as a 4-byte integer. The native format is defined by either of the following:

- The database vendor
- The database driver vendor in the case of a driver with an independent protocol architecture such as a Type 3 JDBC driver

The native format is designed for fast transmission and can be decoded by interceptors given some time and effort.

Because a native format does not provide complete protection from interceptors, you may want to use data encryption to provide a more secure transmission of data. For example, you may want to use data encryption in the following scenarios:

• You have offices that share confidential information over an intranet.
• You send sensitive data, such as credit card numbers, over a database connection.
• You need to comply with government or industry privacy and security requirements.

Data encryption is achieved by using a protocol for managing the security of message transmission, such as Secure Sockets Layer (SSL). Some database systems, such as DB2 for z/OS, implement their own data encryption protocol. The way the database-specific protocols work and the performance penalties associated with them are similar to SSL.

In the world of database applications, **SSL** is an industry-standard protocol for sending encrypted data over database connections. SSL secures the integrity of your data by encrypting information and providing client/server authentication.

From a performance perspective, SSL introduces an additional processing layer, as shown in Figure 2-10.

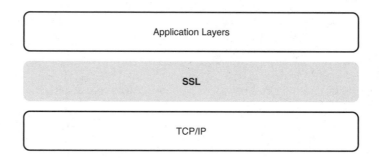

Figure 2-10   SSL: an additional processing layer

The SSL layer includes two CPU-intensive phases: SSL handshake and encryption.

When encrypting data using SSL, the database connection process includes extra steps between the database driver and the database to negotiate and agree

upon the encryption/decryption information that will be used. This is called the
SSL handshake. An SSL handshake results in multiple network round trips as
well as additional CPU to process the information needed for every SSL connection made to the database.

During an SSL handshake, the following steps take place, as shown in Figure 2-11:

1. The application via a database driver sends a connection request to the
   database server.

2. The database server returns its certificate and a list of supported encryption methods (cipher suites).

3. A secure, encrypted session is established when both the database driver
   and the server have agreed on an encryption method.

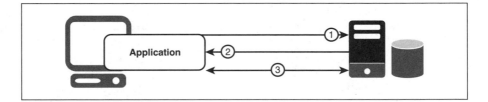

Figure 2-11   SSL handshake

Encryption is performed on each byte of data transferred; therefore, the
more data being encrypted, the more processing cycles occur, which means
slower network throughput.

SSL supports symmetric encryption methods such as DES, RC2, and Triple
DES. Some of these symmetric methods cause a larger performance penalty than
others, for example, Triple DES is slower than DES because larger keys must be
used to encrypt/decrypt the data. Larger keys mean more memory must be referenced, copied, and processed. You cannot always control which encryption
method your database server uses, but it is good to know which one is used so
that you can set realistic performance goals.

Figure 2-12 shows an example of how an SSL connection can affect throughput. In this example, the same benchmark was run twice using the same application, JDBC driver, database server, hardware, and operating system. The only
variable was whether an SSL connection was used.

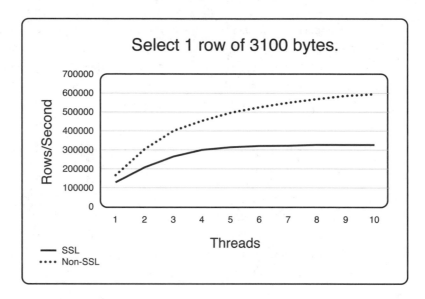

Figure 2-12   Rows per second: SSL versus non-SSL

Figure 2-13 shows the CPU associated with the throughput of this example. As you can see, CPU use increases when using an SSL connection.

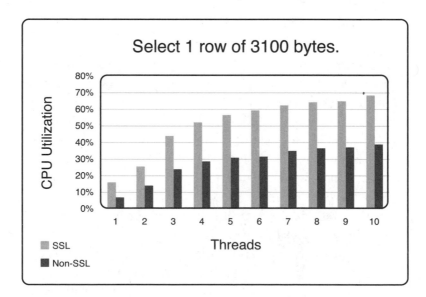

Figure 2-13   CPU utilization: SSL versus non-SSL

> ### Performance Tip
>
> To limit the performance penalty associated with data encryption, consider establishing a connection that uses encryption for accessing sensitive data such as an individual's tax ID number, and another connection that does not use encryption for accessing data that is less sensitive, such as an individual's department and title. There is one caveat here: Not all database systems allow this. Oracle and Microsoft SQL Server are examples of database systems that do. Sybase is an example of either all connections to the database use encryption or none of them do.

Static SQL Versus Dynamic SQL

At the inception of relational database systems and into the 1980s, the only portable interface for applications was embedded SQL. At that time, there was no common function API such as a standards-based database API, for example, ODBC. **Embedded SQL** is SQL statements written within an application programming language such as C. These statements are preprocessed by a SQL preprocessor, which is database dependent, before the application is compiled. In the preprocessing stage, the database creates the access plan for each SQL statement. During this time, the SQL was embedded and, typically, always static.

In the 1990s, the first portable database API for SQL was defined by the SQL Access Group. Following this specification came the ODBC specification from Microsoft. The ODBC specification was widely adopted, and it quickly became the de facto standard for SQL APIs. Using ODBC, SQL did not have to be embedded into the application programming language, and precompilation was no longer required, which allowed database independence. Using SQL APIs, the SQL is not embedded; it is dynamic.

What is static SQL and dynamic SQL? **Static SQL** is SQL statements in an application that do not change at runtime and, therefore, can be hard-coded into the application. **Dynamic SQL** is SQL statements that are constructed at runtime; for example, the application may allow users to enter their own queries. Thus, the SQL statements cannot be hard-coded into the application.

Static SQL provides performance advantages over dynamic SQL because static SQL is preprocessed, which means the statements are parsed, validated, and optimized only once.

If you are using a standards-based API, such as ODBC, to develop your application, static SQL is probably not an option for you. However, you can achieve a similar level of performance by using either statement pooling or stored procedures. See "Statement Pooling," page 29, for a discussion about how statement pooling can improve performance.

A **stored procedure** is a set of SQL statements (a subroutine) available to applications accessing a relational database system. Stored procedures are physically stored in the database. The SQL statements you define in a stored procedure are parsed, validated, and optimized only once, as with static SQL.

Stored procedures are database dependent because each relational database system implements stored procedures in a proprietary way. Therefore, if you want your application to be database independent, think twice before using stored procedures.

Note

Today, a few tools are appearing on the market that convert dynamic SQL in a standards-based database application into static SQL. Using static SQL, applications achieve better performance and decreased CPU costs. The CPU normally used to prepare a dynamic SQL statement is eliminated.

The Network

The network, which is a component of the database middleware, has many factors that affect performance: database protocol packets, network packets, network hops, network contention, and packet fragmentation. See "Network," in Chapter 4 (page 86) for details on how to understand the performance implications of the network and guidelines for dealing with them.

In this section, let's look at one important fact about performance and the network: database application performance improves when communication between the database driver and the database is optimized.

With this in mind, you should always ask yourself: How can I reduce the information that is communicated between the driver and the database? One important factor in this optimization is the size of database protocol packets.

The size of database protocol packets sent by the database driver to the database server must be equal to or less than the maximum database protocol packet size allowed by the database server. If the database server accepts a maximum packet size of 64KB, the database driver must send packets of 64KB or less. Typically, the larger the packet size, the better the performance, because fewer packets are needed to communicate between the driver and the database. Fewer packets means fewer network round trips to and from the database.

For example, if the database driver uses a packet size of 32KB and the database server's packet size is configured for 64KB, the database server must limit its packet size to the smaller 32KB packet size used by the driver—increasing the number of packets sent over the network to return the same amount of data to the client (as shown in Figure 2-14).

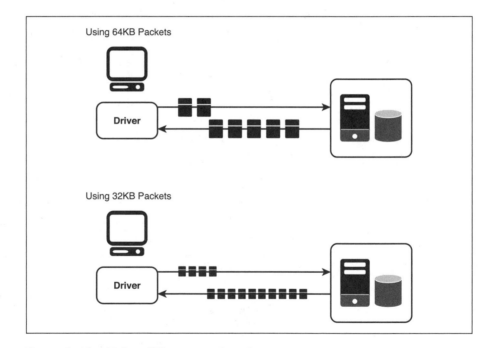

Figure 2-14   Using different packet sizes

This increase in the number of packets also means an increase in packet overhead. High packet overhead reduces throughput, or the amount of data that is transferred from sender to receiver over a period of time.

You might be thinking, "But how can I do anything about the size of database protocol packets?" You can use a database driver that allows you to configure their size. See "Runtime Performance Tuning Options," page 62, for more information about which performance tuning options to look for in a database driver.

The Database Driver

The database driver, which is a component of the database middleware, can degrade the performance of your database application because of the following reasons:

- The architecture of the driver is not optimal.
- The driver is not tunable. It does not have runtime performance tuning options that allow you to configure the driver for optimal performance.

See Chapter 3, "Database Middleware: Why It's Important," for a detailed description of how a database driver can improve the performance of your database application.

In this section, let's look at one important fact about performance and a database driver: The architecture of your database driver matters. Typically, the most optimal architecture is database wire protocol.

Database wire protocol drivers communicate with the database directly, eliminating the need for the database's client software, as shown in Figure 2-15.

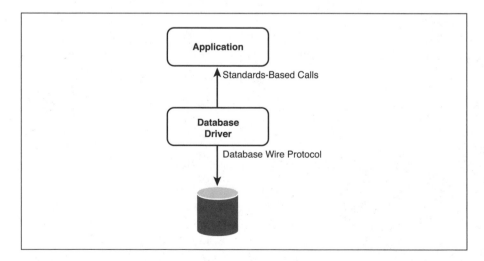

Figure 2-15   Database wire protocol architecture

Using a wire protocol database driver improves the performance of your database application because it does the following:

- Decreases latency by eliminating the processing required in the client software and the extra network traffic caused by the client software.
- Reduces network bandwidth requirements from extra transmissions. That is, database wire protocol drivers optimize network traffic because they can control interaction with TCP.

We go into more detail about the benefits of using a database wire protocol driver in "Database Driver Architecture," page 55.

Know Your Database System

You may think your database system supports all the functionality that is specified in the standards-based APIs (such as ODBC, JDBC, and ADO.NET). That is likely not true. Yet, the driver you use may provide the functionality, which is often a benefit to you. For example, if your application performs bulk inserts or updates, you can improve performance by using arrays of parameters. Yet, not all database systems support arrays of parameters. In any case, if you use a database driver that supports them, you can use this functionality even if the database system does not support it, which 1) results in performance improvements for bulk inserts or updates, and 2) eliminates the need for you to implement the functionality yourself.

The trade-off of using functionality that is not natively supported by your database system is that emulated functionality can increase CPU use. You must weigh this trade-off against the benefit of having the functionality in your application.

The protocol of your database system is another important implementation detail that you should understand. Throughout this chapter, we discussed design decisions that are affected by the protocol used by your database system of choice: cursor-based or streaming. Explanations of these two protocols can be found in "One Connection for Multiple Statements" on page 16.

Table 2-3 lists some common functionality and whether it is natively supported by five major database systems.

Table 2-3   Database System Native Support

Functionality	DB2	Microsoft SQL Server	MySQL	Oracle	Sybase ASE
Cursor-based protocol	Supported	Supported	Not supported	Supported	Not supported
Streaming protocol	Not supported	Not supported	Supported	Not supported	Supported
Prepared statements	Native	Native	Native	Native	Not supported
Arrays of parameters	Depends on version	Depends on version	Not supported	Native	Not supported
Scrollable cursors[1]	Supported	Supported	Not supported	Not supported	Depends on version
Auto-commit mode	Not supported	Not supported	Native	Native	Native
LOB locators	Native	Native	Not supported	Native	Not supported

[1] See Table 2-2, page 36, for more information about how these database systems support scrollable cursors.

Using Object-Relational Mapping Tools

Most business applications access data in relational databases. However, the relational model is designed for efficiently storing and retrieving data, not for the object-oriented model often used for business applications.

As a result, new object-relational mapping (ORM) tools are becoming popular with many business application developers. Hibernate and Java Persistence API (JPA) are such tools for the Java environment, and NHibernate and ADO.NET Entity Framework are such tools for the .NET environment.

Object-relational mapping tools map object-oriented programming objects to the tables of relational databases. When using relational databases with objects, typically, an ORM tool can reduce development costs because the tool does the object-to-table and table-to-object conversions needed. Otherwise, these conversions must be written in addition to the application development. ORM tools allow developers to focus on the business application.

From a design point of view, you need to know that when you use object-relational mapping tools you lose much of the ability to tune your database application code. For example, you are not writing the SQL statements that are sent to the database; the ORM tool is creating them. This can mean that the SQL statements could be more complex than ones you would write, which can result in performance issues. Also, you don't get to choose the API calls used to return data, for example, SQLGetData versus SQLBindCol for ODBC.

To optimize application performance when using an ORM tool, we recommend that you tune your database driver appropriately for use with the database your application is accessing. For example, you can use a tool to log the packets sent between the driver and the database and configure the driver to send a packet size that is equal to the packet size of that configured on the database. See Chapter 4, "The Environment: Tuning for Performance," for more information.

Summary

Many factors affect performance. Some are beyond your control, but thoughtful design of your application and the configuration of the database middleware that connects your application to the database server can result in optimal performance.

If you are going to design only one aspect of your application, let it be database connections, which are performance-expensive. Establishing a connection can take up to ten network round trips. You should assess whether connection pooling or one connection at a time is more appropriate for your situation.

When designing your database application, here are some important questions to ask: Are you retrieving only the minimum amount of data that you need? Are you retrieving the most efficient data type? Would a prepared statement save you some overhead? Could you use a local transaction instead of a more performance-expensive distributed transaction?

Lastly, make sure that you are using the best database driver for your application. Does your database driver support all the functionality that you want to use in your application? For example, does your driver support statement pooling? Does the driver have runtime performance tuning options that you can configure to improve performance? For example, can you configure the driver to reduce network activity?

CHAPTER THREE

Database Middleware: Why It's Important

Database middleware is important to performance because it plays a significant role in how your database applications perform. Whether your database application services a doctor viewing X-rays, a person getting money from an ATM, a customer waiting for a credit card transaction to process at a department store, or a handyman waiting for a paint color to match at a building supply store, the performance of your application depends on your database middleware and how efficiently the data is moved at high speeds with high user counts.

In fact, as we stated in Chapter 1, "Performance Isn't What It Used to Be," in a well-tuned environment, 75% to 95% of the time necessary to process a data request is spent in the database middleware, so if the database middleware is not optimally tuned, performance suffers.

In this chapter, we define database middleware, discuss how it can affect performance, and focus on one important component of database middleware: database drivers.

What Is Database Middleware?

Database middleware is all the components that handle the communication between an application and the database management software. Database middleware handles the application's data request until that request is handed to the database, and in the other direction, it handles the database's response until it is handed to the application.

The components of database middleware might include the following:

- Database client software such as Oracle Net8 or DB2 Connect
- JDBC or ODBC database drivers
- Driver Manager for ODBC or JDBC
- ADO.NET data providers
- Java Virtual Machine (JVM) in a JDBC-enabled database application
- TCP/IP network or other libraries loaded into the application's address space when it connects to a database such as SSL libraries for data encryption

Figure 3-1 shows an example of a deployed ODBC-enabled database application and the middleware it uses.

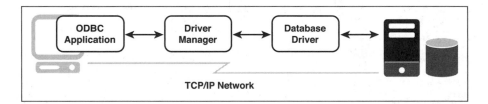

Figure 3-1   Database middleware example

How Database Middleware Affects Application Performance

Database applications typically fall into four basic categories:

- Applications that return a small result and a single row, such as an ATM transaction—often referred to as online transaction processing (OLTP) applications. For example, this might be a Select statement that retrieves one row with two columns.

- Applications that return a large result and a single row, such as purchase order applications. For example, this might be a `Select` statement that retrieves one row with 30 columns.
- Applications that return a small result and many rows, such as a report with a list of part numbers—often referred to as drill-down applications. For example, this might be a `Select` statement that retrieves 100 rows with one column.
- Applications that return a large result and many rows, such as reporting applications—often referred to as business intelligence applications. For example, this might be a `Select` statement that retrieves 10,000 rows with 30 columns.

The performance issues you might see in an application can depend on the amount of data your application requests. The more data an application requests, the more data the database driver must retrieve from the database and return to the application. More data can equate to a longer response time. The first three types of applications in the preceding list may have many of the same performance issues. The performance issues are likely caused by poorly tuned database middleware because in these types of applications, *most of the response time is spent in the database middleware.*

For business intelligence applications (applications that report, analyze, and present data), you will see different performance issues depending on whether the application is generating a report or doing expensive online analytical processing (OLAP) analysis. In the case of a report, most of the response time is spent in the database middleware. For OLAP, most of the response time is spent in the database, not the middleware.

In this chapter, we focus on database drivers—what they are, what they do, and how they affect performance. See Chapter 4, "The Environment: Tuning for Performance," for information about how your runtime environment, network, operating system, and hardware can affect performance.

Database Drivers

A **database driver** is a software component that an application uses on demand to gain access to a database using a standards-defined method.

Database drivers are a key component of your database application deployment, and they can affect the performance of your database application. You might be thinking that a driver is a driver is a driver. But that isn't true.

Here are two major reasons a database driver can degrade the performance of your database application:

- The architecture of the driver is not optimal.
- The driver is not tunable. It does not have runtime performance tuning options that allow you to configure the driver for optimal performance. The type of options that we are talking about are ones that you can adjust to match your application and environment. For example, if your application retrieves large objects, look for a driver option that allows you to configure how much active memory the driver uses to cache a large object.

What Does a Database Driver Do?

The standards-based API specifications define the required functionality that a database driver must implement to be compliant. All drivers are not created equal; some drivers on the market are implemented with only the required functionality, and some are implemented with much, much more. You may be surprised at how many tasks database drivers perform. The following list provides a brief description of the tasks. Remember that not all drivers implement all this functionality:

- Translate a standards-based API (such as ODBC or JDBC) into a low-level set of database API requests (such as to a proprietary database wire protocol)
- Provide thread safety to the application when making database API requests
- Provide a full state machine regarding environment context for making database connections and statements for executing SQL queries
- Handle all data conversion from a proprietary database format of data into native language data types
- Buffer database query results from the network into the application's buffers
- Manage the TCP/IP connection from the client to the database server
- Provide load balancing to various database servers
- Provide failover to backup database servers if fatal errors occur
- Map errors from database-specific codes into standard errors
- Provide data translation from client code pages to and from database-specific code pages
- Take cross-database SQL and translate it to database-specific SQL

- Optimize database stored procedure requests from character-based SQL to database-specific RPC calls
- Optimize data access to ensure scalability
- Control the state of the network port to the database to ensure only one active statement is being processed
- Emulate functionality not present in the database (for example, scrollable cursors, arrays of parameters, prepared statements)
- Batch queries in chunks to get maximum throughput
- Expose database options as configuration options
- Manage database transaction states, including coordinating with distributed transaction coordinators
- Provide connection pooling for the application
- Provide network authentication and data encryption across the network

The way all this functionality is implemented in a database driver is key to how well the driver performs. Even when two database drivers implement all the same functionality, the performance of the database drivers may be quite different when used with your database applications. If you are experiencing less than optimal performance with the database driver you are using, consider evaluating another database driver. See Chapter 9, "Developing Good Benchmarks," for information about how to test database drivers in your environment.

When selecting a driver for your database application, make sure that the driver's functionality meets the requirements of your application. For example, if you are implementing a Unicode application, make sure the database driver you choose supports Unicode. **Unicode** is a standard encoding that is used to support multilingual character sets.

Database Driver Architecture

Four distinct architectures exist for database drivers: bridge, client-based, database wire protocol, and independent protocol. Choose a database driver that is implemented with an architecture that provides the best performance for your application.

Bridge Architecture

A **bridge** is a database driver that bridges between an existing database connectivity standard and a new one, as shown in Figure 3-2. For example, when Sun Microsystems, Inc. released the JDBC specification, Sun wanted to encourage developers to use JDBC, but not many JDBC drivers were on the market at the time. However, hundreds of ODBC drivers to almost every data source were available, so Sun Microsystems, Inc. released a single JDBC/ODBC bridge that gave Java developers access to all the data sources that the ODBC drivers supported.

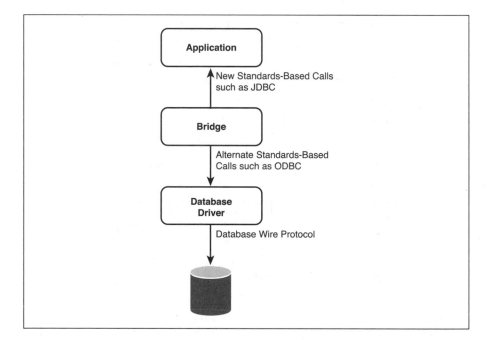

Figure 3-2   Database driver bridge architecture

Many JDBC/ODBC bridges are available on the market; these are called Type 1 JDBC drivers. The book *JDBC API Tutorial and Reference* states that Type 1 drivers are "generally less desirable solutions."[1] Unless no other solution meets the requirements of your database application, you should consider using a database driver with a more optimal architecture.

Following are the disadvantages of using bridges:

- Often they cannot fully implement a new standard because they are constrained by the definition of the alternate standard.
- They can pose security risks.
- Many implementations struggle to function optimally under high user counts.

---

[1] Fisher, Maydene, Jon Ellis, and Jonathan Bruce. *JDBC API Tutorial and Reference*, Third Edition. Addison-Wesley, 2003.

Database Client-Based Architecture

Client-based database drivers communicate with the database through the database's client software, as shown in Figure 3-3. This software is the database vendor's proprietary software, such as Oracle Net8 or OpenClient for Sybase. Many ODBC drivers and ADO.NET data providers on the market use this architecture. In the JDBC world, only a few drivers, known as Type 2 drivers, use this architecture. *JDBC API Tutorial and Reference* states that Type 2 drivers are "generally less desirable solutions."

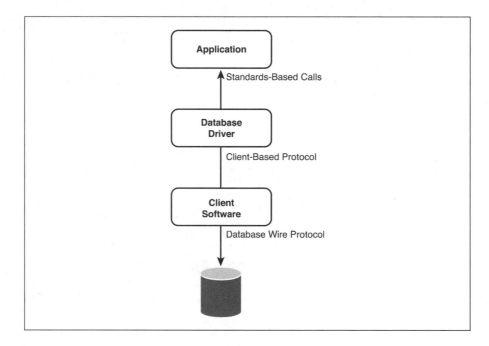

Figure 3-3   Database client-based architecture

Following are the disadvantages of using client-based drivers:

- You must install, configure, and maintain database client software on every computer that needs database connectivity.
- You may have to install and support a different version of the client software for each version of the database system you are using.
- The database driver must be developed with the restrictions of the client software, which may be either functional or quality restrictions. For example, if your application is designed to run on a 64-bit Linux operating

system, but the database vendor does not offer its database client software on that operating system, the database driver vendor cannot develop a 64-bit Linux driver.

- In the case of Java and ADO.NET, the database driver/provider must make calls to the client software, which is Java native libraries or ADO.NET unmanaged code. See the following section, "Database Wire Protocol Architecture," for details.

Database Wire Protocol Architecture

Database wire protocol drivers communicate with the database directly, eliminating the need for the database's client software, as shown in Figure 3-4.

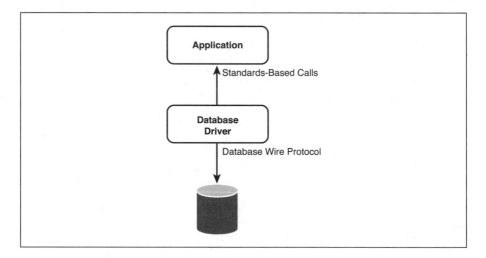

Figure 3-4   Database wire protocol architecture

Today, few ODBC drivers and ADO.NET data providers on the market use this architecture. Many JDBC drivers, known as Type 4 drivers, use this architecture.

Databases have a proprietary API that allows other software components to communicate with them. In a client-based architecture, the client software makes the wire protocol calls to the database. In a database wire protocol architecture, the database drivers generate the required wire protocol calls, thereby communicating directly with the database.

The benefits of choosing a database driver that has a database wire protocol architecture are many. First, the database driver can be installed with your database application and can immediately connect to the database without configuring other software. Second, you do not have to install, configure, and maintain database client software. Third, performance is improved because a database wire protocol driver does both of the following:

- Decreases latency by eliminating the processing required in the client software and the extra network traffic caused by the client software.
- Reduces network bandwidth requirements from extra transmissions. That is, database wire protocol drivers can optimize network traffic because they can control interaction with TCP.

Regarding Java and ADO.NET, another important advantage exists when you use a database wire protocol driver/provider: The driver/provider does not have to make calls to the client software. What does this mean?

- For Java, this means the driver can use Pure Java code and not make calls to the native libraries. The Pure Java standard is a set of programs, rules, and certifications used in the design process to ensure that Java executables live up to the WORA (write once, run always) principles. A Pure Java program relies only on the Java Language specifications. Using native methods in a Java program means that you lose the benefits of the Java runtime, such as security, platform independence, garbage collection, and easy class loading. Specific external functionality is provided by the Java core APIs, such as JDBC.
- For ADO.NET, this means the provider can use 100% managed code. The benefit of 100% managed code is that it runs in the Common Language Runtime (CLR), which provides services such as automatic memory management and lifetime control of objects, platform neutrality, and cross-language integration. Managed code also provides improved versioning facilities as well as easier deployment. In contrast, unmanaged code, which includes all code written before the .NET Framework was introduced, does not run inside the .NET environment and cannot use .NET managed facilities. Performance is decreased because the CLR must perform additional security checks.

Performance Examples

Figure 3-5 compares the performance of a wire protocol database driver to a client-based driver. In these examples, each benchmark was run twice using the same database server, hardware, and operating system. The only variable was the database driver. The drivers tested were from different vendors. The benchmarks measured the throughput and scalability of a database application.

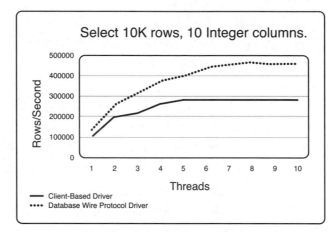

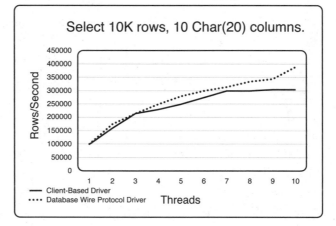

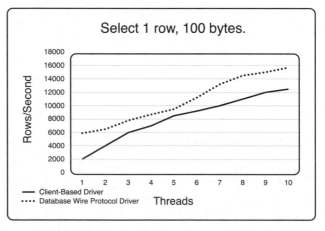

Figure 3-5   Comparing the performance of a wire protocol driver to a client-based driver

As you can see in these graphs, in most cases, the throughput and scalability of the database wire protocol driver is greater than that of the client-based driver.

Independent Protocol Architecture

Independent protocol database drivers translate the standards-based API calls into a database-independent protocol, which is then translated to the database wire protocol by a server. This architecture has both a database driver client and server component, as shown in Figure 3-6.

A few ODBC and JDBC drivers, and ADO.NET data providers on the market use this architecture. In the JDBC world, these drivers are known as Type 3 drivers.

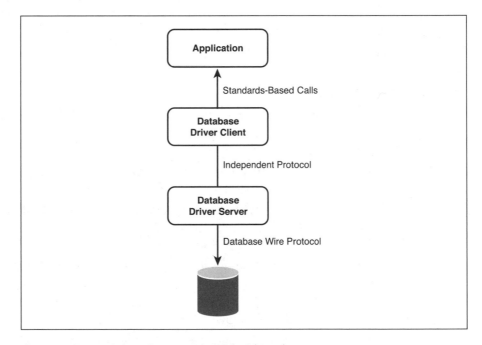

Figure 3-6   Independent protocol architecture

Typically, this type of architecture provides advanced security features such as the latest SSL encryption, access to a more varied set of data sources such as SQL to VSAM files, and centralized management and monitoring.

Independent protocol database drivers have many of the same benefits as database wire protocol drivers. The server-side component of the independent protocol drivers offers extra value that goes beyond the scope of this book.

One main disadvantage exists for this type of driver: a client and server component must be installed, configured, and maintained, unlike the database wire protocol drivers. However, you may be willing to pay this price if you cannot find a database wire protocol driver to access the data source of your choice.

Runtime Performance Tuning Options

Database drivers that offer runtime performance tuning options are ideal to use in your database application deployment because they provide options that you can configure to increase response time, throughput, and scalability. Some important options to look for are ones that allow you to optimize the driver for the following:

- Retrieving large objects
- Reducing network activity
- Performing bulk operations

Retrieving Large Objects

If your application retrieves large objects, such as pictures, XML, or long text, you would benefit from using a database driver that you can tune to optimize for this use. Access to the data types that store large objects often results in performance issues with your database application, typically caused by memory bottlenecks. If memory issues occur and your database driver does not provide appropriate performance-tuning options, your application is stuck with nonoptimal performance. See the section, "Memory," page 107, for information about memory bottlenecks.

Ideally, architects of applications that access large objects will deploy a database driver with their application that allows for configuration of how much active memory the driver uses to cache a large object, how long the object is cached, and when the object becomes available to the client. With these types of configuration options, you can control memory usage—how much and for how long data is in memory and when and whether the data is sent to disk.

Reducing Network Activity

To achieve maximum performance and the least amount of activity on the network, the database protocol packet size used by the database driver should be configurable so that it can be set to match the packet size set on the database. If the database driver uses a packet size smaller than the database's, the database has to limit its packet size to the smaller size used by that driver. This results in an increase in the number of packets sent over the network to return data to the client. An increase in the number of packets equates to an increase in packet overhead, and high packet overhead reduces throughput. See the section "Network," page 86.

Performing Bulk Operations

In data warehouse applications, loading bulk data into tables is common. To accomplish this task, you can use the database vendor's proprietary tools or write your own tool. But what if you are loading data into Oracle, DB2, and MySQL? You probably have to use three different ways (or tools) to load the data. In addition, if you want to operate within a standards-based API to accomplish the task, you might be out of luck unless you choose database drivers that implement this functionality in a standard way.

Today, we are seeing some database drivers that have bulk load functionality implemented as defined in the standards-based APIs. This is good news because you can write your bulk load applications using the standards-based API bulk interfaces and then just plug in the database drivers to do the work for you. This solution provides a simple, consistent, nonproprietary way to load data.

Configuring Database Drivers/Data Providers

The method for configuring a database driver for use with database applications depends on the driver you are using. In this section, we give examples of how to configure ODBC drivers, JDBC drivers, and ADO.NET data providers from DataDirect Technologies. You configure other vendors' drivers in a similar way. Refer to your driver's technical documentation for details.

ODBC Drivers

After you install the driver, you need to configure a data source or use a connection string to connect to the database. If you want to use a data source but need to change some of its values, you can either modify the data source or override its values through a connection string.

Configuring a Data Source on Windows

On Windows, data sources are stored in the Windows Registry. You can configure and modify data sources through the ODBC Administrator using a driver Setup dialog box. Figure 3-7 shows an example of an Oracle Setup dialog box.

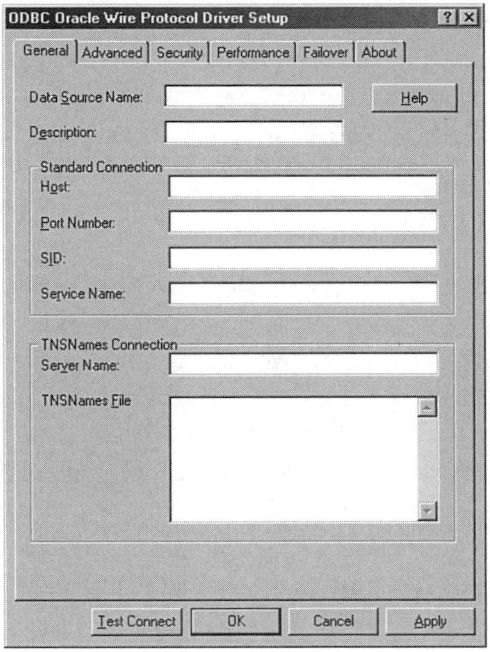

Figure 3-7   Example of Setup dialog box on Windows

Configuring a Data Source on UNIX/Linux

On UNIX and Linux, data sources are stored in the system information file (by default, odbc.ini). You can configure and modify data sources directly by editing the system information file and storing default connection values there. The system information file is divided into two sections.

At the beginning of the file is a section named [ODBC Data Sources] containing data_source_name=installed-driver pairs. For example:

```
Oracle Wire Protocol=DataDirect 5.3 Oracle Wire Protocol
```

The driver uses this section to match a data source to the appropriate installed driver.

The [ODBC Data Sources] section also includes data source definitions. The default odbc.ini contains a data source definition for each driver. Each data source definition begins with a data source name in square brackets, such as [Oracle Wire Protocol]. The data source definitions contain connection string attribute=value pairs with default values. You can modify these values as appropriate for your system.

The second section of the file is named [ODBC] and includes several key-words:

```
[ODBC]
IANAAppCodePage=4
InstallDir=ODBCHOME
UseCursorLib=0
Trace=0
TraceFile=odbctrace.out
TraceDll=ODBCHOME/lib/odbctrac.so
```

The InstallDir keyword must be included in this section. The value of this keyword is the path to the installation directory under which the /lib and /mes-sages directories are contained. The installation process automatically writes your installation directory to the default odbc.ini.

For example, if you choose an installation location of /opt/odbc, the follow-ing line is written to the [ODBC] section of the default odbc.ini:

```
InstallDir=/opt/odbc
```

Here is an example of a default Oracle Wire Protocol driver system informa-tion file:

```
[ODBC Data Sources]
Oracle Wire Protocol=DataDirect 5.3 Oracle Wire Protocol

[Oracle Wire Protocol]
Driver=ODBCHOME/lib/ivora23.so
Description=DataDirect 5.3 Oracle Wire Protocol
AlternateServers=
ApplicationUsingThreads=1
ArraySize=60000
AuthenticationMethod=1
CachedCursorLimit=32
CachedDescLimit=0
CatalogIncludesSynonyms=1
CatalogOptions=0
ConnectionRetryCount=0
ConnectionRetryDelay=3
DefaultLongDataBuffLen=1024
```

```
DescribeAtPrepare=0
EnableDescribeParam=0
EnableNcharSupport=0
EnableScrollableCursors=1
EnableStaticCursorsForLongData=0
EnableTimestampWithTimeZone=0
EncryptionMethod=0
GSSClient=native
HostName=<Oracle_server>
HostNameInCertificate=
KeyPassword=
KeyStore=
KeyStorePassword
LoadBalancing=0
LocalTimeZoneOffset=
LockTimeOut=-1
LogonID=
Password=
PortNumber=<Oracle_server_port>
ProcedureRetResults=0
ReportCodePageConversionErrors=0
ReportRecycleBin=0
ServerName=<server_name in tnsnames.ora>
ServerType=0
ServiceName=
SID=<Oracle_System_Identifier>
TimestampeEscapeMapping=0
TNSNamesFile=<tnsnames.ora_filename>
TrustStore=
TrustStorePassword=
UseCurrentSchema=1
ValidateServerCertificate=1
WireProtocolMode=1

[ODBC]
IANAAppCodePage=4
InstallDir=ODBCHOME
```

```
UseCursorLib=0
Trace=0
TraceFile=odbctrace.out
TraceDll=ODBCHOME/lib/odbctrac.so
```

Connecting to a Database Using a Connection String

If you want to use a connection string to connect to a database, or if your application requires it, you must specify either a DSN (data source name), a File DSN, or a DSN-less connection in the string. The difference is whether you use the DSN=, FILEDSN=, or DRIVER= keyword in the connection string, as described in the ODBC specification. A DSN or FILEDSN connection string tells the driver where to find the default connection information. Optionally, you may specify attribute=value pairs in the connection string to override the default values stored in the data source. These attribute=value pairs are the specifics of the connection, such as which database server to connect to and whether the driver uses connection failover and Kerberos. You can find the connection options supported by the database driver in the driver's technical documentation.

The DSN connection string has the following form:

```
DSN=data_source_name[;attribute=value[;attribute=value]...]
```

The FILEDSN connection string has this form:

```
FILEDSN=filename.dsn[;attribute=value[;attribute=value]...]
```

The DSN-less connection string specifies a driver instead of a data source. You must enter all connection information in the connection string because there is no data source storing the information.

The DSN-less connection string has the following form:

```
DRIVER=[{]driver_name[}][;attribute=value[;attribute=value]
    ...]
```

JDBC Drivers

After you install the driver, you can connect to the database in one of the following ways: with a connection URL through the JDBC Driver Manager or with a Java Naming Directory Interface (JNDI) data source. The examples we use in this section are for a DataDirect Technologies JDBC driver.

Using the JDBC Driver Manager

One way to connect to a database is through the JDBC Driver Manager by using the `DriverManager.getConnection` method. This method uses a string containing a connection URL. The following code fragment shows an example of using the JDBC Driver Manager to connect to Microsoft SQL Server:

```
Connection conn = DriverManager.getConnection
  ("jdbc:datadirect:sqlserver://server1:1433;User=test;
  Password=secret");
```

REGISTERING THE JDBC DRIVER   Registering the DataDirect JDBC drivers with the JDBC Driver Manager allows the JDBC Driver Manager to load them. To register a JDBC driver with the JDBC Driver Manager, you must specify the name of the driver. Note that if you are using Java SE 6, you do not need to register the drivers. Java SE 6 automatically registers the drivers with the JDBC Driver Manager.

You can register the DataDirect JDBC drivers with the JDBC Driver Manager using any of the following methods:

• **Method 1**—Set the Java system property `jdbc.drivers` using the Java -D option. The `jdbc.drivers` property is defined as a colon-separated list of driver class names. For example:

```
java -Djdbc.drivers=com.ddtek.jdbc.db2.DB2Driver:
com.ddtek.jdbc.sqlserver.SQLServerDriver
```

registers the DataDirect JDBC DB2 driver and the DataDirect JDBC Microsoft SQL Server driver.

• **Method 2**—Set the Java property `jdbc.drivers` from within your Java application or applet. To do this, include the following code fragment in your Java application or applet, and call `DriverManager.getConnection`:

```
Properties p = System.getProperties();
p.put ("jdbc.drivers",
"com.ddtek.jdbc.sqlserver.SQLServerDriver");
System.setProperties (p);
```

• **Method 3**—Explicitly load the driver class using the standard `Class.forName` method. To do this, include the following code fragment in your application or applet and call `DriverManager.getConnection`:

```
Class.forName("com.ddtek.jdbc.sqlserver.SQLServerDriver");
```

SPECIFYING CONNECTION URLs The connection URL format used with the Driver Manager is as follows:

```
jdbc:datadirect:drivername:
//hostname:port[;property=value[;...]]
```

where:
- *drivername* is the name of the driver, such as `sqlserver`.
- *hostname* is the IP address or TCP/IP host name of the server to which you are connecting.
- *port* is the number of the TCP/IP port.
- *property=value* specifies connection properties. The connection properties supported by the database driver can be found in the driver's technical documentation.

Using a JDBC Data Source

A JDBC data source is a Java object—specifically a `DataSource` object—that defines connection information needed for a JDBC driver to connect to the database. Each JDBC driver vendor provides its own data source implementation for this purpose.

The main advantage of using a data source is that it works with the JNDI naming service, and it is created and managed apart from applications that use it. Because the connection information is defined outside the application, it requires minimal effort to reconfigure your infrastructure when a change is made. For example, if the database is moved to another database server and uses another port number, the administrator needs only to change the relevant properties of the data source (`DataSource` object). The applications using the database do not need to change because they only refer to the logical name of the data source.

DataDirect Technologies ships a data source class for each of its JDBC drivers. Each DataDirect data source class implements the following JDBC interfaces:

- `javax.sql.DataSource`
- `javax.sql.ConnectionPoolDataSource`, which allows your applications to use connection pooling

- `javax.sql.XADataSource`, which allows your applications to use distributed transactions through the Java Transaction API (JTA)

Applications can call a DataDirect JDBC data source using a logical name to retrieve the `javax.sql.DataSource` object. This object loads the specified driver and can establish a connection to the database.

Once the data source has been registered with JNDI, your JDBC application can use it, as shown in the following example:

```
Context ctx = new InitialContext();
DataSource ds = (DataSource)ctx.lookup("EmployeeDB");
Connection conn = ds.getConnection("scott", "tiger");
```

In this example, the JNDI environment is initialized first. Next, the initial naming context is used to find the logical name of the data source (`EmployeeDB`). The `Context.lookup()` method returns a reference to a Java object, which is narrowed to a `javax.sql.DataSource` object. Finally, the `DataSource.getConnection()` method is called to establish a connection with the database.

ADO.NET Data Providers

After you install the data provider, you can connect from your application to your database with a connection string. You can configure the connection string either by using the common programming model or by using the provider-specific objects.

Each DataDirect Technologies data provider uses a connection string to provide information needed to connect to a specific database. The connection information is defined by connection string options.

The connection options have the following form:

```
option=value
```

Each connection string option value pair is separated by a semicolon. For example:

```
Host=Accounting1;Port=50000;User ID=johng;Password=test01;
Database=Test
```

You can find the connection options supported by the data provider in the provider's technical documentation.

Using the Common Programming Model

The following example illustrates connecting to a DB2 database from an application developed in Visual Studio 2008 using C# and the common programming model:

1. Check the beginning of your application. Ensure that the ADO.NET namespaces are present.

```
// Access DB2 using factory
using System.Data;
using System.Data.Common;
```

2. Add the connection information of your server and exception handling code, and close the connection.

```
DbProviderFactory factory=DbProviderFactories("DDTek.DB2");
DbConnection Conn = factory.createConnection();
Conn.CommandText = "Host=Accounting1;Port=50000;User ID=johng;
   Password=test01;Database=test";

try
{
    Conn.Open();
    Console.WriteLine("Connection successful!");
}
catch (Exception ex)
{
    // Connection failed
    Console.WriteLine(ex.Message);
}
// Close the connection
Conn.Close();
```

Using the Provider-Specific Objects

The following example uses the provider-specific objects to connect to a database using the DB2 data provider from an application developed in Visual Studio 2008 using C#:

1. In the Solution Explorer, right-click **References**, and then select **Add Reference**.

2. Select the DB2 data provider in the component list of the Add Reference dialog box.

3. Click **OK**. The Solution Explorer now includes DDTek.DB2, the assembly name of the DB2 data provider.

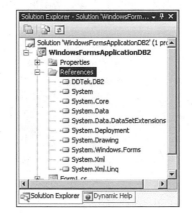

4. Add the data provider's namespace to the beginning of your application, as shown in the following C# code fragment:

```
// Access DB2
using System.Data;
using DDTek.DB2;
```

5. Add the connection information for your server and exception handling code, and close the connection, as shown in the following C# code fragment:

```
DB2Connection DBConn = new
DB2Connection("Host=Accounting1;Port=50000;User ID=johng;
Password=test01;Database=Test01");
   try
   {
     DBConn.Open();
     Console.WriteLine ("Connection successful!");
   }

   // Display any exceptions
   catch (DB2Exception ex)
```

```
    {
        // Connection failed
        Console.WriteLine(ex.Message);
        return;
    }
```
6. Close the connection.

```
    // Close the connection
    Conn.Close();
```

Summary

In a well-tuned environment, 75% to 95% of the time it takes to process a data request is spent in the database middleware; this includes all the components that handle the communication between an application and the database management software. Perhaps the most important component of middleware is the database driver.

Your database driver can degrade performance if it does not include configurable options to tune performance or if its architecture is not optimal. The most optimal architecture for a driver is database wire protocol, which provides the following advantages:

- Elimination of the need for client software installation, configuration, and maintenance on each computer needing database connectivity
- Elimination of restrictions of the client software, whether functional or quality
- Decrease in latency by eliminating the processing and network traffic required by the client software
- Reduction of network bandwidth requirements from extra transmissions because the driver can control interaction with TCP

Additionally, database drivers that offer runtime performance tuning options are ideal to use in your database application deployment. Some important options to look for are ones that allow you to optimize the driver for the following:

- Retrieving large objects
- Reducing network activity
- Performing bulk operations

CHAPTER FOUR

The Environment: Tuning for Performance

The performance of your database application, whether that is measured by response time, throughput, or scalability, is affected by many things, each of which can be a limiting factor to overall performance. In Chapter 3, "Database Middleware: Why It's Important," we explained that the database driver is only one component of your database middleware and that multiple environment layers also work with the database driver to handle the communication between a database application and the database management software. This chapter describes how those environment layers, shown in Figure 4-1, can influence performance and how to optimize performance for data requests and responses that flow through these layers. In addition, this chapter provides details about how your database driver and specific application design and coding techniques can optimize your hardware resources and relieve performance bottlenecks.

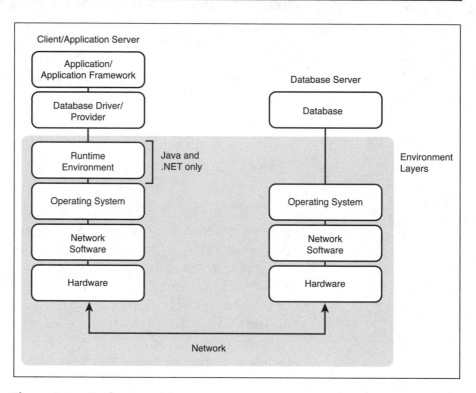

Figure 4-1   Environment layers

The influence of the environment can be significant, as shown by the following real-world example. A major business software company thoroughly tested a new database application on a local area network (LAN), and performance was acceptable according to all the benchmarks that were run. Surprisingly, when the database application was deployed in the production environment, which involved network travel over a wide area network (WAN), overall response time dropped by half. Puzzled about the performance, developers placed the actual machines used in the testing environment into the production environment; performance was still compromised. After troubleshooting the database application in the production environment, the developers discovered that the network traffic over the WAN passed through multiple network nodes with lower MTUs, which caused network packet fragmentation. See the section, "Avoiding Network Packet Fragmentation," page 98, for more information about packet fragmentation.

In this chapter, we'll talk about how the following environment layers affect performance and what you can do about it:

- Runtime environment (Java and .NET)
- Operating system
- Network
- Hardware

Runtime Environment (Java and .NET)

What do a Java Virtual Machine (JVM) and the .NET Common Language Runtime (CLR) have in common? They're both runtime environments for applications. Whereas a JVM is a runtime environment for the Java language, the .NET CLR, as part of the .NET Framework, operates as a runtime environment for multiple languages on Windows platforms. They also significantly impact the performance of your database applications.

JVM

IBM, Sun Microsystems, Oracle (BEA), and others manufacture their own JVMs. However, all JVMs are not created equal. Although vendors who produce JVMs using the "Java" trademark must adhere to the JVM specification published by Sun Microsystems, Inc., there are differences in the way those JVMs are implemented—differences that affect performance.

For example, Figure 4-2 shows the results of a benchmark that measures the throughput and scalability of a database application with different JVMs. The benchmark was run multiple times using the same JDBC driver, database server, hardware, and operating system. The only variable in this scenario is the choice of JVM. The JVMs tested were manufactured by different vendors, but were the same version of JVM and had comparable configurations. As you can see in Figure 4-2, where each line represents a benchmark run with a different JVM, the throughput and scalability of JVMs can vary significantly.

Not only does your choice of JVM matter for performance, but how that JVM is configured matters. Each JVM has tuning options that can impact your application's performance. For example, Figure 4-3 shows the results of a benchmark that used the same JDBC driver, database server, hardware, operating system, and JVM. The benchmark compares the throughput and scalability of a database application. However, the JVM was first configured to run in client mode and then configured to run in server mode. (See the section, "Client Versus Server Mode," page 82, for more information.) As you can see, the throughput and scalability of the JVM running in server mode dramatically outperformed the JVM running in client mode.

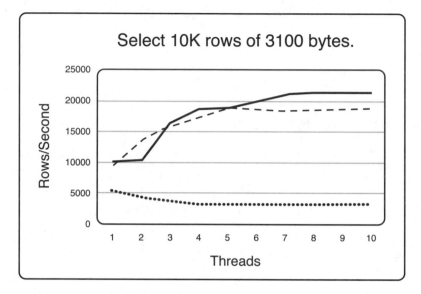

Figure 4-2   Comparing different JVMs

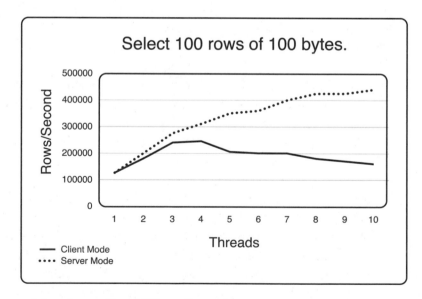

Figure 4-3   Comparing JVM configurations

You can tune the performance of your database application by setting the following common JVM options:

- Garbage collection
- Client versus server mode

Performance Tip

Choose a JVM that gives your database application the best performance. In addition, tuning options, such as those for garbage collection and client versus server mode, can improve performance.

Garbage Collection

While C++ requires direct control over when memory is allocated and freed, Java makes this process more automatic. As a Java application runs, it creates Java objects that it uses for varying lengths of time. When the Java application is finished with an object, it stops referencing it. The JVM allocates memory for Java objects from a reserved pool of memory known as the **Java heap**. This means that at any one time, the heap may have allocated memory for the following:

- Live objects that are being used by the application
- Dead objects that are no longer used (no longer referenced) by the application

Because the heap maintains memory for both types of objects and new objects are created constantly, eventually the heap runs low on memory. When this occurs, the JVM runs a routine known as a **garbage collector** to clean up dead objects and reclaim memory so that the heap has enough memory to allocate to new objects.

Why does garbage collection matter to performance? Different JVMs use different garbage collection algorithms, but most garbage collectors halt the allocation of objects while the garbage collector performs its collection routine, effectively "freezing" any application work running at the same time. Depending on the garbage collection algorithm used, this pause in work may persist as long as several seconds. When the garbage collector is finished with its collection, it lets the allocation of objects resume. For most database applications, lengthy collection pauses can negatively affect performance and scalability.

The most important options that control garbage collection are these:

- Heap size
- Generation heap size
- Garbage collection algorithm used by the JVM

The **heap size** controls how much memory is allocated to the overall Java heap. The heap size also controls how often the JVM performs garbage collection.

Finding the ideal heap size is a balancing act. When the heap size is set to a large value, garbage collection occurs less frequently, but collection pauses are longer because there's more heap to scan. In contrast, small heap sizes cause garbage collection to occur more frequently, but result in shorter pauses.

If garbage collection occurs too frequently, performance can be severely impacted. For example, suppose that your application uses a heap size that is too small to handle every live object being used by your application plus new ones that need to be created. Once the maximum heap size is reached, your application attempts to allocate a new object and fails. This failure triggers the garbage collector, which frees up memory. Your application tries again to allocate a new object. If the garbage collector failed to recover enough memory the first time, the second attempt fails, triggering the garbage collector to run again. Even if the garbage collector reclaims enough memory to satisfy the immediate request, the wait won't be long before another allocation failure occurs, triggering yet another garbage collection cycle. As a result, instead of servicing your application, the JVM constantly scavenges the heap for memory.

Performance Tip

As a general rule, try increasing the heap size so that garbage collection is not triggered as frequently, keeping in mind that you don't want to run out of physical memory (RAM). See the section, "Memory," page 107, for information about how running out of RAM affects performance. If garbage collection pauses seem unnecessarily long, try decreasing the heap size.

Older JVMs often treat the heap as one big repository, requiring the garbage collector to inspect each object in the heap to determine whether it is a dead object and can be cleaned up. Newer JVMs use **generational garbage collection** to separate objects into different memory pools within the heap based on the object's lifetime.

Some Java objects are short lived, such as local variables; others are long-lived, such as connections. Generational garbage collection divides the heap into Young and Old generations, as shown in Figure 4-4. New objects are allocated from the Young generation and, if they live long enough, eventually migrate to the Old generation. Figure 4-4 also shows another generation called the Permanent generation, which holds the JVM's class and method objects.

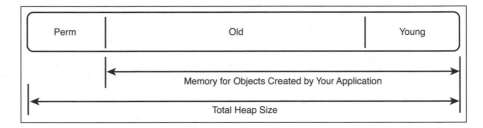

Figure 4-4   Heap generations

When the Young generation becomes full, the garbage collector looks for surviving objects while cleaning up short-lived objects. It moves surviving objects into a reserved area of the Young generation called a survivor space. If that survivor is still being used by the next collection, it's considered tenured. In this case, the collector moves the object into the Old generation. When the Old generation becomes full, the garbage collector cleans up any unused objects. Because the Young generation typically occupies a smaller heap space than the Old generation, garbage collection occurs more frequently in the Young generation, but collection pauses are shorter.

Similar to the way that the overall heap size affects garbage collection, the heap sizes of the generations affect garbage collection.

Performance Tip

As a general rule, set the size of the Young generation to be one-fourth that of the Old generation. You may want to increase the size of the Young generation if your application generates large numbers of short-lived objects.

Different JVMs use different garbage collection algorithms. A few let you tune which algorithm is used. Each algorithm has its own performance implications.

For example, an Incremental garbage collection algorithm performs its collection work a little at a time instead of trying to work its way through the entire heap, which results in shorter garbage collection pauses but reduces throughput.

Client Versus Server Mode

As a way to improve performance, many JVMs use Just-in-Time (JIT) compilers to compile and optimize code as it executes. The compiler that the JVM uses depends on the mode in which the JVM runs:

- Client mode uses a JIT compiler that is optimized for applications that are short running, need fast startup times, and require minimum memory, such as GUI applications. Many JVMs use this mode as the default.
- Server mode uses a JIT compiler that instructs the JVM to perform more extensive run-time optimization for applications that are long running and use substantial memory, such as database applications. Therefore, after startup, the JVM executes slowly until it has had enough time to optimize the code. After that, performance is considerably faster.

Performance Tip

Tune your JVM to use server mode. For database applications that run for weeks or months at a time, slower execution during the first few hours is a small price to pay for better performance later on.

.NET CLR

The CLR provides automatic garbage collection in much the same way as a JVM. When your application creates a new object, the CLR allocates memory to it from a pool of memory known as the **CLR heap**. The CLR also uses generational garbage collection. The CLR has three generations: generation 0, generation 1, and generation 2. When the garbage collector performs a collection in any of its generations, it cleans up objects that are no longer used and reclaims the memory allocated to them. Objects that survive a collection are progressively promoted to the next generation. For example, objects that survive a collection in generation 1 are moved to generation 2 during the next collection.

Unlike a JVM, the CLR doesn't provide tuning options that allow you to tune garbage collection. The CLR doesn't let you set a maximum limit on the heap size. Instead, the CLR heap size depends on how much memory can be allocated from the operating system. In addition, the CLR automatically adjusts the sizes of the generations according to its own optimization criteria.

If you can't tune garbage collection in the CLR, how can you ensure that garbage collection works in favor of your application's performance? The way your application code is designed and coded largely affects how efficiently garbage collection is performed.

Performance Tip

To optimize garbage collection in the CLR, make sure that your application closes connections as soon as the user is finished with them, and correctly and consistently use the Dispose method to free an object's resources. See the section, "Disconnecting Efficiently," page 196, for more information.

Operating System

Another factor in the environment that affects performance is the operating system. This is not to claim that one operating system is better than another—just that you need to be aware that any operating system change, no matter how minor, can increase or decrease performance, sometimes dramatically. For example, when testing an application that applied a recommended Windows update, we saw performance plummet when the database driver made CharUpper calls. In our benchmark, 660 queries per second throughput dropped to a mere 11 queries per second—an astounding 98% decrease.

Often, we see performance differences when running the same benchmark on different operating systems. For example, on UNIX/Linux, a database driver may use mblen(), a standard C library function, to determine the length in bytes of a multibyte character; on Windows, it may use the equivalent function, IsDBCSLeadByte(). Our benchmarks have shown that when an application used mblen() on Linux, the processing of mblen() appropriated 30% to 35% of the total CPU time. When run on Windows, IsDBCSLeadByte() used only 3% to 5% of the total CPU time.

It's also helpful to know which byte order, or **endianness**[1], is used by the operating system on the database client to store multibyte data in memory, such as long integers, floating point numbers, and UTF-16 characters. The endianness

---

[1] The term endianness was adopted from the novel *Gulliver's Travels* by Jonathan Swift, first published in 1726. In the novel, a shipwrecked castaway, Gulliver, tangled with a sovereign state of diminutive Lilliputians who were split into two intractable factions: Big-Endians who opened their soft-boiled eggs at the larger end, and Little-Endians who broke their eggs at the smaller end.

of the operating system is determined by the processor that the operating system runs on. Processors use either of the following byte-order conventions:

- **Big endian** machines store data in memory "big-end" first. The first byte is the biggest (most significant).
- **Little endian** machines store data in memory "little-end" first. The first byte is the smallest (least significant).

For example, let's consider the integer 56789652, which is 0x03628a94 in hexadecimal. On a big endian machine, the 4 bytes in memory at address 0x18000 start with the leftmost hexadecimal digit. In contrast, on a little endian machine, the 4 bytes start with the rightmost hexadecimal digit.

Big Endian

```
18000  18001  18002  18003
0x03   0x62   0x8a   0x94
```

Little Endian

```
18000  18001  18002  18003
0x94   0x8a   0x62   0x03
```

Intel's 80x86 processors and their clones are little endian. Sun Microsystem's SPARC, Motorola's 68K, and the PowerPC families are big endian. Java Virtual Machines (JVMs) are big endian as well. Some processors even have a bit in the register that allows you to select which endianness you want the processor to use.

Performance Tip

If possible, match the endianness of the operating system on the database client to that of the database server. If they match, the database driver doesn't need to perform extra work to convert the byte order of multibyte data.

For example, suppose you have an accounting application that allows you to prepare financial statements such as balance sheets, income statements, cash flows, and general ledger accounts. The application runs on Windows XP and retrieves data from a Microsoft SQL Server database running on Windows NT. The database driver doesn't need to convert the byte order of long integers because the exchange between the machines is a match: little endian to little endian. What if you installed the application on a UNIX operating system running on a Solaris machine? You would see a drop in performance because the database driver must convert long integers retrieved from the database server from little endian to big endian, as shown in Figure 4-5. Similarly, if your application runs on a Windows machine and the database server switched to a UNIX operating system running on a Solaris machine, the database driver would need to perform byte-order conversion for long integers because of the mismatch. In many cases, you can't do anything about a mismatch, but it's helpful to know that, when all other things are equal, an endianness mismatch impacts performance.

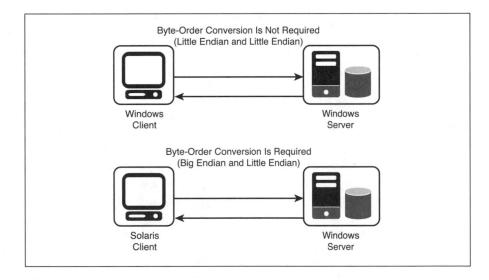

Figure 4-5   Endianness of processor determines whether byte-order conversion is required

To complicate matters, the database system doesn't always send data in the endianness of the operating system of the database server machine. Some database systems always send data either in big endian or little endian. Others send data using the same endianness of the database server machine. Still others send data using the same endianness of the database client machine. Table 4-1 lists the endianness that some common database systems use to send data.

Table 4-1   Endianness Database Systems Use to Send Data

Database Systems	Endianness
DB2	Endianness of database server machine
MySQL	Little endian
Oracle	Big endian
Microsoft SQL Server	Little endian
Sybase ASE	Endianness of database client machine

For example, suppose your application connects to an Oracle database that runs on a Windows machine. Oracle, which typically sends data big endian, must accommodate the little endian operating system it runs on and convert the byte order of multibyte data. Once again, you may not be able to change the endianness of your database client, database server, and database system to align, but it's helpful to know how endianness impacts performance if you have a choice.

Network

If your database application communicates to the database system over the network, which is part of the database middleware, you need to understand the performance implications of the network. In this section, we describe those performance implications and provide guidelines for dealing with them.

Database Protocol Packets

To request and retrieve information, database drivers and database servers transfer **database protocol packets** over a network (typically, TCP/IP).[2] Each database vendor defines a protocol for communication with the database system, a format that only that database system understands. For example, Microsoft SQL Server uses communication encoded with the Tabular Data Stream (TDS) protocol, and IBM DB2 uses communication encoded with the Distributed Relational Database Architecture (DRDA) protocol.

The way database drivers communicate to the database depends on their architecture. Some database drivers communicate to the database server directly using a database-specific protocol. Other drivers communicate using a driver-specific protocol that is translated into a database-specific protocol by a server component. Still other drivers require database vendor client libraries to com-

---

[2] If an application is running on the same machine as the database, the database driver uses the network in a loop-back mode or does not use the network at all and communicates directly with the database using shared memory.

municate with the database server. See the section, "Database Driver Architecture," page 55, for more information about database driver architecture.

When an application makes a standards-based API request, such as executing a `Select` statement to retrieve data, the database driver transforms that API request into zero, one, or multiple requests to the database server. The database driver[3] packages the requests into database protocol packets and sends them to the database server, as shown in Figure 4-6. The database server also uses database protocol packets to transfer the requested data to the driver.

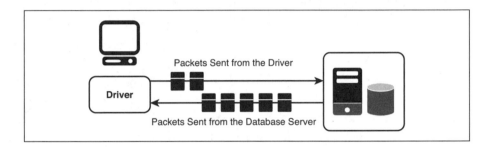

Figure 4-6   Database protocol packets

One important principle to understand: The relationship between application API requests and the number of database protocol packets sent to the database is not one to one. For example, if an ODBC application fetches result set rows one at a time using the `SQLFetch` function, not every execution of `SQLFetch` results in database protocol packets being sent to or from the database. Most drivers optimize retrieving results from the database by prefetching multiple rows at a time. If the requested result set row already exists in a driver result set cache because the driver retrieved it as an optimization on a previous `SQLFetch` execution, a network round trip to the database server would be unnecessary.

This book repeatedly demonstrates that database application performance improves when communication between the database driver and the database is optimized. With this in mind, one question you should always ask is this: How can I reduce the amount of information that is communicated between the database driver and the database? One important factor for this optimization is the size of database protocol packets.

The size of database protocol packets sent by the database driver to the database server must be equal to or less than the maximum database protocol packet size allowed by the database server. For example, if the database server accepts a

---

[3] Generally, we state that the database driver sends the database protocol packets to the database server. However, for drivers that have a client-based architecture, this task is performed by the database client (Net8 for Oracle, for example).

maximum packet size of 64KB, the database driver must send packets of 64KB or less. Typically, the larger the packet size, the better the performance, because fewer packets are needed to communicate between the driver and the database. Fewer packets means fewer network round trips to and from the database.

> ### Note
>
> Although most database applications experience better performance when sending and receiving fewer packets, this is not always the case, as explained in the section, "Configuring Packet Size," page 92.

For example, if the database driver uses a packet size of 32KB and the database server's packet size is configured for 64KB, the database server must limit its packet size to the smaller 32KB packet size used by the driver. As shown in Figure 4-7, this increases the number of packets sent over the network to retrieve the same amount of data to the client.

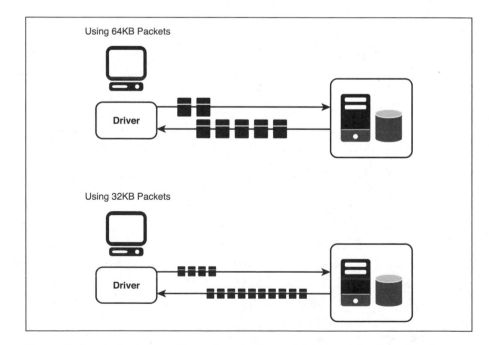

Figure 4-7   Packet size affects the number of database protocol packets required

The increase in the number of packets also means an increase in packet overhead. High packet overhead reduces throughput, or the amount of data that is transferred from sender to receiver over a period of time.

Why does packet overhead reduce throughput? Each packet stores extra bytes of information in the packet header, which limits the amount of data that can be transported in each packet. The smaller the packet size, the more packets are required to transport data. For example, a 64KB packet with a packet header of 30 bytes equals a total of three 32KB packets, each with 30-byte packet headers, as shown in Figure 4-8. The extra CPU required to disassemble packets for transport and reassemble them when they reach their destination reduces the overall transmission speed of the raw data. Fewer packets require less disassembly and reassembly, and ultimately, use less CPU.

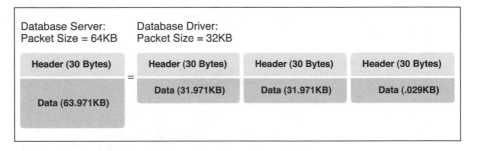

Figure 4-8   64KB database protocol packets compared to 32KB packets

Network Packets

Once database protocol packets are created, the database driver hands over the packets to TCP/IP for transfer to the database server. TCP/IP transfers the data in **network packets**. If the size of the database protocol packet is larger than the defined size of the network packet, TCP/IP breaks up the communication into even smaller network packets for transmission over the network and reassembles them at their destination.

Think of it like this: The database protocol packet is like a case of diet soda, which can be too difficult to carry over a long distance. TCP/IP breaks up that case into four 6 packs, or network packets, that can be easily carried over the network. When all four 6 packs reach their destination, they are reassembled into a case.

Similar to database protocol packets, the fewer the network packets, the better the performance. In contrast to database protocol packets, you can't configure the size of network packets.

Each network node (any machine connected to the network such as a client, server, router, and so on) has at least one network adapter for each network it connects to. The network packet size is determined by a **maximum transmission unit (MTU)** setting[4] for the network adapter in the operating system of the sending network node. The MTU is the maximum packet size that can be sent across a particular network link and is a characteristic of the network type. By default, the MTU setting is set to the MTU of the network type. You can set the MTU setting to another value, but that value cannot exceed the MTU of the network type.

For example, if the network packet size is 1500 bytes (MTU for Ethernet networks), TCP/IP breaks up the database protocol packet into as many 1500-byte network packets as needed to transfer the data across the network, as shown in Figure 4-9.

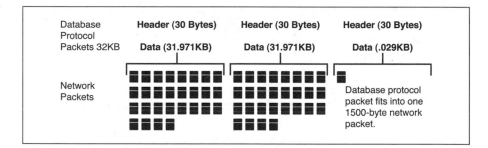

Figure 4-9   Database protocol packets divided into network packets

See the section, "Understanding Maximum Transmission Unit (MTU)," page 99, for details about how MTU affects network packets.

Database drivers and database servers only deal with database protocol packets, not network packets. Once network packets reach their destination, such as a database server, the operating system of the database server reassembles them into database protocol packets that deliver the communication to the database. To understand how this happens, let's take a closer look at network packets and how a network such as TCP/IP works.

Like a busy highway with a limited number of lanes, a network has a limited amount of bandwidth to handle network traffic between computers. By breaking up communication into network packets, TCP/IP can control the flow of traffic.

---

[4] The name of this setting depends on the operating system. Refer to your operating system documentation for details.

Like cars merging onto a highway, network packets can merge into traffic along with packets sent from other computers instead of hogging the road, so to speak.

The header of each network packet contains information about the following:

- Where the network packet comes from
- Where the network packet is going
- How the network packet will be reassembled with other network packets into a database protocol packet
- How to check the network packet content for errors

Because each network packet essentially contains its own shipping instructions, not all network packets associated with a single message may travel the same path. As traffic conditions change, network packets may be dynamically routed through different paths in the network. For example, if Path A is overloaded with traffic, network packets may be routed through Path B, reducing the congestion bottleneck as shown in Figure 4-10.

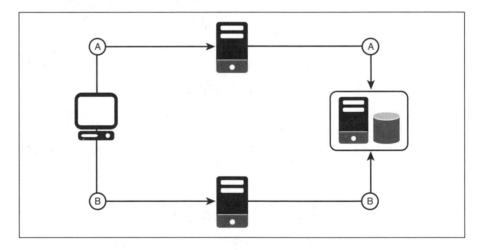

Figure 4-10   Network packets may travel different paths as a result of dynamic routing

Network packets can even arrive at their destination out of sequence. For example, network packets traveling Path B may arrive at their destination before those traveling on Path A. When all packets reach their destination, the operating system of the receiving computer reassembles the network packets into a database protocol packet.

Configuring Packet Size

Remember that larger packet sizes typically provide the best performance because fewer packets are needed to retrieve data, and fewer packets means fewer network round trips to and from the database. Therefore, it's important to use a database driver that allows you to configure the packet size of database protocol packets. See the section, "Runtime Performance Tuning Options," page 62, for more information about performance tuning options to look for in a database driver. In addition, many database servers can be configured to use packet sizes that are larger than the default.

If network packets are really the way that data is transported over the network and the MTU of the network controls the size of network packets, why does a larger database protocol packet size improve performance? Let's compare the following examples. In both examples, a database driver sends 25KB of data to the database server, but Example B uses a larger database protocol packet size than Example A. Because a larger database protocol packet size is used, the number of network round trips is reduced. More importantly, actual network traffic is reduced.

Example A: Database Protocol Packet Size = 4KB

Using a 4KB database protocol packet, as shown in Figure 4-11, the database driver creates seven 4KB database protocol packets (assuming a 30-byte packet header) to send 25KB of data to the database server (6 packets transporting 3.971KB of data and 1 packet transporting 0.199KB of data).

Figure 4-11   4KB database protocol packet size

If the MTU of the network path is 1500 bytes, as shown in Figure 4-12, the database protocol packets are divided into network packets for transport across the network (total of 19 network packets). The first 6 database protocol packets are each divided into three 1500-byte network packets. The data contained in the last database protocol packet fits within one 1500-byte network packet.

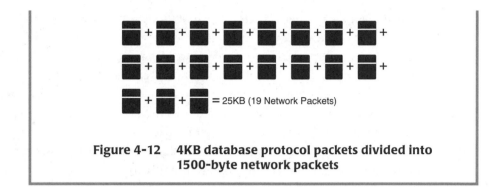

**Figure 4-12   4KB database protocol packets divided into
1500-byte network packets**

Now let's look at Example B, which uses a larger database protocol packet
size.

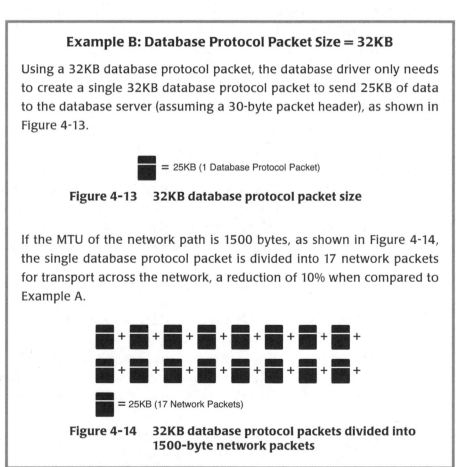

Example B: Database Protocol Packet Size = 32KB

Using a 32KB database protocol packet, the database driver only needs
to create a single 32KB database protocol packet to send 25KB of data
to the database server (assuming a 30-byte packet header), as shown in
Figure 4-13.

Figure 4-13   32KB database protocol packet size

If the MTU of the network path is 1500 bytes, as shown in Figure 4-14,
the single database protocol packet is divided into 17 network packets
for transport across the network, a reduction of 10% when compared to
Example A.

**Figure 4-14   32KB database protocol packets divided into
1500-byte network packets**

Although a larger packet size is typically the best choice for performance, this isn't always the case. If your application sends queries that only retrieve small result sets, a small packet size can work well. For example, an ATM banking application typically sends and receives many packets that contain a small amount of data, such as a withdrawal amount, a deposit amount, and a new balance. A result set that contains only one or two rows of data may not completely fill a larger packet. In this case, using larger packets wouldn't improve performance. In contrast, a reporting application that retrieves large result sets with thousands of rows performs best when using larger packets.

Performance Tip

If your application sends queries that retrieve large amounts of data, tune your database server packet size to the maximum size, and tune your database driver to match the maximum size used by the database server.

Analyzing the Network Path

Often, we talk about database access as if the client is always local to the database server, perhaps in the same building connected by a LAN. However, in today's distributed computing environment, the reality is that a user working from a client desktop in New York may retrieve data stored in a database that is located in California, or Europe, for that matter.

For example, a database application may send a data request that travels across a LAN, often through one or multiple routers, across a WAN, and through more routers to reach the target database. Because the world's most popular WAN is the Internet, an application may also need to communicate through one or multiple Internet service provider (ISP) routers. Then the data that is retrieved from the database must travel back along a similar path before users even see it on their desktops.

Whether your database application accesses a database server locally on a LAN or your data requests follow a more complicated path, how do you determine if network packets associated with your database application are using the most efficient path?

You can use the tracert command (Windows) and the traceroute command (UNIX/Linux) to find out which network nodes the network packets travel through on their way to a destination. In addition, by default, these commands display a sampling of the **latency**, the time delay it takes to make a network round trip to each node along the traced path.

Example A: Using the `tracert` Command on Windows

This example traces the path that network packets take from a database client in North America to a database server in Europe. Let's execute the `tracert` command:

```
tracert belgserver-01
```

Notice that the trace report shows that network packets make three network hops. (The fourth network node in the list is the destination.)

```
Tracing route to belgserver-01 (10.145.11.263)
over a maximum of 30 hops:

  1      <1 ms      <1 ms      <1 ms      10.40.11.215
  2       1 ms       3 ms       3 ms      10.40.11.291
  3     113 ms     113 ms     113 ms      10.98.15.222
  4     120 ms     117 ms     119 ms      10.145.16.263
```

Example B: Using the `traceroute` Command on UNIX/Linux

This example traces the path that network packets take on the return trip. Let's execute the `traceroute` command:[5]

```
traceroute nc-sking
```

Similar to the trace report shown in Example A, this trace report shows that network packets make three network hops.

```
Traceroute to nc-sking (10.40.4.263), 30 hops max,
40 byte packets

  1     10.139.11.215     <1 ms     <1 ms     <1 ms
  2     10.139.11.291      2 ms      1 ms      1 ms
  3     10.40.11.254     182 ms    190 ms    194 ms
  4     10.40.4.263      119 ms    112 ms    120 ms
```

---

[5] The traceroute command supports different options depending on your operating system. Refer to the command reference of your operating system documentation for command options.

After you have traced the paths going to and from the database server, let's look at what the trace report can tell you.

- Is the path taken by network packets from the client to the database server comparable to that taken on the return trip? The physical path through the network may be different in each direction, but is one path significantly slower than the other? For example, if a particular router is a bottleneck because of network congestion, you may want to change your network topology so that network packets can take a different path.

- On either path, how many network hops separate the client and database server? Can any of these network hops be eliminated? For example, if the client is assigned to a different network subnet than the database server, can the machines be reassigned to the same subnet? See the following section for details about reducing network hops.

- On either path, does packet fragmentation occur? See "Avoiding Network Packet Fragmentation," page 98, for details about detecting packet fragmentation and strategies for avoiding it.

Reducing Network Hops and Contention

There's a saying that goes something like this: "The road to success is not straight." However, when referring to data access, this adage does not necessarily apply. Shorter network paths with fewer network hops typically provide better performance than longer paths with many network hops because each intermediate network node must process each network packet that passes through that node on its way to its destination.

This processing involves checking the packet header for destination information and looking up the destination in its routing tables to determine the best path to take. In addition, each intermediate network node checks the size of the packet to determine whether the packet needs to be fragmented. On longer paths, for example, from LAN to WAN, a data request is more likely to encounter varying MTU sizes that cause packet fragmentation (see "Avoiding Network Packet Fragmentation," page 98).

A database application typically shares the network with other types of network traffic. At any one time, different users may request files and Internet content, send e-mail, use streaming video/voice, perform backups, and so on. When the traffic load is light, the network operates at top form and performance may be great. However, when large numbers of users request connections and make other network requests at the same time, the network can become overloaded with too many network packets. If network packets sent by your database application pass through an intermediate network node that is overloaded with network traffic, application performance can be negatively affected.

Sometimes network congestion from normal business traffic is made worse by poorly planned network topology or bandwidth changes. For example, if network packets are forced to pass through a single gateway router to reach their destination, packets must wait in the router's queue for processing, causing a packet backup at the gateway. In this case, is it possible to change your network topology by adding additional router access to the destination network? Similarly, differences in bandwidth from LAN to WAN can cause a communication slowdown, much like a 4-lane highway merging into a 2-lane highway.

One way to reduce network hops and network contention is to create a dedicated path for your database application using a **private data network**, which can be implemented using a network switch to a dedicated network adapter, a leased T1 connection, or some other type of dedicated connection. For example, as shown in Figure 4-15, clients have full public access to the corporate network, including e-mail and the Internet, while enjoying private direct access to the database server.

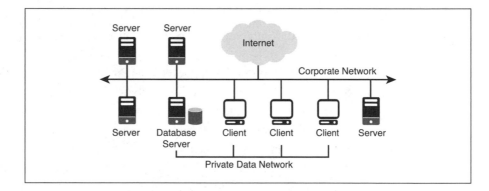

Figure 4-15   Private data network

Even when the client and database server are in proximity to one another, don't assume that network packets take a direct point-to-point path. For example, consider the case of a real-world company whose business depended on critical bulk updates that executed periodically during the course of the day. Performance was poor despite the fact that the client and database server machines were installed side by side in the same room.

The network path analysis revealed that when the application requested data, network packets associated with requests typically made as many as 17 network hops before reaching the database server. Although the client and database server machines resided in the same location, they were assigned to different corporate network subnets. In this case, reassigning the machines to the same network subnet reduced the number of network hops from 17 to 1, and the average response time for bulk updates decreased from 30 seconds to 5 seconds, an amazing performance gain of 500%.

Note

A **virtual private network (VPN)** emulates a private data network for applications that transfer data over the Internet. It doesn't eliminate network hops but provides a secure extension of a private network and reduces network contention.

Avoiding Network Packet Fragmentation

Before we go forward, let's recap some of what we've already learned about how database drivers and database servers use the network to request and send data:

- Database drivers and database servers communicate by sending database protocol packets.
- If the size of the database protocol packet is larger than the defined size of the network packet, TCP/IP divides the database protocol packets into as many network packets as needed for transmission over the network.
- The MTU is the maximum network packet size that can be sent across a particular network link and is a characteristic of the network type.
- Packet size is important for both types of packets because the fewer the packets, the better the performance.

Packet fragmentation occurs when a network packet is too large to traverse a network link as determined by the network link's MTU. For example, if a network link's MTU is 1500 bytes, it cannot transport a 1700-byte packet. An oversized packet must be divided into smaller packets that are able to traverse the link, or the communication must be re-sent using smaller packets.

In most modern systems, packet fragmentation is not automatic but occurs as a result of a process known as **path MTU discovery**, a technique for determining the **path MTU**, which is the lowest MTU of any network node along a particular network route. Because packet fragmentation requires additional communication between network nodes to negotiate the correct packet size and significant CPU processing to divide communication into smaller packets and reassemble them, it degrades performance. The following sections explain why packet fragmentation has a negative impact on performance and provide guidelines for detecting and resolving packet fragmentation.

Understanding Maximum Transmission Unit (MTU)

MTU is the maximum packet size that can be sent across a particular network link as determined by the network type. See Table 4-2 for the MTU values of some common network types.

Table 4-2   MTU Values of Common Network Types

Network	MTU
16 MB/second Token Ring	17914
4 MB/second Token Ring	4464
FDDI	4352
Ethernet	1500
IEEE 802.3/802.2	1492
PPPoE (WAN miniport)	1480
X.25	576

Each network node has one or multiple network adapters installed, one for each network it connects to. The operating system on each node provides an MTU setting for each network adapter. The MTU setting determines the size of network packets sent from that node. By default, this MTU setting is set to the MTU of the network type and can be set to another value, but that value cannot exceed the MTU of the network type. For example, if a network node is connected to an Ethernet network, the MTU setting for that machine's network adapter must be set to a value of 1500 (MTU for Ethernet networks) or less.

How does MTU affect network packets? Let's consider a simple example where only two network nodes, a client and database server, send and receive network packets as shown Figure 4-16. In this case, Node A has an MTU setting of 1500, meaning that it sends 1500-byte packets across the network to Node B.

Similarly, Node B has an MTU setting of 1500 and sends 1500-byte packets on the return trip to Node A.

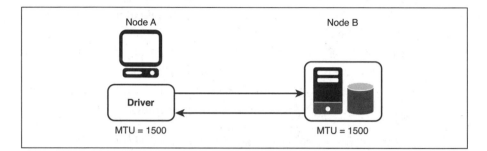

Figure 4-16   Simple example of MTU

Now let's look at a more complex example where network packets are routed by an intermediate network node to the database server, as shown in Figure 4-17. In this case, Node A has an MTU setting of 1500, Node B has an MTU setting of 1492, and Node C has an MTU setting of 1500.

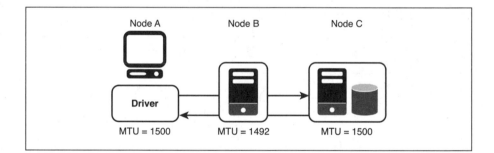

Figure 4-17   Complex example of MTU

The maximum packet size that can be sent across the network depends on the network link, or the part of the network, that the packet is being sent across, as shown in Table 4-3.

Table 4-3   Maximum Packet Size

Network Link	Maximum Packet Size
Node A to Node B	1500 bytes
Node B to Node C	1492 bytes
Node C to Node B	1500 bytes
Node B to Node A	1492 bytes

If a network node receives an oversized network packet, the network node discards that packet and sends a message to the sending network node with information about a packet size that will fit. The sending network node resends the original communication, dividing it into smaller packets. The communication required to notify the sending network node that fragmentation must occur and the resending of the communication in smaller packets increases traffic along that network route. In addition, significant CPU processing is required to divide the communication into smaller packets for transport and reassemble them when they reach their destination.

To understand how this process works, let's step through the example shown in Figure 4-18.

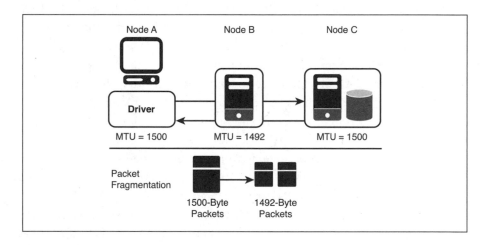

Figure 4-18   Packet fragmentation example

1. As the result of a data request, Node A sends multiple 1500-byte packets to Node C.
2. Each time Node B receives a 1500-byte packet, it discards the packet and sends a message to Node A, telling Node A that it cannot pass along a packet larger than 1492 bytes.
3. Node A resends each communication, breaking it into as many 1492-byte packets as needed.
4. When Node B receives each 1492-byte packet, it passes the packets to Node C.

> **Performance Tip**
>
> In most cases, you can avoid packet fragmentation by configuring the MTU setting of the client and the database server to be the same as the path MTU, the lowest MTU of any network node along the path. For example, using the scenario in Figure 4-18, if you configure the MTU setting of the client and database server to be a value of 1492, packet fragmentation would not occur.

VPNs Magnify Packet Fragmentation

Configuring the MTU setting to the path MTU doesn't always avoid packet fragmentation. For example, when VPN tunneling is used, the problem of packet fragmentation is magnified because of additional packet overhead.

VPNs are routinely used to connect remote machines over the Internet to corporate LANs, creating a secure path between two endpoints. Communication within the VPN path is encrypted so that other users of the Internet cannot intercept and inspect or modify communications. The security protocol that performs the encryption, typically Internet Protocol Security Protocol (IPSec), encapsulates, or wraps, each network packet in a new, larger packet while adding its own IPSec headers to the new packet. Often, the larger packet size caused by this encapsulation results in packet fragmentation.

For example, suppose the MTU of a VPN network link is 1500 bytes and the MTU setting of the VPN client is set to the path MTU, a value of 1500. Although this configuration is ideal for LAN access, it presents a problem for VPN users. IPSec cannot encapsulate a 1500-byte packet because the packet is already as large as the VPN network link will accept. In this case, the original communication is re-sent using smaller packets that IPSec can encapsulate. Changing the MTU setting on the client to a value of 1420 or less gives adequate leeway for IPSec encapsulation and avoids packet fragmentation.

> **Performance Tip**
>
> A one-size-fits-all MTU doesn't exist. If most of your users are VPN users, change the MTU setting along the network path to accommodate your VPN users. However, remember that reducing the MTU for your LAN users will cause their application performance to suffer.

LAN versus WAN

Because communication across a WAN typically requires more network hops than communication across a LAN, your application is more likely to encounter varying MTU sizes, resulting in packet fragmentation. In addition, if data has to travel over VPN within a WAN, packet fragmentation further reduces the MTU size. If you are unable to avoid packet fragmentation by setting the client and the database server to the path MTU (see "Understanding Maximum Transmission Unit (MTU)," page 99), it becomes even more important to reduce the number of network round trips between the client and server to preserve performance.

Detecting and Resolving Network Packet Fragmentation

If you don't have privy knowledge of the MTUs of every network node along the network path, how can you tell if packet fragmentation occurs? Operating system commands, such as the ping command (Windows) and the traceroute command (UNIX/Linux), can help you determine if packets are being fragmented along a particular network path. In addition, with a little persistence and detective work, you can determine the optimal packet size for the network path, a size that doesn't require packet fragmentation.

For example, suppose your client is a Windows XP machine, and data requests are made from this machine to a UNIX database server located in London. You know from the following trace report that three network hops are involved to reach the server:

```
Tracing route to UK-server-03 [10.131.15.289]
over a maximum of 30 hops:

  1    <1 ms    <1 ms    <1 ms   10.30.4.241
  2    <1 ms    <1 ms    <1 ms   10.30.4.245
  3   112 ms   111 ms   111 ms   10.168.73.37
  4   113 ms   112 ms   116 ms   10.131.15.289
```

Therefore, the network path looks similar to the configuration shown in Figure 4-19. If the MTU of the client is set to a value of 1500, the client sends 1500-byte packets across the network. The MTU of the other network nodes is unknown.

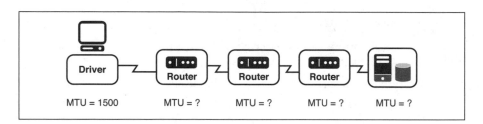

Figure 4-19   Network analysis of MTU

In the following examples, we use the ping (Windows) and traceroute (UNIX/Linux) commands to determine if packet fragmentation occurs along this network path for a 1500-byte packet, and we find the optimal packet size for the network path.

Example A: Detecting Packet Fragmentation on Windows

1. At a command prompt, enter the ping command to test the connection between the client and database server. The -f flag turns on a "do not fragment" (DF) field in the header of the packet, forcing the ping command to fail if the packet needs to be fragmented at any network node along the path. The -1 flag sets the packet size. For example:

   ```
   ping UK-server-03 -f -1 1500
   ```

   If packet fragmentation is needed, the ping command fails with the following message, which indicates that the packet was not fragmented because the DF field was set:

   ```
   Packet needs to be fragmented but DF set
   ```

2. Reissue the ping command repeatedly, each time lowering the size of the packet in logical increments (for example, 1500, 1475, 1450, 1425, 1400, and so on) until a message is returned indicating that the command was successful.

For example, the following code shows that the `ping` command was successful when executed with a packet size of 1370 bytes:

```
Pinging UK-server-03 [10.131.15.289] with 1370 bytes of
  data

Reply from 10.131.15.289: bytes=1370 time=128ms TTL=1
Reply from 10.131.15.289: bytes=1370 time=128ms TTL=1
Reply from 10.131.15.289: bytes=1370 time=128ms TTL=1
Reply from 10.131.15.289: bytes=1370 time=128ms TTL=1

Ping statistics for 10.131.15.289:
    Packets: Sent = 4, Received = 4, Lost = 0 (0% loss)
Approximate round trip times in milli-seconds:
    Minimum = 128ms, Maximum = 128ms, Average = 128ms
```

3. Once you have a packet size that works for the entire path, configure the MTU setting of the client and database server to that value (if possible).

Example B: Detecting Packet Fragmentation on UNIX/Linux

1. At a prompt, enter the `traceroute` command.[6] The -F flag forces the command to fail if packet fragmentation occurs. The integer sets the packet size.

    ```
    traceroute UK-server-03 -F 1500
    ```

    If packet fragmentation occurs, the command fails with the following message:

    ```
    !F
    ```

2. Reissue the `traceroute` command repeatedly, each time lowering the size of the packet in logical increments (for example, 1500, 1475, 1450, 1425, 1400, and so on) until a message is returned indicating that the `traceroute` command was successful.

---

[6] The `traceroute` command supports different options depending on your operating system. Refer to the command reference of your operating system documentation for command options.

> The following example shows that the traceroute command was successful when executed with a packet size of 1370 bytes:
>
> ```
> Traceroute to UK-server-03 (10.131.15.289), 4 hops max,
> 1370 byte packets
>
>     1    10.139.11.215      <1 ms      <1 ms      <1 ms
>     2    10.139.11.291       2 ms       1 ms       1 ms
>     3    10.40.11.254      182 ms     190 ms     194 ms
>     4    10.40.4.263       119 ms     112 ms     120 ms
> ```

Increasing Network Bandwidth

Bandwidth is the capacity of a network connection to transport network packets. The greater the capacity, the more likely that good performance will result, although overall performance also depends on factors such as latency. Increasing bandwidth is similar to widening a congested 2-lane highway into a 4- or 6-lane highway. The highway can handle more traffic, relieving bottlenecks.

Upgrading to a large-capacity network adapter is one of the easiest and cheapest investments you can make to improve the performance of your network. While bandwidth capacity has dramatically increased over the years, the costs associated with the hardware that provide it have dramatically fallen. Today, you can easily purchase a 1GB network adapter for less than $40. Assuming there are no other network constraints, upgrading from a 100Mbps network adapter to a 1GB network adapter can result in as much as a 7% to 10% performance gain. For the price and ease of effort, that's a great return on investment.

Hardware

Clearly, how your database is configured can conserve or consume hardware resources, but our focus in this section is on how database driver and specific application design and coding techniques can optimize your hardware resources and relieve performance bottlenecks in the following hardware resources:

- Memory
- Disk
- CPU (processor)
- Network adapter

In addition, we'll talk about how a hot new trend in database computing known as virtualization can magnify hardware-related performance problems.

Memory

A computer has a finite amount of **Random Access Memory (RAM)** or physical memory, and, as a general rule, more RAM is better. As the computer runs its processes, it stores code and data for quick access in blocks of RAM known as **pages**. The amount of data that can be stored on a single page depends on the processor platform.

When a computer runs out of RAM, it takes advantage of virtual memory to ensure that work processes smoothly. **Virtual memory** allows the operating system to free up space in RAM by copying pages stored in RAM that have not been used recently into a file that resides on disk. This file is called a **page file (swap file)**, and the process of writing to the file is known as **paging**. If an application needs that page again for any reason, the operating system swaps it back out of the page file into RAM.

When RAM is being used to capacity, paging occurs more frequently. Because disk I/O is much slower than RAM, excessive paging causes a drastic performance slowdown. Excessive paging also can interfere with other processes that require the same disk, causing disk contention (see the section, "Disk," page 110, for more information). In fact, memory bottlenecks often masquerade as disk issues. If you suspect that the disk is being read from or written to excessively, the first thing you should do is rule out a memory bottleneck.

A **memory leak** can also result in excessive paging, steadily using up RAM, and then virtual memory, until the page file size reaches its maximum. Depending on how critical a memory leak is, virtual memory can be used up within a period of weeks, days, or hours. Memory leaks often are created when applications use resources, but they don't release the resources when they are no longer required.

Table 4-4 lists some common causes for memory bottlenecks and their recommended solutions.

Table 4-4   Causes and Solutions of Memory Bottlenecks

Cause	Solution
Insufficient physical memory (RAM)	Add more RAM.
Poorly optimized application code or database driver causing excessive memory use	Analyze and tune your application or database driver to minimize memory use. See "Tuning Your Application and Database Driver to Minimize Memory Use," page 109, for more information.

Detecting Memory Bottlenecks

The primary symptom of a memory bottleneck is a sustained, high rate of page faults. A **page fault** occurs when an application requests a page, but the system can't find the page at the requested location in RAM.

Two types of page faults can occur:

- **Soft page faults** can occur when the requested page is located elsewhere in RAM. A soft page fault's effect on performance is negligible because disk I/O is not required to find the page.
- **Hard page faults** occur when the requested page is located in virtual memory. The operating system must swap the page out of virtual memory and place it back into RAM. Because of the disk I/O involved, hard page faults slow performance if they occur frequently.

To detect a memory bottleneck, gather information about your system to answer the following questions:

- **How often are requested pages triggering a page fault?** This information gives you an idea of the number of total page faults, both soft and hard page faults, that occur over a period of time.
- **How many pages are retrieved from disk to satisfy page faults?** Compare this information to the preceding information to determine how many hard page faults occur out of the total number of page faults.
- **Does the memory use of any individual application or process climb steadily and never level off?** If so, that application or process is probably leaking memory. In pooled environments, detecting memory leaks is more difficult because pooled connections and prepared statements hold onto memory and can make it appear as if your application is leaking memory even when it isn't. If you run into memory issues when using connection pooling, try tuning the connection pool to reduce the number of connections in the pool. Similarly, try tuning the statement pool to reduce the number of prepared statements in the pool.

For information about tools that can help you troubleshoot memory use, see "The Environment," page 272.

Tuning Your Application and Database Driver to Minimize Memory Use

Here are some general guidelines to minimize memory use:

- **Reduce the number of open connections and prepared statements**—Open connections use memory on the client and on the database server. Make sure that your application closes connections immediately after it's finished with them. If your application uses connection pooling and the database server (or application server) starts to experience memory problems, try tuning the connection pool to reduce the number of connections in the pool. Alternatively, if your database system and database driver supports reauthentication, you may be able to use it to minimize the number of connections required to service your application.

    Using statement pooling with connection pooling complicates the memory situation exponentially. On the database client, client resources that correlate to each pooled statement are stored in memory. On the database server, each pooled connection has a statement pool associated with it that's also maintained in memory. For example, if your application uses 5 pooled connections along with 20 prepared statements, each statement pool associated with those 5 connections may potentially contain all 20 prepared statements. That's 5 connections $\times$ 20 prepared statements = 100 prepared statements, all maintained in memory on the database server. If you use statement pooling and the client or database server starts to experience memory problems, try tuning the statement pool to reduce the number of prepared statements in the pool. See "Using Statement Pooling with Connection Pooling," page 238, for more information.

- **Do not leave transactions active for too long**—The database must write every modification made by a transaction to a log that is stored in memory on the database server. If your application uses transactions that update large amounts of data without committing modifications at regular intervals, the application can consume a substantial amount of database memory. Committing a transaction flushes the contents of the log and releases memory used by the database server. See "Managing Commits in Transactions," page 22, for guidelines on committing active transactions.

- **Avoid retrieving large amounts of data from the database server**—When the database driver retrieves data from the database server, it typically stores that data in a result set that is maintained in memory on the client. If your application executes queries that retrieve millions of rows, memory can be used up quickly. Always formulate your SQL queries to retrieve only the data you need.

Similarly, retrieving long data—such as large XML data, long varchar/text, long varbinary, Clobs, and Blobs—can be problematic for memory. Suppose your application executes a query that retrieves hundreds of rows, and those rows happen to contain a Blob. If the database system does not support true LOBs, the database driver will probably emulate this functionality and retrieve the entire Blob across the network and place it in memory on the client. See "Data Retrieval," page 30, for more information.

* **Avoid scrollable cursors unless you know your database system fully supports them**—Scrollable cursors let you go both forward and backward through a result set. Because of limited support for server-side scrollable cursors in many database systems, database drivers often emulate scrollable cursors, storing rows from a scrollable result set in memory on the client or application server. Large scrollable result sets can easily consume memory. See "Using Scrollable Cursors," page 36, for more information.

* **If memory is a limiting factor on your database server, application server, or client, tune your database driver to compensate for that limiting factor**—Some database drivers provide tuning options that allow you to choose how and where some memory-intensive operations are performed. For example, if your client excessively pages to disk because of large result sets, you may want to decrease the size of the fetch buffer, the amount of memory used by the driver to store results retrieved from the database server. Decreasing the fetch buffer size reduces memory consumption, but it means more network round trips, so you need to be aware of the trade-off.

Disk

When an operation reads or writes to disk, performance suffers because disk access is extremely slow. The easiest way to avoid accessing the disk (or disk controller in the case of multiple disks) is to use memory. For example, consider the case of an application that retrieves large result sets. If your client or application server has ample memory and your database driver supports this tuning option, you could increase the size of the fetch buffer on the client to avoid the result set being written to disk. However, remember that if you routinely stretch memory to its limit, paging to disk occurs more frequently. In addition to slowing performance, excessive paging can interfere with other processes that require the same disk, causing disk contention.

Disk contention occurs when multiple processes or threads try to access the same disk simultaneously. The disk limits how many processes/threads can access it and how much data it can transfer. When these limits are reached, processes may have to wait to access the disk. Often, CPU activity is suspended until disk access completes.

If you suspect that disk access occurs more often than it should, the first thing you should do is rule out a memory bottleneck. Once you've ruled out a memory bottleneck, make sure your application avoids unnecessary disk reads and writes so that disk contention rarely happens.

Performance Tip

As a general rule, your application should only access the disk in the following cases: to retrieve database metadata into memory and to write changes to disk, such as in the case of committing transactions.

Table 4-5 lists some common causes for disk bottlenecks and their recommended solutions.

Table 4-5   Causes and Solutions of Disk Bottlenecks

Cause	Solution
Excessive paging caused by a memory bottleneck	Detect and resolve the memory bottleneck. See "Memory," page 107, for more information.
Excessive reads or writes to disk, possibly causing disk contention	Analyze and tune your application to avoid unnecessary disk reads or writes. See "Tuning Your Application to Avoid Unnecessary Disk Reads/Writes," page 112, for more information.

Detecting Disk Bottlenecks

To detect a disk bottleneck, gather information about your system to answer the following questions:

- **Is excessive paging occurring?** A memory bottleneck can resemble a disk bottleneck so it's important to rule out a memory problem before you make any disk improvements. See "Detecting Memory Bottlenecks," page 108, for information about detecting memory bottlenecks.

- **How often is the disk busy?** If your disk has a sustained rate of disk activity of 85% or more for a sustained period of time and a persistent disk queue, you may have a disk bottleneck.

Tuning Your Application to Avoid Unnecessary Disk Reads/Writes

Here are some general guidelines to help your application avoid unnecessary disk reads and writes:

- **Avoid stretching memory to its limit**—Once memory is used up, paging to disk occurs. See "Memory," page 107, for information about detecting and avoiding a memory bottleneck.
- **Avoid using auto-commit mode for transactions**—When using transactions, the database writes every modification made by a transaction to a log that is stored in database memory. A commit tells the database to make those changes permanent. In response, the database writes the changes to disk and flushes the log. In auto-commit mode, transactions are committed automatically by the database, or if the database doesn't support auto-commit mode, by the database driver. You can minimize disk access by using manual commits. See "Managing Commits in Transactions," page 22, for more information.

CPU (Processor)

The CPU is the brain of your database server (or application server), performing most of the calculations and logic required to retrieve data or modify database tables. When the CPU is overly busy, it processes work slowly and may even have jobs waiting in its run queue. When the CPU is too busy to respond to work requests, performance of the database server or application server rapidly hits a ceiling. For example, Figure 4-20 shows benchmark runs of the same driver on different machines with different CPU capacity. As you can see, when run on the machine that is not CPU-bound, performance steadily climbed. On a machine that is CPU bound, performance is capped by the CPU.

Table 4-6 lists some common causes for CPU bottlenecks and their recommended solutions.

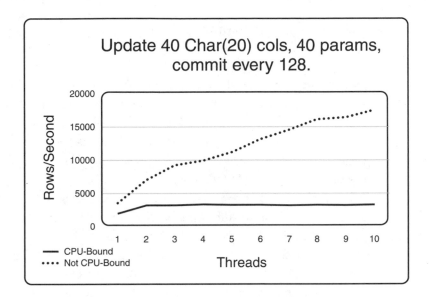

Figure 4-20   CPU-bound versus non-CPU-bound

Table 4-6   Causes and Solutions of CPU Bottlenecks

Cause	Solution
Insufficient CPU capacity	Add multiple processors or upgrade to a more powerful processor.
Inefficient database driver	See "Database Drivers," page 53, for information on why it's important to choose a good database driver.
Poorly optimized application code or database driver	Analyze and tune your application and database driver to minimize CPU use. See "Tuning Your Application or Database Driver to Minimize CPU Use," page 114, for more information.

Detecting CPU Bottlenecks

To detect a CPU bottleneck, gather information about your system to answer the following questions:

- **How much time does the CPU spend executing work?** If the processor is busy 80% or higher for sustained periods, it can be a source of trouble. If you detect high CPU use, drill down to individual processes to determine if any one application is using more than its fair share of CPU cycles. If so, look more closely at how that application is designed and coded as described in "Tuning Your Application or Database Driver to Minimize CPU Use," page 114.

• **How many processes or threads are waiting to be serviced in the CPU's run queue?** A single queue is used for CPU requests, even on computers with multiple processors. If all processors are busy, threads must wait until CPU cycles are free to perform work. Processes waiting in the queue for sustained periods indicate a CPU bottleneck.

• **What is the rate that processes or threads are switched by the operating system to perform work for other waiting threads?** A **context switch** is the process of storing and restoring the state (context) of a CPU so that multiple processes can share a single CPU resource. Each time the CPU stops running one process and starts running another, a context switch occurs. For example, if your application is waiting for a row lock to release so that it can update data, the operating system may switch the context so that the CPU can perform work on behalf of another application while your application is waiting for the lock to release. Context switching requires significant processor time, so excessive context switches and high CPU use tend to go hand in hand.

For information about tools that can help you troubleshoot CPU use, see Chapter 10, "Troubleshooting Performance Issues."

Tuning Your Application or Database Driver to Minimize CPU Use

Here are some general guidelines to help your application or database driver to minimize CPU use:

• **Maximize query plan reuse**—When a new SQL statement is sent to the database, the database compiles a query plan for that statement and stores it for future reference. Each time a SQL statement is submitted to the database, the database looks for a matching SQL statement and query plan. If a query plan isn't found, the database creates a new query plan for the statement. Each time the database creates a new query plan, it uses CPU cycles. To maximize query plan reuse, consider using statement pooling. For more information about statement pooling, see "Using Statement Pooling," page 236.

• **Ensure connection pools and statement pools are tuned correctly**—Pooling can conserve CPU if tuned correctly, but if not, your pooling environment may use more CPU than expected. As a general rule, when the database has to create a new connection or prepared statement, CPU processing becomes expensive. See Chapter 8, "Connection Pooling and Statement Pooling," for information about configuring your pooling environment.

- **Avoid context switching by reducing network round trips**—Each data request that results in a network round trip triggers a context switch. Context switching requires significant processor time, so excessive context switches and high CPU use tend to go hand in hand. Reducing the number of network round trips also reduces the number of context switches. Application design and coding practices that reduce network round trips include connection pooling, statement pooling, avoiding auto-commit mode in favor of manual commits, using local transactions instead of distributed transactions where appropriate, and using batches or arrays of parameters for bulk inserts.

- **Minimize data conversions**—Choose database drivers that convert data efficiently. For example, some database drivers don't support Unicode, a standard encoding that is used for multilingual character sets. If your database driver doesn't support Unicode, more data conversion is required to work with Unicode data, resulting in higher CPU use.

  In addition, choose data types that process efficiently. When you are working with data on a large scale, select the data type that can be processed most efficiently. Retrieving and returning certain data types across the network can increase or decrease network traffic. See "Choosing the Right Data Type," page 34, for details on which data types process more efficiently than others.

- **Be aware that emulated functionality can increase CPU use**—Database drivers sometimes emulate functionality if the database system doesn't support it. While this provides the benefit of interoperability, you should remember that emulated behavior typically uses more CPU because the database driver or the database must perform extra steps to satisfy the behavior. For example, if your application uses scrollable cursors against Oracle, which doesn't support scrollable cursors, CPU use on both the client/application server and database server will be higher than against a database system that does support scrollable cursors, such as DB2. For more information about the type of functionality that drivers emulate, see "Know Your Database System," page 47.

• **Use data encryption with caution**—Data encryption methods, such as SSL, are CPU-intensive because they require extra steps between the database driver and the database system, to negotiate and agree upon the encryption/decryption information to be used in addition to the process of encrypting the data. To limit the performance penalty associated with data encryption, consider establishing separate connections for encrypted and nonencrypted data. For example, one connection can use encryption for accessing sensitive data such as an individual's tax ID number, while the other connection can forgo encryption for data that is less sensitive, such as an individual's department and title. However, not all database systems allow this. With some database systems, such as Sybase ASE, either all connections to the database use encryption or none of them do. See "Data Encryption across the Network," page 39, for more information.

• **If CPU is a limiting factor on your database server, application server, or client, tune your database driver to compensate for that limiting factor**— Some database drivers provide tuning options that allow you to choose how and where some CPU-intensive operations are performed. For example, Sybase ASE creates stored procedures for prepared statements, a CPU-intensive operation to create the stored procedure, but not to execute it. If your application executes a prepared statement only once, not multiple times, the database server uses more CPU than necessary. Choosing a driver that allows you to tune whether Sybase ASE creates a stored procedure for a prepared statement could improve performance significantly by conserving CPU.

Network Adapter

Computers that are connected to a network have at least one network adapter that sends and receives network packets across the network. Network adapters are designed for a specific network type, such as Ethernet, token-ring, and so on. Differences in the speed of network adapters at either end of the network can cause performance issues. For example, a 64-bit network adapter sends data faster than a 32-bit network adapter can process it.

A sluggish network can indicate that you need more bandwidth, the capacity to send and receive network packets. Increasing bandwidth is similar to widening a congested 2-lane highway into a 4- or 6-lane highway. The highway can handle more traffic, relieving bottlenecks.

Table 4-7 lists some common causes for network bottlenecks and their recommended solutions.

Table 4-7   Causes and Solutions of Network Bottlenecks

Cause	Solution
Insufficient bandwidth	Add more network adapters or upgrade your network adapter. See "Increasing Network Bandwidth," page 106, for more information about upgrading your network adapter.
	Distribute client connections across multiple network adapters.
	Reduce network traffic by configuring the database driver to use the maximum database protocol packet size allowed by the database server. See "Configuring Packet Size," page 92, for more information.
Inefficient database driver	See "Database Drivers," page 53, for information on why it's important to choose a good database driver.
Poorly optimized application code or database driver	Analyze and tune your application and database driver to use the network efficiently. See "Tuning Your Application or Database Driver to Use the Network Efficiently," page 118, for more information.

Detecting a Network Bottleneck

What is the rate at which network packets are sent and received using the network adapter? Comparing this rate to the total bandwidth of your network adapter can tell you if the network traffic load is too much for your network adapter. To allow room for spikes in traffic, you should use no more than 50% of capacity.

For information about tools that can help you troubleshoot network use, see "The Environment," page 272.

Tuning Your Application or Database Driver to Use the Network Efficiently

Here are some general guidelines to help your application and database driver use the network efficiently:

- **Reduce the number of network round trips**—Reducing network round trips reduces your application's reliance on the network, which improves performance. Application design and coding practices that reduce network round trips include connection pooling, statement pooling, avoiding auto-commit mode in favor of manual commits, using local transactions instead of distributed transactions where appropriate, and using batches or arrays of parameters for bulk inserts.

- **Tune your database driver to optimize communication across the network**—Some database drivers provide tuning options that allow you to optimize network traffic. For example, if your database driver supports it, you can increase the size of database protocol packets, which ultimately improves performance because it results in fewer network packets being sent across the network. See "Configuring Packet Size," page 92, for more information.

- **Avoid retrieving large amounts of data from the database server**—The more data that must be transferred across the network, the more network packets are required to transfer the data. For example, data such as XML files, Blobs, and Clobs can be very large. Just as retrieving thousands of rows of character data can be a drain on performance, retrieving long data across the network is slow and resource intensive because of the size of the data. Avoid retrieving it unless you have a compelling reason to do so. See "Data Retrieval," page 30, for more information.

  If you can't avoid retrieving data that generates large amounts of network traffic, your application can still control the amount of data being sent from the database by limiting the number of rows sent across the network and reducing the size of each row sent across the network. See "Limiting the Amount of Data Returned," page 34, for more information.

- **Be aware that large result sets can delay your application's response time if you are using a streaming protocol database**—Sybase ASE, Microsoft SQL Server, and MySQL are examples of streaming protocol databases. These database systems process the query and send results until there are no more results to send; the database is uninterruptable. Therefore, the network connection is "busy" until all results are returned (fetched) to the application. Large result sets can suspend the availability of the network for longer times than small result sets. If you're using a streaming protocol database, it's even more important to reduce the amount of data retrieved from the database server. See "How One Connection for Multiple Statements Works," page 17, for more information about streaming protocol databases versus cursor-based protocol databases.

- **Avoid scrollable cursors unless you know your database system fully supports them**—Scrollable cursors provide the ability to go both forward and backward through a result set. Because of limited support for server-side scrollable cursors in many database systems, database drivers often emulate scrollable cursors, storing rows from a scrollable result set in memory on the client or application server. A large result set can result in large amounts of data being transferred over the network. See "Using Scrollable Cursors," page 36, for more information.

Virtualization

You may have heard talk about a recent trend in database computing known as virtualization. **Virtualization** allows companies to consolidate server resources by allowing multiple operating system instances to run at the same time on a single physical computer. A single server can run 4, 8, 16, or even more virtual operating systems. In 2007, the number of companies offering virtualization management solutions increased from 6 to 50, a staggering 866% increase. It's not hard to figure out why.

Over the past 10 years, hardware has become less expensive and more powerful. To keep pace with computing demands, companies have acquired large numbers of server machines, but they often find themselves low on the space, power, and air conditioning required to store and maintain them. It's estimated that in an unvirtualized environment, only 8% to 10% of the capacity of a server is used. Using virtualization, companies can get more work out of fewer machines, easing and sometimes eliminating the costs associated with housing multiple servers. For example, imagine an IT's data center that maintains 50 servers stored in a crowded, subleased server space. By creating 5 virtual servers on only 10 servers, that data center can move to a smaller space and get rid of an expensive sublease without sacrificing business capability.

What does virtualization mean to the performance of database applications? First, it's important to choose a database driver that supports virtualization technologies. Next, you need to be aware that it becomes easier to stretch hardware resources such as network, memory, CPU, and disk use to their limits; the probability that your database application will be affected by performance issues caused by hardware constraints is amplified.

Finally, it's important to understand that virtualized environments make it harder to detect where performance bottlenecks actually originate because of the increased complexity of the environment. In addition, there's no overarching tool that is operating system-agnostic to analyze resource use in virtualized environments (although companies are rushing to develop virtualization management tools that allow you to monitor activity and resource use). For example, Figure 4-21 shows a virtualized machine that runs four operating systems and hosts four applications. If Application A and Application C routinely generate a spike in network traffic at the same time every day, the network adapter of the virtualized machine may not be able to handle the increase in network requests. The increase can affect the performance of not only Application A and C, but also the performance of Application B and D.

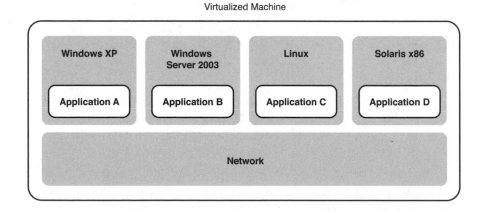

Figure 4-21   Virtualized machine running multiple operating systems and database applications

The soundest advice we can give is to invest in the best hardware you can afford. Software tools to help you troubleshoot performance issues in virtualized environments demand a steep learning curve and, ultimately, will cost more than the best hardware. In the example shown in Figure 4-21, if we provide each virtualized machine with its own dedicated network adapter, our performance bottleneck is resolved.

In a few cases, it may not be feasible to add or upgrade hardware resources to expand those that are being overworked. For example, each computer has a physical limit on the amount of memory it can address. When hardware becomes the limiting factor for performance, using an efficient database driver becomes even more important. See "Database Drivers," page 53, for more information about choosing an efficient database driver.

Summary

The environment in which your database application runs affects its performance. In the Java environment, performance can vary between JVMs from different manufacturers, so it's important to choose a JVM that gives your application the best performance. You can further improve performance by tuning JVM settings for heap size and garbage collection. In contrast, the .NET CLR doesn't provide the same tuning ability for garbage collection, and efficient garbage collection largely depends on your application code.

Any operating system change, even a minor one, can affect performance more than you would think. One often overlooked factor is the endianness of the operating system, as determined by the computer's processor. If possible, try to align the endianness of the operating system on the database client with that of the operating system on the database server.

Database clients and database servers communicate over a network, typically TCP/IP. How efficiently your database application uses that network affects performance. Following are key techniques for ensuring the best performance over the network:

- Reducing network round trips
- Tuning the size of database protocol packets
- Reducing the number of network hops between network destinations
- Avoiding network packet fragmentation

Hardware resources such as memory, disk I/O, CPU, and the network adapter can be a limiting factor for performance. To conserve hardware resources, you often can tune the database driver or use specific application design and coding techniques. In virtualized environments, it's easier to stretch hardware resources to their limits and harder to detect where bottlenecks originate. Investing in the best hardware that you can afford will save you in the long run.

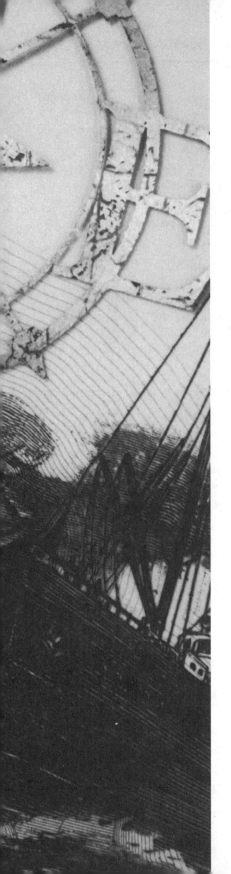

CHAPTER FIVE

ODBC Applications: Writing Good Code

Developing performance-optimized ODBC applications is not easy. Microsoft's *ODBC Programmer's Reference* does not provide information about performance. In addition, ODBC drivers and the ODBC Driver Manager don't return warnings when applications run inefficiently. This chapter describes some general guidelines for coding practices that improve ODBC application performance. These guidelines have been compiled by examining the ODBC implementations of numerous shipping ODBC applications. In general, the guidelines described in this chapter improve performance because they accomplish one or more of the following goals:

- Reduce network traffic
- Limit disk I/O
- Optimize application-to-driver interaction
- Simplify queries

If you've read the other coding chapters (Chapters 6 and 7), you'll notice that some of the information here resembles those chapters. While there are some similarities, this chapter focuses on specific information about coding for ODBC.

Managing Connections

Typically, creating a connection is one of the most performance-expensive operations that an application performs. Developers often assume that establishing a connection is a simple request that results in the driver making a single network round trip to the database server to validate a user's credentials. In reality, a connection involves many network round trips between the driver and the database server. For example, when a driver connects to Oracle or Sybase ASE, that connection may require seven to ten network round trips. In addition, the database establishes resources on behalf of the connection, which involves performance-expensive disk I/O and memory allocation.

Your time will be well spent if you sit down and design how to handle connections before implementing them in your application. Use the guidelines in this section to manage your connections more efficiently.

Connecting Efficiently

Database applications use either of the following methods to manage connections:

- Obtain a connection from a connection pool.
- Create a new connection one at a time as needed.

When choosing a method to manage connections, remember the following facts about connections and performance:

- Creating a connection is performance expensive.
- Open connections use a substantial amount of memory on both the database server and the database client.
- Opening numerous connections can contribute to an out-of-memory condition, which causes paging of memory to disk and, thus, overall performance degradation.

Using Connection Pooling

If your application has multiple users and your database server provides sufficient database resources, using connection pooling can provide significant performance gains. Reusing a connection reduces the number of network round trips needed to establish a physical connection between the driver and the database. The performance penalty is paid up front at the time the connection pool is populated with connections. As the connections in the pool are actually used by the application, performance improves significantly. Obtaining a connection becomes one of the fastest operations an application performs instead of one of the slowest.

Although obtaining connections from a pool is efficient, when your application opens and closes connections impacts the scalability of your application. Open connections just before the user needs them, not sooner, to minimize the time that the user owns the physical connection. Similarly, close connections as soon as the user no longer needs them.

To minimize the number of connections required in a connection pool to service users, you can switch a user associated with a connection to another user if your database driver supports a feature known as reauthentication. Minimizing the number of connections conserves memory and can improve performance. See "Using Reauthentication with Connection Pooling," page 232. See Chapter 8, "Connection Pooling and Statement Pooling," for details about connection pooling.

Establishing Connections One at a Time

Some applications are not good candidates for using connection pooling, particularly if connection reuse is limited. See "When Not to Use Connection Pooling," page 15, for examples.

> **Performance Tip**
>
> If your application does not use connection pooling, avoid connecting and disconnecting multiple times throughout your application to execute SQL statements because of the performance hit your application pays for opening connections. You don't need to open a new connection for each SQL statement your application executes.

Using One Connection for Multiple Statements

When you're using a single connection for multiple statements, your application may have to wait for a connection if it connects to a streaming protocol database. In streaming protocol databases, only one request can be processed at a time over a single connection; other requests on the same connection must wait for the preceding request to complete. Sybase ASE, Microsoft SQL Server, and MySQL are examples of streaming protocol databases.

In contrast, when connecting to cursor-based protocol databases, the driver tells the database server when to work and how much data to retrieve. Several cursors can use the network, each working in small slices of time. Oracle and DB2 are examples of cursor-based protocol databases. For a more detailed explanation of streaming versus cursor-based protocol databases, see "One Connection for Multiple Statements," page 16.

The advantage of using one connection for multiple statements is that it reduces the overhead of establishing multiple connections, while allowing multiple statements to access the database. The overhead is reduced on both the database server and client machines. The disadvantage is that the application may have to wait to execute a statement until the single connection is available. See "One Connection for Multiple Statements," page 16, for guidelines on using this model of connection management.

Obtaining Database and Driver Information Efficiently

Remember that creating a connection is one of the most performance-expensive operations that an application performs.

> **Performance Tip**
>
> Because of the performance hit your application pays for opening connections, once your application is connected, you should avoid establishing additional connections to gather information about the driver and the database, such as supported data types or database versions, using SQLGetInfo and SQLGetTypeInfo. For example, some applications establish a connection and then call a routine in a separate DLL or shared library that reconnects and gathers information about the driver and the database.

How often do databases change their supported data types or database version between connections? Because this type of information typically doesn't change between connections and isn't a large amount of information to store, you may want to retrieve and cache the information so the application can access it later.

Managing Transactions

To ensure data integrity, all statements in a transaction are committed or rolled back as a unit. For example, when you use a computer to transfer money from one bank account to another, the request involves a transaction—updating values stored in the database for both accounts. If all parts of that unit of work succeed, the transaction is committed. If any part of that unit of work fails, the transaction is rolled back.

Use the guidelines in this section to help you manage transactions more efficiently.

Managing Commits in Transactions

Committing (and rolling back) transactions is slow because of the disk I/O and, potentially, the number of network round trips required. What does a commit actually involve? The database must write to disk every modification made by a transaction to the database. This is usually a sequential write to a journal file (or log); nevertheless, it involves expensive disk I/O.

In ODBC, the default transaction commit mode is auto-commit. In auto-commit mode, a commit is performed for every SQL statement that requires a request to the database (Insert, Update, Delete, and Select statements). When auto-commit mode is used, your application doesn't control when database work is committed. In fact, commits commonly occur when there's actually no real work to commit.

Some databases, such as DB2, don't support auto-commit mode. For these databases, the database driver, by default, sends a commit request to the database after every successful operation (SQL statement). The commit request equates to a network round trip between the driver and the database. The round trip to the database occurs even though the application didn't request the commit and even if the operation made no changes to the database. For example, the driver makes a network round trip even when a Select statement is executed.

Let's look at the following ODBC code, which doesn't turn off auto-commit mode. Comments in the code show when commits occur if the driver or the database performs commits automatically:

```
/* For conciseness, this code omits error checking */

/* Allocate a statement handle */
rc = SQLAllocHandle(SQL_HANDLE_STMT, hdbc, &hstmt);
```

```
/* Prepare an INSERT statement for multiple executions */
strcpy (sqlStatement, "INSERT INTO employees " +
    "VALUES (?, ?, ?)");
rc = SQLPrepare((SQLHSTMT)hstmt, sqlStatement, SQL_NTS);

/* Bind parameters */
rc = SQLBindParameter(hstmt, 1, SQL_PARAM_INPUT,
                      SQL_C_SLONG, SQL_INTEGER, 10, 0,
                      &id, sizeof(id), NULL);
rc = SQLBindParameter(hstmt, 2, SQL_PARAM_INPUT,
                      SQL_C_CHAR, SQL_CHAR, 20, 0,
                      name, sizeof(name), NULL);
rc = SQLBindParameter(hstmt, 3, SQL_PARAM_INPUT,
                      SQL_C_SLONG, SQL_INTEGER, 10, 0,
                      &salary, sizeof(salary), NULL);

/* Set parameter values before execution */
id = 20;
strcpy(name, "Employee20");
salary = 100000;
rc = SQLExecute(hstmt);

/* A commit occurs because auto-commit is on */

/* Change parameter values for the next execution */
id = 21;
strcpy(name, "Employee21");
salary = 150000;
rc = SQLExecute(hstmt);

/* A commit occurs because auto-commit is on */

/* Reset parameter bindings */
rc = SQLFreeStmt((SQLHSTMT)hstmt, SQL_RESET_PARAMS);
strcpy(sqlStatement, "SELECT id, name, salary " +
    "FROM employees");
```

```
/* Execute a SELECT statement. A prepare is unnecessary
   because it's executed only once. */
rc = SQLExecDirect((SQLHSTMT)hstmt, sqlStatement, SQL_NTS);

/* Fetch the first row */
rc = SQLFetch(hstmt);
while (rc != SQL_NO_DATA_FOUND) {

/* All rows are returned when fetch
   returns SQL_NO_DATA_FOUND */

   /* Get the data for each column in the result set row */
   rc = SQLGetData (hstmt, 1, SQL_INTEGER, &id,
                    sizeof(id), NULL);
   rc = SQLGetData (hstmt, 2, SQL_VARCHAR, &name,
                    sizeof(name), NULL);
   rc = SQLGetData (hstmt, 3, SQL_INTEGER, &salary,
                    sizeof(salary), NULL);
   printf("\nID: %d Name: %s Salary: %d", id, name, salary);

   /* Fetch the next row of data */
   rc = SQLFetch(hstmt);
   }

/* Close the cursor */
rc = SQLFreeStmt ((SQLHSTMT)hstmt, SQL_CLOSE);

/* Whether a commit occurs after a SELECT statement
   because auto-commit is on depends on the driver.
   It's safest to assume a commit occurs here.    */

/* Prepare the UPDATE statement for multiple executions */
strcpy (sqlStatement,
        "UPDATE employees SET salary = salary * 1.05" +
        "WHERE id = ?");
```

```
rc = SQLPrepare ((SQLHSTMT)hstmt, sqlStatement, SQL_NTS);

/* Bind parameter */
rc = SQLBindParameter(hstmt, 1, SQL_PARAM_INPUT,
                      SQL_C_LONG, SQL_INTEGER, 10, 0,
                      &index, sizeof(index), NULL);

for (index = 0; index < 10; index++) {

   /* Execute the UPDATE statement for each
      value of index between 0 and 9 */
   rc = SQLExecute (hstmt);

/* Because auto-commit is on, a commit occurs each time
   through loop for a total of 10 commits */
   }

/* Reset parameter bindings */
rc = SQLFreeStmt ((SQLHSTMT)hstmt, SQL_RESET_PARAMS);

/* Execute a SELECT statement. A prepare is unnecessary
   because it's only executed once. */
strcpy(sqlStatement, "SELECT id, name, salary" +
   "FROM employees");
rc = SQLExecDirect ((SQLHSTMT)hstmt, sqlStatement, SQL_NTS);

/* Fetch the first row */
rc = SQLFetch(hstmt);
while (rc != SQL_NO_DATA_FOUND) {

/* All rows are returned when fetch
   returns SQL_NO_DATA_FOUND */
```

```
/* Get the data for each column in the result set row */
rc = SQLGetData (hstmt, 1, SQL_INTEGER, &id,
               sizeof(id), NULL);
rc = SQLGetData (hstmt, 2, SQL_VARCHAR, &name,
               sizeof(name), NULL);
rc = SQLGetData (hstmt,3,SQL_INTEGER,&salary,
               sizeof(salary), NULL);
 printf("\nID: %d Name: %s Salary: %d", id, name, salary);

 /* Fetch the next row of data */
 rc = SQLFetch(hstmt);
 }

/* Close the cursor */
rc = SQLFreeStmt ((SQLHSTMT)hstmt, SQL_CLOSE);

/* Whether a commit occurs after a SELECT statement
   because auto-commit is on depends on the driver.
   It's safest to assume a commit occurs here.     */
```

Performance Tip

Because of the significant amount of disk I/O on the database server required to commit every operation and the extra network round trips that occur between the driver and the database server, it's a good idea to turn off auto-commit mode in your application and use manual commits instead. Using manual commits allows your application to control when database work is committed, which provides dramatically better performance. To turn off auto-commit mode, use the SQLSetConnectAttr function, for example, SQLSetConnectAttr(hstmt, SQL_ATTR_AUTOCOMMIT, SQL_AUTOCOMMIT_OFF).

For example, let's look at the following ODBC code. It's identical to the previous ODBC code except that it turns off auto-commit mode and uses manual commits:

```
/* For conciseness, this code omits error checking */

/* Allocate a statement handle */
rc = SQLAllocStmt((SQLHDBC)hdbc, (SQLHSTMT *)&hstmt);

/* Turn auto-commit off */
rc = SQLSetConnectAttr (hdbc, SQL_AUTOCOMMIT,
                        SQL_AUTOCOMMIT_OFF);

/* Prepare an INSERT statement for multiple executions */
strcpy (sqlStatement, "INSERT INTO employees" +
  "VALUES (?, ?, ?)");
rc = SQLPrepare((SQLHSTMT)hstmt, sqlStatement, SQL_NTS);

/* Bind parameters */
rc = SQLBindParameter(hstmt, 1, SQL_PARAM_INPUT,
                      SQL_C_SLONG, SQL_INTEGER, 10, 0,
                      &id, sizeof(id), NULL);
rc = SQLBindParameter(hstmt, 2, SQL_PARAM_INPUT,
                      SQL_C_CHAR, SQL_CHAR, 20, 0,
                      name, sizeof(name), NULL);
rc = SQLBindParameter(hstmt, 3, SQL_PARAM_INPUT,
                      SQL_C_SLONG, SQL_INTEGER, 10, 0,
                      &salary, sizeof(salary), NULL);

/* Set parameter values before execution */
id = 20;
strcpy(name,"Employee20");
salary = 100000;
rc = SQLExecute(hstmt);

/* Change parameter values for the next execution */
id = 21;
strcpy(name,"Employee21");
```

```
salary = 150000;
rc = SQLExecute(hstmt);

/* Reset parameter bindings */
rc = SQLFreeStmt(hstmt, SQL_RESET_PARAMS);

/* Manual commit */
rc = SQLEndTran(SQL_HANDLE_DBC, hdbc, SQL_COMMIT);

/* Execute a SELECT statement. A prepare is unnecessary
   because it's only executed once. */
strcpy(sqlStatement, "SELECT id, name, salary" +
   "FROM employees");
rc = SQLExecDirect((SQLHSTMT)hstmt, sqlStatement, SQL_NTS);

/* Fetch the first row */
rc = SQLFetch(hstmt);
while (rc != SQL_NO_DATA_FOUND) {

/* All rows are returned when fetch
   returns SQL_NO_DATA_FOUND */

   /* Get the data for each column in the result set row */
   rc = SQLGetData (hstmt, 1, SQL_INTEGER, &id,
                    sizeof(id), NULL);
   rc = SQLGetData (hstmt, 2, SQL_VARCHAR, &name,
                    sizeof(name), NULL);
   rc = SQLGetData (hstmt, 3, SQL_INTEGER, &salary,
                    sizeof(salary), NULL);
   printf("\nID: %d Name: %s Salary: %d", id, name, salary);

   /* Fetch the next row of data */
   rc = SQLFetch(hstmt);
   }
```

```
/* Close the cursor */
rc = SQLFreeStmt ((SQLHSTMT)hstmt, SQL_CLOSE);

strcpy (sqlStatement,
        "UPDATE employees SET salary = salary * 1.05" +
        "WHERE id = ?");

/* Prepare the UPDATE statement for multiple executions */
rc = SQLPrepare ((SQLHSTMT)hstmt, sqlStatement, SQL_NTS);

/* Bind parameter */
rc = SQLBindParameter(hstmt, 1, SQL_PARAM_INPUT,
                      SQL_C_SLONG, SQL_INTEGER, 10, 0,
                      &index, sizeof(index), NULL);

for (index = 0; index < 10; index++) {

   /* Execute the UPDATE statement for each
      value of index between 0 and 9 */
   rc = SQLExecute (hstmt);
   }

/* Manual commit */
rc = SQLEndTran(SQL_HANDLE_DBC, hdbc, SQL_COMMIT);

/* Reset parameter bindings */
rc = SQLFreeStmt ((SQLHSTMT)hstmt, SQL_RESET_PARAMS);

/* Execute a SELECT statement. A prepare is unnecessary
   because it's only executed once. */
strcpy(sqlStatement, "SELECT id, name, salary" +
   "FROM employees");
rc = SQLExecDirect ((SQLHSTMT)hstmt, sqlStatement, SQL_NTS);
```

```
/* Fetch the first row */
rc = SQLFetch(hstmt);
while (rc != SQL_NO_DATA_FOUND) {

/* All rows are returned when fetch
   returns SQL_NO_DATA_FOUND */

   /* Get the data for each column in the result set row */
   rc = SQLGetData (hstmt, 1, SQL_INTEGER, &id,
                    sizeof(id), NULL);
   rc = SQLGetData (hstmt, 2, SQL_VARCHAR, &name,
                    sizeof(name), NULL);
   rc = SQLGetData (hstmt,3,SQL_INTEGER,&salary,
                    sizeof(salary), NULL);
   printf("\nID: %d Name: %s Salary: %d", id, name, salary);

   /* Fetch the next row of data */
   rc = SQLFetch(hstmt);
   }

/* Close the cursor */
rc = SQLFreeStmt ((SQLHSTMT)hstmt, SQL_CLOSE);

/* Manual commit */
rc = SQLEndTran (SQL_HANDLE_DBC, hdbc, SQL_COMMIT);
```

See "Managing Commits in Transactions," page 22, for information on when to commit work if you've turned off auto-commit mode.

Choosing the Right Transaction Model

Which type of transaction should you use: local or distributed? A local transaction accesses and updates data on a single database. A distributed transaction accesses and updates data on multiple databases; therefore, it must be coordinated among those databases.

Be aware that the default transaction behavior of many COM+ components uses distributed transactions, so changing that default transaction behavior to local transactions as shown can improve performance.

```
// Disable MTS Transactions.
XACTOPT options[1] = {XACTSTAT_NONE,"NOT SUPPORTED"};
hr = Itxoptions->SetOptions(options);
```

See "Transaction Management," page 21, for more information about performance and transactions.

Executing SQL Statements

Use the guidelines in this section to help you select which ODBC functions will give you the best performance when executing SQL statements.

Using Stored Procedures

Database drivers can call stored procedures on the database using either of the following methods:

- Execute the procedure the same way as any other SQL statement. The database parses the SQL statement, validates argument types, and converts arguments into the correct data types.
- Invoke a Remote Procedure Call (RPC) directly in the database. The database skips the parsing and optimization that executing a SQL statement requires.

Performance Tip
Call stored procedures by invoking an RPC with parameter markers for arguments instead of using literal arguments. Because the database skips the parsing and optimization required in executing the stored procedure as a SQL statement, performance is significantly improved.

Remember that SQL is always sent to the database as a character string. For example, consider the following stored procedure call, which passes a literal argument to the stored procedure:

```
{call getCustName (12345)}
```

Although the argument to getCustName() is an integer, the argument is passed inside a character string to the database, namely {call getCustName (12345)}. The database parses the SQL statement, isolates the single argument value of 12345, and converts the string 12345 into an integer value before executing the procedure as a SQL language event. Using an RPC on the database, your application can pass the parameters to the RPC. The driver sends a database protocol packet that contains the parameters in their native data type formats, skipping the parsing and optimization required to execute the stored procedure as a SQL statement. Compare the following examples.

Example A: Not Using a Server-Side RPC

The stored procedure getCustName is not optimized to use a server-side RPC. The database treats the SQL stored procedure execution request as a normal SQL language event, which includes parsing the statement, validating argument types, and converting arguments into the correct data types before executing the procedure.

```
strcpy (sqlStatement,"{call getCustName (12345)}");
rc = SQLPrepare((SQLHSTMT)hstmt, sqlStatement, SQL_NTS);
rc = SQLExecute(hstmt);
```

Example B: Using a Server-Side RPC

The stored procedure `getCustName` is optimized to use a server-side RPC. Because the application avoids literal arguments and calls the procedure by specifying arguments as parameters, the driver optimizes the execution by invoking the stored procedure directly on the database as an RPC. The SQL language processing by the database is avoided, and execution time is faster.

```
strcpy (sqlStatement,"{call getCustName (?)}");
rc = SQLPrepare((SQLHSTMT)hstmt, sqlStatement, SQL_NTS);
rc = SQLBindParameter(hstmt, 1, SQL_PARAM_INPUT,
                      SQL_C_LONG, SQL_INTEGER, 10, 0,
                      &id, sizeof(id), NULL);
id = 12345;
rc = SQLExecute(hstmt);
```

Why doesn't the driver parse and automatically change the SQL stored procedure call when it encounters a literal argument so that it can execute the stored procedure using an RPC? Consider this example:

```
{call getCustname (12345)}
```

The driver doesn't know if the value 12345 represents an integer, a decimal, a smallint, a bigint, or another numeric data type. To determine the correct data type for packaging the RPC request, the driver must make an expensive network round trip to the database server. The overhead needed to determine the true data type of the literal argument far outweighs the benefit of trying to execute the request as an RPC.

Using Statements Versus Prepared Statements

Most applications have a certain set of SQL statements that are executed multiple times and a few SQL statements that are executed only once or twice during the life of the application. Choose the `SQLExecDirect` function or the `SQLPrepare`/`SQLExecute` functions depending on how frequently you plan to execute the SQL statement.

The SQLExecDirect function is optimized for a SQL statement that is only executed once. In contrast, the SQLPrepare/SQLExecute functions are optimized for SQL statements that use parameter markers and are executed multiple times. Although the overhead for the initial execution of a prepared statement is high, the advantage is realized with subsequent executions of the SQL statement.

Using the SQLPrepare/SQLExecute functions typically results in at least two network round trips to the database server:

- One network round trip to parse and optimize the statement
- One or more network round trips to execute the statement and retrieve results

---

Performance Tip

If your application makes a request only once during its life span, using the SQLExecDirect function is a better choice than using the SQLPrepare/SQLExecute function because SQLExecDirect results in only a single network round trip. Remember, reducing network communication typically provides the most performance gain. For example, if you have an application that runs an end-of-day sales report, send the query that generates the data for that report to the database using the SQLExecDirect function, not the SQLPrepare/SQLExecute function.

See "SQL Statements," page 27, for more information about statements versus prepared statements.

Using Arrays of Parameters

Updating large amounts of data typically is done by preparing an Insert statement and executing that statement multiple times, resulting in many network round trips.

Performance Tip

To reduce the number of network round trips when updating large amounts of data, you can send multiple Insert statements to the database at a time using the SQLSetStmtAttr function with the following arguments: SQL_ATTR_PARAMSET_SIZE sets the array size of the parameter, SQL_ATTR_PARAMS_PROCESSED_PTR assigns a variable filled by SQLExecute (containing the number of rows that are inserted), and SQL_ATTR_PARAM_STATUS_PTR points to an array in which status information for each row of parameter values is retrieved.

With ODBC 3.*x*, calls to SQLSetStmtAttr with the SQL_ATTR_PARAMSET_SIZE, SQL_ATTR_PARAMS_PROCESSED_PTR, and SQL_ATTR_PARAM_STATUS_PTR arguments supersede the ODBC 2.*x* call to SQLParamOptions.

Before executing the statement, the application sets the value of each data element in the bound array. When the statement is executed, the driver tries to process the entire array contents using one network round trip. For example, let's compare the following examples.

Example A: Executing a Prepared Statement Multiple Times

A prepared statement is used to execute an Insert statement multiple times, requiring 101 network round trips to perform 100 Insert operations: 1 round trip to prepare the statement and 100 additional round trips to execute its iterations.

```
rc = SQLPrepare (hstmt, "INSERT INTO DailyLedger (...)" +
    "VALUES (?,?,...)", SQL_NTS);
// bind parameters
...
do {
// read ledger values into bound parameter buffers
...
rc = SQLExecute (hstmt);
// insert row
} while ! (eof);
```

Example B: Arrays of Parameters

When arrays of parameters are used to consolidate 100 Insert operations, only two network round trips are required: one to prepare the
statement and another to execute the array. Although arrays of parameters use more CPU cycles, performance is gained by reducing the number of network round trips.

```
SQLPrepare (hstmt, "INSERT INTO DailyLedger (...)" +
    "VALUES (?,?,...)", SQL_NTS);
SQLSetStmtAttr (hstmt, SQL_ATTR_PARAMSET_SIZE, (UDWORD)100,
    SQL_IS_UINTEGER);
SQLSetStmtAttr (hstmt, SQL_ATTR_PARAMS_PROCESSED_PTR,
    &rows_processed, SQL_IS_POINTER);
// Specify an array in which to retrieve the status of
// each set of parameters.
SQLSetStmtAttr(hstmt, SQL_ATTR_PARAM_STATUS_PTR,
    ParamStatusArray, SQL_IS_POINTER);
// pass 100 parameters per execute
// bind parameters
...
do {
// read up to 100 ledger values into
// bound parameter buffers.
...
rc = SQLExecute (hstmt);
// insert a group of 100 rows
} while ! (eof);
```

Using the Cursor Library

The ODBC cursor library is a component of Microsoft Data Access Components
(MDAC) and is used to implement static cursors (one type of scrollable cursor)
for drivers that normally don't support them.

<table>
<tr><td>

Performance Tip

If your ODBC driver supports scrollable cursors, don't code your application to load the ODBC cursor library. Although the cursor library provides support for static cursors, the cursor library also creates temporary log files on the user's local disk drive. Because of the disk I/O required to create these temporary log files, using the ODBC cursor library slows performance.

</td></tr>
</table>

What if you don't know whether your driver supports scrollable cursors? Using the following code ensures that the ODBC cursor library is only used when the driver doesn't support scrollable cursors:

```
rc = SQLSetConnectAttr (hstmt, SQL_ATTR_ODBC_CURSORS,
    SQL_CUR_USE_IF_NEEDED, SQL_IS_INTEGER);
```

Retrieving Data

Retrieve only the data you need, and choose the most efficient method to retrieve that data. Use the guidelines in this section to optimize your performance when retrieving data.

Retrieving Long Data

Retrieving long data—such as large XML data, long varchar/text, long varbinary, Clobs, and Blobs—across a network is slow and resource intensive. Most users really don't want to see long data. For example, consider the user interface of an employee directory application that allows the user to look up an employee's phone extension and department, and optionally, view an employee's photograph by clicking the name of the employee.

Employee	Phone	Dept
Harding	X4568	Manager
Hoover	X4324	Sales
Taft	X4569	Sales
Lincoln	X4329	Tech

Retrieving each employee's photograph would slow performance unnecessarily. If the user does want to see the photograph, he can click the employee name and the application can query the database again, specifying only the long columns in the `Select` list. This method allows users to retrieve result sets without paying a high performance penalty for network traffic.

Although excluding long data from the `Select` list is the best approach, some applications do not formulate the `Select` list before sending the query to the driver (that is, some applications use SELECT * FROM *table* ...). If the `Select` list contains long data, the driver is forced to retrieve that long data, even if the application never requests the long data from the result set. When possible, use a method that does not retrieve all columns of the table. For example, consider the following code:

```
rc = SQLExecDirect (hstmt, "SELECT * FROM employees" +
                   "WHERE SSID = '999-99-2222'", SQL_NTS);
rc = SQLFetch (hstmt);
```

When a query is executed, the driver has no way to determine which result columns the application will use; an application may fetch any result column that is retrieved. When the driver processes a `SQLFetch` or `SQLExtendedFetch` request, it retrieves at least one, and often multiple, result rows from the database across the network. A result row contains all the column values for each row. What if one of the columns includes long data such as an employee photograph? Performance would slow considerably.

> **Performance Tip**
>
> Because retrieving long data across the network negatively affects performance, design your application to exclude long data from the Select list.

Limiting the `Select` list to contain only the name column results in a faster performing query at runtime. For example:

```
rc = SQLExecDirect (hstmt, "SELECT name FROM employees" +
                   "WHERE SSID = '999-99-2222'", SQL_NTS);
rc = SQLFetch(hstmt);
rc = SQLGetData(hstmt, 1, ...);
```

Limiting the Amount of Data Retrieved

If your application executes a query that retrieves five rows when it needs only two, application performance suffers, especially if the unnecessary rows include long data.

Performance Tip

One of the easiest ways to improve performance is to limit the amount of network traffic between the driver and the database server—optimally by writing SQL queries that instruct the driver to retrieve from the database only the data that the application requires.

Make sure that your `Select` statements use a `Where` clause to limit the amount of data that is retrieved. Even when using a `Where` clause, a `Select` statement that does not adequately restrict its request could retrieve hundreds of rows of data. For example, if you want data from the employees table for each manager hired in recent years, your application could execute the following statement, and subsequently, filter out the rows of employees who are not managers:

```
SELECT * FROM employees
WHERE hiredate > 2000
```

However, suppose the employees table contains a column that stores photographs of each employee. In this case, retrieving extra rows is extremely expensive to your application performance. Let the database filter the request for you and avoid sending extra data that you don't need across the network. The following query uses a better approach, limiting the data retrieved and improving performance:

```
SELECT * FROM employees
WHERE hiredate > 2003 AND job_title='Manager'
```

Sometimes applications need to use SQL queries that generate a large amount of network traffic. For example, consider an application that displays information from support case histories, which each contains a 10MB log file. Does the user really need to see the entire contents of the log file? If not, performance would improve if the application displayed only the first 1MB of the log file.

> **Performance Tip**
>
> When you cannot avoid retrieving data that generates a large amount of network traffic, your application can still control the amount of data being sent from the database to the driver by limiting the number of rows sent across the network and reducing the size of each row sent across the network.

Suppose you have a GUI-based application, and each screen can display no more than 20 rows of data. It's easy to construct a query that may retrieve a million rows, such as SELECT * FROM employees, but it's hard to imagine a scenario where a query that retrieves a million rows would be useful. When designing applications, it's good practice to call the SQLSetStmtAttr function with the SQL_ATTR_MAX_ROWS option as a fail-safe to limit the number of rows that a query can retrieve. For example, if an application calls SQLSetStmt(SQL_ATTR_MAX_ROWS, 10000, 0), no query will retrieve more than 10,000 rows.

In addition, calling the SQLSetStmtAttr function with the SQL_ATTR_MAX_LENGTH option limits the bytes of data that can be retrieved for a column value with the following data types:

- Binary
- Varbinary
- Longvarbinary
- Char
- Varchar
- Longvarchar

For example, consider an application that allows users to select from a repository of technical articles. Rather than retrieve and display the entire article, the application can call SQLSetStmtAttr(SQL_ATTR_MAX_LENGTH, 153600, 0) to retrieve only the first 150KB of text to the application—enough to give users a reasonable preview of the article.

Using Bound Columns

Data can be retrieved from the database using either the SQLBindCol function or the SQLGetData function. When SQLBindCol is called, it associates, or binds, a variable to a column in the result set. Nothing is sent to the database.

SQLBindCol tells the driver to remember the addresses of the variables, which the driver will use to store the data when it is actually retrieved. When SQLFetch is executed, the driver places the data into the addresses of the variables specified by SQLBindCol. In contrast, SQLGetData returns data directly into variables. It's commonly called to retrieve long data, which often exceeds the length of a single buffer and must be retrieved in parts.

> ### Performance Tip
>
> Retrieving data using the SQLBindCol function instead of using the SQLGetData function reduces the number of ODBC calls, and ultimately the number of network round trips, improving performance.

The following code uses the SQLGetData function to retrieve data:

```
rc = SQLExecDirect (hstmt, "SELECT <20 columns>" +
                    "FROM employees" +
                    "WHERE HireDate >= ?", SQL_NTS);
do {
rc = SQLFetch (hstmt);
// call SQLGetData 20 times
} while ((rc == SQL_SUCCESS) || (rc == SQL_SUCCESS_WITH_INFO));
```

If the query retrieves 90 result rows, 1,891 ODBC calls are made (20 calls to SQLGetData × 90 result rows + 91 calls to SQLFetch).

The following code uses the SQLBindCol function instead of SQLGetData:

```
rc = SQLExecDirect (hstmt, "SELECT <20 columns>" +
                    "FROM employees" +
                    "WHERE HireDate >= ?", SQL_NTS);
// call SQLBindCol 20 times
do {
rc = SQLFetch (hstmt);
} while ((rc == SQL_SUCCESS) || (rc ==   SQL_SUCCESS_WITH_INFO));
```

The number of ODBC calls is reduced from 1,891 to 111 (20 calls to SQLBindCol + 91 calls to SQLFetch). In addition to reducing the number of calls required, many drivers optimize how SQLBindCol is used by binding result information directly from the database into the user's buffer. That is, instead of the driver retrieving information into a container and then copying that information to the user's buffer, the driver requests that the information from the database be placed directly into the user's buffer.

Using **SQLExtendedFetch** Instead of **SQLFetch**

Most ODBC drivers now support SQLExtendedFetch for forward-only cursors. Yet, most ODBC applications continue to use SQLFetch to fetch data.

> **Performance Tip**
>
> Using the SQLExtendedFetch function instead of SQLFetch to fetch data reduces the number of ODBC calls, and ultimately the number of network round trips, and simplifies coding. Using SQLExtendedFetch results in better performance and more maintainable code.

Again, consider the same example we used in the section, "Using Bound Columns," page 145, but using SQLExtendedFetch instead of SQLFetch:

```
rc = SQLSetStmtOption (hstmt, SQL_ROWSET_SIZE, 100);
// use arrays of 100 elements
rc = SQLExecDirect (hstmt, "SELECT <20 columns>" +
                    "FROM employees" +
                    "WHERE HireDate >= ?", SQL_NTS);
// call SQLBindCol 1 time specifying row-wise binding
do {
rc = SQLExtendedFetch (hstmt, SQL_FETCH_NEXT, 0,
    &RowsFetched, RowStatus);
} while ((rc == SQL_SUCCESS) || (rc == SQL_SUCCESS_WITH_INFO));
```

The number of ODBC calls made by the application has been reduced from 1,891 to 4 (1 SQLSetStmtOption + 1 SQLExecDirect + 1 SQLBindCol + 1 SQLExtendedFetch). Besides reducing the ODBC call load, some ODBC drivers can retrieve data from the server in arrays, further improving the performance by reducing network traffic.

For ODBC drivers that do not support SQLExtendedFetch, your application can enable forward-only cursors using the ODBC cursor library by calling SQLSetConnectAttr. Using the cursor library won't improve performance, but it also won't decrease application response time when using forward-only cursors because no logging is required. For scrollable cursors, it's a different story (see "Using the Cursor Library," page 141). In addition, using the cursor library when SQLExtendedFetch is not supported natively by the driver simplifies code because the application can always depend on SQLExtendedFetch being available. The application doesn't require two algorithms (one using SQLExtendedFetch and one using SQLFetch).

Determining the Number of Rows in a Result Set

ODBC defines two types of cursors:

- Forward-only
- Scrollable (static, keyset-driven, dynamic, and mixed)

Scrollable cursors let you go both forward and backward through a result set. However, because of limited support for server-side scrollable cursors in many database systems, ODBC drivers often emulate scrollable cursors, storing rows from a scrollable result set in a cache on the machine where the driver resides (client or application server).

Unless you are certain that the database natively supports using a scrollable result set, do not call the SQLExtendedFetch function to find out how many rows the result set contains. For drivers that emulate scrollable cursors, calling SQLExtendedFetch causes the driver to retrieve all results across the network to reach the last row. This emulated model of scrollable cursors provides flexibility for the developer but comes with a performance penalty until the client cache of rows is fully populated. Instead of calling SQLExtendedFetch to determine the number of rows, count the rows by iterating through the result set or obtain the number of rows by submitting a Select statement with the Count function. For example:

```
SELECT COUNT(*) FROM employees
```

Unfortunately, there's no easy way to tell if a database driver uses native server-side scrollable cursors or emulates this functionality. For Oracle or

MySQL, you know the driver emulates scrollable cursors, but for other databases, it's more complicated. See "Using Scrollable Cursors," page 36, for details about which common databases support server-side scrollable cursors and how database drivers emulate scrollable cursors.

> **Performance Tip**
>
> In general, do not write code that relies on the number of result rows from a query because drivers often must retrieve all rows in a result set to determine how many rows the query will return.

Choosing the Right Data Type

When designing your database schema, it's obvious that you need to think about the impact of storage requirements on the database server. Less obvious, but just as important, you need to think about the network traffic required to move data in its native format to and from the ODBC driver. Retrieving and sending certain data types across the network can increase or decrease network traffic.

> **Performance Tip**
>
> For multiuser, multivolume applications, billions, or even trillions, of network packets can move between the driver and the database server over the course of a day. Choosing data types that are processed efficiently can incrementally provide a measurable gain in performance.

See "Choosing the Right Data Type," page 34, for information about which data types are processed faster than others.

Updating Data

Use the guidelines in this section to manage your updates more efficiently.

Using `SQLSpecialColumns` to Optimize Updates and Deletes

Many databases have hidden columns, named **pseudo-columns,** that represent a unique key associated with every row in a table. Typically, pseudo-columns in a

SQL statement provide the fastest way to access a row because they usually point to the exact location of the physical record.

Performance Tip

Use SQLSpecialColumns to identify the most optimal columns, typically pseudo-columns, to use in the Where clause for updating data.

Some applications, such as an application that forms a Where clause consisting of a subset of the column values retrieved in the result set, cannot be designed to take advantage of positioned updates and deletes. Some applications may formulate the Where clause by using searchable result columns or by calling SQLStatistics to find columns that may be part of a unique index. These methods usually work but can result in fairly complex queries. For example:

```
rc = SQLExecDirect (hstmt, "SELECT first_name, last_name," +
                    "ssn, address, city, state, zip" +
                    "FROM employees", SQL_NTS);
// fetch data using complex query
...
rc = SQLExecDirect (hstmt, "UPDATE employees SET address = ?" +
                    "WHERE first_name = ? AND last_name = ?" +
                    "AND ssn = ? AND address = ? AND city = ? AND" +
                    "state = ? AND zip = ?", SQL_NTS);
```

Many databases support pseudo-columns that are not explicitly defined in the table definition but are hidden columns of every table (for example, ROWID for Oracle). Because pseudo-columns are not part of the explicit table definition, they're not retrieved when SQLColumns is called. To determine if pseudo-columns exist, your application must call SQLSpecialColumns. For example:

```
...
rc = SQLSpecialColumns (hstmt, SQL_BEST_ROWID, ...);
...
```

```
rc = SQLExecDirect (hstmt, "SELECT first_name, last_name," +
                    "ssn, address, city, state, zip," +
                    "ROWID FROM employees", SQL_NTS);
// fetch data and probably "hide" ROWID from the user
...
rc = SQLExecDirect (hstmt, "UPDATE employees SET address = ?" +
                    "WHERE ROWID = ?", SQL_NTS);
// fastest access to the data!
```

If your data source doesn't contain pseudo-columns, the result set of SQLSpecialColumns consists of the columns of the most optimal unique index on the specified table (if a unique index exists). Therefore, your application doesn't need to call SQLStatistics to find the smallest unique index.

Using Catalog Functions

Catalog functions retrieve information about a result set, such as the number and type of columns. Because catalog functions are slow compared to other ODBC functions, using them frequently can impair performance. Use the guidelines in this section to optimize performance when selecting and using catalog functions.

Minimizing the Use of Catalog Functions

Compared to other ODBC functions, catalog functions that generate result sets are slow. To retrieve all result column information mandated by the ODBC specification, an ODBC driver often must perform multiple or complex queries to retrieve the result set for a single call to a catalog function.

Performance Tip

Although it's almost impossible to write an ODBC application without using a catalog function, you can improve performance by minimizing their use.

In addition to avoid executing catalog functions multiple times, you should cache information retrieved from result sets generated by catalog functions. For example, call SQLGetTypeInfo once, and cache the elements of the result set that your application depends on. It's unlikely that any application will use all elements of the result set generated by a catalog function, so the cache of information shouldn't be difficult to maintain.

Avoiding Search Patterns

Catalog functions support arguments that can limit the amount of data retrieved. Using null values or search patterns, such as %A%, for these arguments often generates time-consuming queries. In addition, network traffic can increase because of unnecessary results.

> **Performance Tip**
>
> Always supply as many non-null arguments as possible to result sets that generate catalog functions.

In the following example, an application uses the SQLTables function to determine whether the table named WSTable exists and provides null values for most of the arguments:

```
rc = SQLTables(hstmt, null, 0, null, 0, "WSTable",
               SQL_NTS, null, 0);
```

The driver interprets the request as follows: Retrieve all tables, views, system tables, synonyms, temporary tables, and aliases named WSTable that exist in any database schema in the database catalog.

In contrast, the following request provides non-null values for all arguments, allowing the driver to process the request more efficiently:

```
rc = SQLTables(hstmt, "cat1", SQL_NTS, "johng", SQL_NTS,
               "WSTable", SQL_NTS, "Table", SQL_NTS);
```

The driver interprets the request as follows: Retrieve all tables in catalog "cat1" that are named "WSTable" and owned by "johng." No synonyms, views, system tables, aliases, or temporary tables are retrieved.

Sometimes little is known about the object that you are requesting information for. Any information that the application can provide the driver when calling catalog functions can result in improved performance and reliability.

Using a Dummy Query to Determine Table Characteristics

Sometimes you need information about columns in the database table, such as column names, column data types, and column precision and scale. For example, an application that allows users to choose which columns to select may need to request the names of each column in the database table.

Performance Tip

To determine characteristics about a database table, avoid using the SQLColumns function. Instead, use a dummy query inside a prepared statement that executes the SQLDescribeCol function. Only use the SQLColumns function when you cannot obtain the requested information from result set metadata (for example, using the table column default values).

The following examples show the benefit of using the SQLDescribeCol function over the SQLColumns function.

Example A: SQLColumns Function

A potentially complex query is prepared and executed, the result description information is formulated, the driver retrieves the result rows, and the application fetches the result. This method results in increased CPU use and network communication.

```
rc = SQLColumns (... "UnknownTable" ...);
// This call to SQLColumns will generate a query to the
// system catalogs... possibly a join which must be
// prepared, executed, and produce a result set.
```

```
rc = SQLBindCol (...);
rc = SQLExtendedFetch (...);
// user must retrieve N rows from the server
// N = # result columns of UnknownTable
// result column information has now been obtained
```

Example B: SQLDescribeCol Function

A simple query that retrieves result set information is prepared, but the query is not executed and result rows are not retrieved by the driver. Only information about the result set is retrieved (the same information retrieved by SQLColumns in Example A).

```
// prepare dummy query
rc = SQLPrepare (... "SELECT * FROM UnknownTable" +
    "WHERE 1 = 0" ...);
// query is never executed on the server - only prepared
rc = SQLNumResultCols (...);
for (irow = 1; irow <= NumColumns; irow++) {
    rc = SQLDescribeCol (...)
    // + optional calls to SQLColAttributes
    }
// result column information has now been obtained
// Note we also know the column ordering within the table!
// This information cannot be
// assumed from the SQLColumns example.
```

What if the database server, such as a Microsoft SQL Server server does not support prepared statements by default? The performance of Example A wouldn't change, but the performance of Example B would decrease slightly because the dummy query is evaluated in addition to being prepared. Because the Where clause of the query always evaluates to FALSE, the query generates no result rows and executes the statement without retrieving result rows. So, even with a slight decrease in performance, Example B still outperforms Example A.

Summary

The performance of ODBC applications can suffer if they fail to reduce network traffic, limit disk I/O, simplify queries, and optimize the interaction between the application and driver. Reducing network communication probably is the most important technique for improving performance. For example, when you need to update large amounts of data, using arrays of parameters rather than executing an `Insert` statement multiple times reduces the number of network round trips required to complete the operation.

Typically, creating a connection is the most performance-expensive task your application performs. Connection pooling can help you manage your connections efficiently, particularly if your application has numerous users. Regardless of whether your application uses connection pooling, make sure that your application closes connections immediately after the user is finished with them.

Making smart choices about how to handle transactions can also improve performance. For example, using manual commits instead of auto-commit mode provides better control over when work is committed. Similarly, if you don't need the protection of distributed transactions, using local transactions can improve performance.

Inefficient SQL queries slow the performance of ODBC applications. Some SQL queries don't filter data, causing the driver to retrieve unnecessary data. Your application pays a huge penalty in performance when that unnecessary data is long data, such as data stored as a Blob or Clob. Even well-formed SQL queries can be more or less effective depending on how they are executed. For example, using `SQLExtendedFetch` instead of `SQLFetch` and using `SQLBindCol` instead of `SQLGetData` reduces ODBC calls and improves performance.

CHAPTER SIX

JDBC Applications: Writing Good Code

Developing performance-optimized JDBC applications is not easy. Database drivers don't throw exceptions to tell you when code is running slow. This chapter describes some general guidelines for coding practices that improve JDBC application performance. These guidelines have been compiled by examining the implementations of numerous shipping JDBC applications. In general, the guidelines described in this chapter improve performance because they accomplish one or more of the following goals:

- Reduce network traffic
- Limit disk I/O
- Optimize application-to-driver interaction
- Simplify queries

If you've read the other coding chapters (Chapters 5 and 7), you'll notice that some of the information here resembles those chapters. While there are some similarities, this chapter focuses on specific information about coding for JDBC.

Managing Connections

Typically, creating a connection is one of the most performance-expensive operations that an application performs. Developers often assume that establishing a connection is a simple request that results in the driver making a single network round trip to the database server to validate a user's credentials. In reality, a connection involves many network round trips between the driver and the database server. For example, when a driver connects to Oracle or Sybase ASE, that connection may require seven to ten network round trips. In addition, the database establishes resources on behalf of the connection, which involves performance-expensive disk I/O and memory allocation.

Your time will be well spent if you sit down and design how to handle connections before implementing them in your application. Use the guidelines in this section to manage your connections more efficiently.

Connecting Efficiently

Database applications use either of the following methods to manage connections:

- Obtain a connection from a connection pool.
- Create a new connection one at a time as needed.

When choosing a method to manage connections, remember the following facts about connections and performance:

- Creating a connection is performance expensive.
- Open connections use a substantial amount of memory on both the database server and the database client.
- Opening numerous connections can contribute to an out-of-memory condition, which causes paging of memory to disk and, thus, overall performance degradation.

Using Connection Pooling

If your application has multiple users and your database server provides sufficient database resources, such as memory and CPU, using connection pooling can provide significant performance gains. Reusing a connection reduces the number of network round trips needed to establish a physical connection between the driver and the database. The performance penalty is paid up front at the time the connection pool is populated with connections. As the connections in the pool are actually used by the application, performance improves significantly. Obtaining a connection becomes one of the fastest operations an application performs instead of one of the slowest.

Although obtaining connections from a pool is efficient, when your application opens and closes connections impacts the scalability of your application. Open connections just before the user needs them, not sooner, to minimize the time that the user owns the physical connection. Similarly, close connections as soon as the user no longer needs them.

To minimize the number of connections required in a connection pool to service users, you can switch a user associated with a connection to another user if your database driver supports a feature known as reauthentication. Minimizing the number of connections conserves memory and can improve performance. See "Using Reauthentication with Connection Pooling," page 232.

See Chapter 8, "Connection Pooling and Statement Pooling," for details about connection pooling.

Establishing Connections One at a Time

Some applications are not good candidates for connection pooling, particularly if connection reuse is limited. See "When Not to Use Connection Pooling," page 15, for examples.

Performance Tip

If your application does not use connection pooling, avoid connecting and disconnecting multiple times throughout your application to execute SQL statements because of the performance hit your application pays for opening connections. You don't need to open a new connection for each SQL statement your application executes.

Using One Connection for Multiple Statements

When you're using a single connection for multiple statements, your application may have to wait for a connection if it connects to a streaming protocol database.

In streaming protocol databases, only one request can be processed at a time over a single connection; other requests on the same connection must wait for the preceding request to complete. Sybase ASE, Microsoft SQL Server, and MySQL are examples of streaming protocol databases.

In contrast, when connecting to cursor-based protocol databases, the driver tells the database server when to work and how much data to retrieve. Several cursors can use the network, each working in small slices of time. Oracle and DB2 are examples of cursor-based protocol databases. For a more detailed explanation of streaming versus cursor-based protocol databases, see "One Connection for Multiple Statements," page 16.

The advantage of using one connection for multiple statements is that it reduces the overhead of establishing multiple connections, while allowing multiple statements to access the database. The overhead is reduced on both the database server and client machines. The disadvantage is that the application may have to wait to execute a statement until the single connection is available. See "One Connection for Multiple Statements," page 16, for guidelines on using this model of connection management.

Disconnecting Efficiently

Each physical connection to the database consumes a substantial amount of memory on both the client and database server.

Performance Tip

Remember to close connections immediately after your application is finished with them—don't wait for the garbage collector to close them for you. This is particularly important if your application uses connection pooling so that connections are returned to the connection pool immediately for other users to use.

For Java applications, the JVM uses garbage collection to automatically identify and reclaim memory allocated to objects that are no longer in use. If you wait for the garbage collector to clean up connections no longer in use, memory is tied up longer than necessary. Regardless of whether you use connection pooling, always remember to explicitly close connections as soon as the user no longer needs them so that connections will release the memory allocated for them.

As a fail-safe for closing open connections, not as a substitute, you can close connections inside a `finally` block, as shown in the following example. Code in the `finally` block always runs, regardless of whether an exception occurs. This code guarantees that any connections you may not have explicitly closed are closed without waiting for the garbage collector.

```
// Open a connection
Connection conn = null;
Statement st = null;
ResultSet rs = null;

try {
    ...
    conn = DriverManager.getConnection(connStr, uid, pwd);
    ...
    st = conn.prepareStatement(sqlString);
    ...
    rs = st.executeQuery();
    ...
    }
catch (SQLException e){
// exception handling code here
                }
finally {
        try {
            if (rs != null)
            rs.close();
            if (st != null)
            st.close();
            if (conn != null)
            conn.close();
            }
catch (SQLException e) {
// exception handling code here
                }
        }
```

Some drivers include the Java finalize() method in their implementation of the Connection object; others don't. In any case, do not rely on a Java finalize() method to close connections because the application must wait on the garbage collector to run the finalize() method. Again, connections that you are no longer using are not closed until the garbage collector detects them, which can tie up memory. In addition, the garbage collector must perform extra steps each time it runs a collection, which slows the collection process and can further delay the time it takes for a connection to close. For more information about how garbage collection works in the JVM, see "Garbage Collection," page 79.

Obtaining Database and Driver Information Efficiently

Remember that creating a connection is one of the most performance-expensive operations that an application performs.

> **Performance Tip**
>
> Because of the performance hit your application pays for opening connections, once your application is connected, avoid establishing additional connections to gather information about the driver and the database, such as supported data types or database version. For example, some applications establish a connection and then call a method in a separate component that reconnects and gathers information about the driver and the database. Applications designed as separate components, such as J2EE shared libraries or Web Services, can share metadata by passing the information as an argument to a routine instead of establishing an additional connection to request that information.

How often do databases change their supported data types or database version between connections? Because this type of information typically doesn't change between connections and isn't a large amount of information to store, you may want to retrieve and cache the information so the application can access it later.

Managing Transactions

To ensure data integrity, all statements in a transaction are committed or rolled back as a unit. For example, when you use a computer to transfer money from one bank account to another, the request involves a transaction—updating values stored in the database for both accounts. If all parts of that unit of work succeed, the transaction is committed. If any part of that unit of work fails, the transaction is rolled back.

Use the guidelines in this section to manage transactions more efficiently.

Managing Commits in Transactions

Committing (and rolling back) transactions is slow because of the disk I/O and, potentially, the number of network round trips required. What does a commit actually involve? The database must write to disk every modification made by a transaction to the database. This is usually a sequential write to a journal file (or log); nevertheless, it involves expensive disk I/O.

In JDBC, the default transaction commit mode is auto-commit. In auto-commit mode, a commit is performed for every SQL statement that requires a request to the database (Insert, Update, Delete, and Select statements). When auto-commit mode is used, your application doesn't control when database work is committed. In fact, commits commonly occur when there's actually no real work to commit.

Some databases, such as DB2, don't support auto-commit mode. For these databases, the database driver, by default, sends a commit request to the database after every successful operation (SQL statement). The commit request equates to a network round trip between the driver and the database. The round trip to the database occurs even though the application didn't request the commit and even if the operation made no changes to the database. For example, the driver makes a network round trip even when a Select statement is executed.

Let's look at the following Java code, which doesn't turn off auto-commit mode. Comments in the code show when commits occur if the driver or the database performs commits automatically.

```
// For conciseness, this code omits error checking

    // Create a Statement object
    stmt = con.createStatement();
```

```
// Prepare an INSERT statement for multiple executions
sql = "INSERT INTO employees VALUES (?, ?, ?)";
prepStmt = con.prepareStatement(sql);

// Set parameter values before execution
prepStmt.setInt(1, 20);
prepStmt.setString(2, "Employee20");
prepStmt.setInt(3, 100000);
prepStmt.executeUpdate();

// A commit occurs because auto-commit is on

// Change parameter values for the next execution
prepStmt.setInt(1, 21);
prepStmt.setString(2, "Employee21");
prepStmt.setInt(3, 150000);
prepStmt.executeUpdate();

// A commit occurs because auto-commit is on

prepStmt.close();

// Execute a SELECT statement. A prepare is unnecessary
// because it's executed only once.
sql = "SELECT id, name, salary FROM employees";

// Fetch the data
resultSet = stmt.executeQuery(sql);
while (resultSet.next()) {

    System.out.println("Id: " + resultSet.getInt(1) +
                    "Name: " + resultSet.getString(2) +
                    "Salary: " + resultSet.getInt(3));
}
System.out.println();
```

```
        resultSet.close();

        // Whether a commit occurs after a SELECT statement
        // because auto-commit is on depends on the driver.
        // It's safest to assume a commit occurs here.

        // Prepare the UPDATE statement for multiple executions
        sql = "UPDATE employees SET salary = salary * 1.05" +
          "WHERE id = ?";
        prepStmt = con.prepareStatement(sql);

        // Because auto-commit is on,
        // a commit occurs each time through loop
        // for total of 10 commits
        for (int index = 0; index < 10; index++) {
          prepStmt.setInt(1, index);
          prepStmt.executeUpdate();
        }

       // Execute a SELECT statement. A prepare is unnecessary
       // because it's only executed once.
       sql = "SELECT id, name, salary FROM employees";

        // Fetch the data
        resultSet = stmt.executeQuery(sql);
        while (resultSet.next()) {

       System.out.println("Id: " + resultSet.getInt(1) +
                      "Name: " + resultSet.getString(2) +
                      "Salary: " + resultSet.getInt(3));
        }
       System.out.println();

        // Close the result set
        resultSet.close();
```

```
// Whether a commit occurs after a SELECT statement
// because auto-commit is on depends on the driver.
// It's safest to assume a commit occurs here.

}
finally {

closeResultSet(resultSet);
closeStatement(stmt);
closeStatement(prepStmt);
}

}
```

Performance Tip

Because of the significant amount of disk I/O on the database server
required to commit every operation and the extra network round trips
that are required between the driver and the database server, it's a good
idea to turn off auto-commit mode in your application and use manual
commits instead. Using manual commits allows your application to control when database work is committed, which provides dramatically better performance. To turn off auto-commit mode, use the Connection
method setAutoCommit(false).

For example, let's look at the following Java code. It's identical to the previous Java code except that it turns off auto-commit mode and uses manual commits.

```
// For conciseness, this code omits error checking

// Turn auto-commit off
con.setAutoCommit(false);

// Create a Statement object
stmt = con.createStatement();
```

```
// Prepare an INSERT statement for multiple executions
sql = "INSERT INTO employees VALUES (?, ?, ?)";
prepStmt = con.prepareStatement(sql);

// Set parameter values before execution
prepStmt.setInt(1, 20);
prepStmt.setString(2, "Employee20");
prepStmt.setInt(3, 100000);
prepStmt.executeUpdate();

// Change parameter values for the next execution
prepStmt.setInt(1, 21);
prepStmt.setString(2, "Employee21");
prepStmt.setInt(3, 150000);
prepStmt.executeUpdate();
prepStmt.close();

// Manual commit
con.commit();

// Execute a SELECT statement. A prepare is unnecessary
// because it's executed only once.
sql = "SELECT id, name, salary FROM employees";

// Fetch the data
resultSet = stmt.executeQuery(sql);
while (resultSet.next()) {

   System.out.println("Id: " + resultSet.getInt(1) +
                  "Name: " + resultSet.getString(2) +
                  "Salary: " + resultSet.getInt(3));
}
System.out.println();
resultSet.close();
```

```
// Prepare the UPDATE statement for multiple executions
sql = "UPDATE employees SET salary = salary * 1.05" +
   "WHERE id = ?";
prepStmt = con.prepareStatement(sql);

// Execute the UPDATE statement for each
// value of index between 0 and 9
for (int index = 0; index < 10; index++) {
   prepStmt.setInt(1, index);
   prepStmt.executeUpdate();
}

// Manual commit
con.commit();

// Execute a SELECT statement. A prepare is unnecessary
// because it's only executed once.
sql = "SELECT id, name, salary FROM employees";

// Fetch the data
resultSet = stmt.executeQuery(sql);
while (resultSet.next()) {

   System.out.println("Id: " + resultSet.getInt(1) +
                  "Name: " + resultSet.getString(2) +
                  "Salary: " + resultSet.getInt(3));
}
System.out.println();

// Close the result set
resultSet.close();

}
finally {
```

```
            closeResultSet(resultSet);
            closeStatement(stmt);
            closeStatement(prepStmt);
        }

    }
```

See "Managing Commits in Transactions," page 22, for information on when to commit work if you've turned off auto-commit mode.

Choosing the Right Transaction Model

Which type of transaction should you use: local or distributed? A local transaction accesses and updates data on a single database. A distributed transaction accesses and updates data on multiple databases; therefore, it must be coordinated among those databases.

Performance Tip

Distributed transactions, as specified by the Java Transaction API (JTA), are substantially slower than local transactions because of the logging and network round trips needed to communicate between all the components involved in the distributed transaction. Unless distributed transactions are required, use local transactions.

If your application will be deployed on an application server, you also need to be aware that the default transactional behavior of many Java application servers is to use distributed transactions. Often, administrators, not developers, are responsible for deploying the application on the application server and may choose the default transaction behavior because they don't fully understand the performance impact of using distributed transactions.

For example, suppose you develop an application that leverages the use of two different jar files. Each jar file connects to a different database to perform work that is completely unrelated. One jar file connects to a database and increments the number of problem tickets in the system. The other jar file connects to another database to update a customer address. When your application is deployed, the application server may ask a tuning question similar to, "Is this component transactional?" The administrator thinks it over and decides that the safest answer is "yes." The administrator just cost your application a significant performance optimization.

What that question really means is, "Does this component access multiple data sources in a logical unit of work?" Obviously, some applications require distributed transactions, but many applications don't need the protection that distributed transactions provide or the overhead associated with them. Be sure to communicate with your application server administrator if you don't want your application to use the default transactional behavior of the application server.

See "Transaction Management," page 21, for more information about performance and transactions.

Executing SQL Statements

Use the guidelines in this section to help you select which JDBC objects and methods will give you the best performance when executing SQL statements.

Using Stored Procedures

Database drivers can call stored procedures on the database using either of the following methods:

- Execute the procedure the same way as any other SQL statement. The database parses the SQL statement, validates argument types, and converts arguments into the correct data types.
- Invoke a Remote Procedure Call (RPC) directly in the database. The database skips the parsing and optimization that executing a SQL statement requires.

> **Performance Tip**
>
> Call stored procedures by invoking an RPC with parameter markers for arguments instead of using literal arguments. Because the database skips the parsing and optimization required in executing the stored procedure as a SQL statement, performance is significantly improved.

Remember that SQL is always sent to the database as a character string. For example, consider the following stored procedure call, which passes a literal argument to the stored procedure:

```
{call getCustName (12345)}
```

Although the argument to getCustName() is an integer, the argument is passed inside a character string to the database, namely {call getCustName (12345)}. The database parses the SQL statement, isolates the single argument value of 12345, and converts the string 12345 into an integer value before executing the procedure as a SQL language event. Using an RPC on the database, your application can pass the parameters to the RPC. The driver sends a database protocol packet that contains the parameters in their native data type formats, skipping the parsing and optimization required to execute the stored procedure as a SQL statement. Compare the following examples.

Example A: Not Using a Server-Side RPC

The stored procedure getCustName isn't optimized to use a server-side RPC. The database treats the SQL stored procedure execution request as a normal SQL language event, which includes parsing the statement, validating the argument types, and converting the arguments into the correct data types before executing the procedure.

```
CallableStatement cstmt =
   conn.prepareCall ("{call getCustName (12345)}");
ResultSet rs = cstmt.executeQuery ();
```

Example B: Using a Server-Side RPC

The stored procedure getCustName is optimized to use a server-side RPC. Because the application avoids literal arguments and calls the procedure by specifying arguments as parameters, the driver optimizes the execution by invoking the stored procedure directly on the database as an RPC. The SQL language processing by the database is avoided, and execution time is faster.

```
CallableStatement cstmt =
   conn.prepareCall ("{call getCustName (?)}");
cstmt.setLong (1, 12345);
ResultSet rs = cstmt.executeQuery();
```

Why doesn't the driver parse and automatically change the SQL stored procedure call when it encounters a literal argument so that it can execute the stored procedure using an RPC? Consider this example:

```
{call getCustname (12345)}
```

The driver doesn't know if the value 12345 represents an integer, a decimal, a smallint, a bigint, or another numeric data type. To determine the correct data type for packaging the RPC request, the driver must make an expensive network round trip to the database server. The overhead needed to determine the true data type of the literal argument far outweighs the benefit of trying to execute the request as an RPC.

Using Statements Versus Prepared Statements

Most applications have a set of SQL statements that are executed multiple times and a few SQL statements that are executed only once or twice during the life of an application. Choose the Statement object or PreparedStatement object depending on how frequently you plan to execute the SQL statement.

The Statement object is optimized for a SQL statement that is executed only once. In contrast, the PreparedStatement object is optimized for SQL statements that are executed multiple times. Although the overhead for the initial execution of a prepared statement is high, the advantage is realized with subsequent executions of the SQL statement.

Using a PreparedStatement object typically results in at least two network round trips to the database server:

- One network round trip to parse and optimize the statement
- One or more network round trips to execute the statement and retrieve results

---

Performance Tip

If your application makes a request only once during its life span, using a Statement object is a better choice than using a PreparedStatement object because the Statement object results in only a single network round trip. Remember, reducing network communication typically provides the most performance gain. For example, if you have an application that runs an end-of-day sales report, send the query that generates the data for that report to the database as a Statement object, not a PreparedStatement object.

Often, database applications use connection pooling, statement pooling, or a combination of both to obtain better performance. How do these features affect whether you should use a Statement or PreparedStatement object?

If you're using JDBC 3.0 and earlier, use the following guidelines:

- If you're using statement pooling and a SQL statement will be executed only once, use a Statement object, which is not placed in the statement pool. This avoids the overhead associated with finding that statement in the pool.
- If a SQL statement will be executed infrequently but may be executed multiple times during the life of a statement pool inside a connection pool, use a PreparedStatement object. Under similar circumstances without statement pooling, use a Statement object.

JDBC 4.0 provides a more granular level of statement pooling. Statement pooling implementations give no weight to a PreparedStatement object that's executed 100 times versus one that's executed only twice. JDBC 4.0 allows applications to hint to the pool manager about whether a prepared statement should be pooled or nonpooled. Prepared statements that are executed multiple times can be pooled to provide optimal performance. Those that are used infrequently can be nonpooled and, consequently, do not affect the pool.

See "SQL Statements," page 27, for more information about using statements versus prepared statements. See "Using Statement Pooling with Connection Pooling," page 238, for information about performance and using statement pooling with connection pooling.

Using Batches Versus Prepared Statements

Updating large amounts of data typically is done by preparing an Insert statement and executing that statement multiple times, resulting in many network round trips to the database server.

Performance Tip

To reduce the number of network round trips when updating large amounts of data, you can send multiple Insert statements to the database at a time using the addBatch() method of the PreparedStatement interface.

For example, let's compare the following examples.

Example A: Executing a Prepared Statement Multiple Times

A prepared statement is used to execute an `Insert` statement multiple times, requiring 101 network round trips to perform 100 `Insert` operations: 1 round trip to prepare the statement and 100 additional round trips to execute its iterations.

```
PreparedStatement ps = conn.prepareStatement(
   "INSERT INTO employees VALUES (?, ?, ?)");
for (n = 0; n < 100; n++) {
   ps.setString(name[n]);
   ps.setLong(id[n]);
   ps.setInt(salary[n]);
   ps.executeUpdate();
}
```

Example B: Using a Batch

When the `addBatch()` method is used to consolidate 100 `Insert` operations, only two network round trips are required: one to prepare the statement and another to execute the batch. Although batches use more CPU cycles, performance is gained by reducing the number of network round trips.

```
PreparedStatement ps = conn.prepareStatement(
   "INSERT INTO employees VALUES (?, ?, ?)");
for (n = 0; n < 100; n++) {
   ps.setString(name[n]);
   ps.setLong(id[n]);
   ps.setInt(salary[n]);
   ps.addBatch();
}
ps.executeBatch();
```

Using **getXXX** Methods to Fetch Data from a Result Set

The JDBC API provides the following methods of fetching data from a result set:

- Generic data type method, such as getObject()
- Specific data type method, such as getInt(), getLong(), and getString()

Because the getObject() method is generic, it provides poor performance when nondefault data type mappings are specified. The driver must perform extra processing to determine the data type of the value being fetched and generate the appropriate mapping. This process is called **boxing**. When boxing occurs, memory is allocated from the Java heap on the database client to create an object, which can force a garbage collection to occur. See "Garbage Collection," page 79, for more information about the impact garbage collection has on performance.

Performance Tip

Use a specific method of fetching data for the data type instead of a generic method. For example, use the getInt() method to fetch an Integer value instead of the getObject() method.

You can also improve performance if you provide the column number of the result column being fetched instead of the column name, such as getString(1), getLong(2), and getInt(3). If column names are specified, the number of network round trips doesn't increase, but costly lookups do. For example, suppose that you specify the following:

```
getString("foo")...
```

If the column name is uppercase in the database, the driver must convert foo to uppercase (FOO) and then compare FOO to all the columns in the column list. That's a costly operation, especially if the result set contains many columns. If the driver can go directly to result column 23, a significant amount of processing is saved.

For example, suppose you have a result set that has 15 columns and 100 rows. You want to retrieve data from only three columns: employee_name (string), employee_number (bigint), and salary (integer). If you specify getString("Employee_Name"), getLong("Employee_Number"), and getInt("Salary"), the driver must convert each column name to the appropriate case of the columns in the database metadata, causing a considerable increase in lookups. In contrast, performance improves significantly if you specify getString(1), getLong(2), and getInt(15).

Retrieving Auto-Generated Keys

Many databases have hidden columns named **pseudo-columns** that store a unique key associated with each row in a table. Typically, using a pseudo-column in a SQL statement is the fastest way to access a row because the pseudo-column usually points to the exact location of the physical record.

Prior to JDBC 3.0, an application could only retrieve the value of a pseudo-column by executing a Select statement immediately after inserting the data. For example, let's look at the following code that retrieves a value from an Oracle ROWID:

```
// insert row
int rowcount = stmt.executeUpdate (
    "INSERT INTO LocalGeniusList (name) VALUES ('Karen')");

// now get the disk address - rowid -
// for the newly inserted row
ResultSet rs = stmt.executeQuery (
    "SELECT rowid FROM LocalGeniusList
    WHERE name = 'Karen'");
```

Retrieving pseudo-columns using this method has two major flaws:

- An additional query is sent over the network and executed on the database server, resulting in increased network communication.
- If the database table doesn't have a primary key, the search condition of the query can't uniquely identify the row. Multiple pseudo-column values could be retrieved, and the application could be unable to determine which value is actually the value for the most recently inserted row.

With JDBC 3.0 and later, you can retrieve auto-generated key information for a row at the same time that the row is inserted into a table. The auto-generated key uniquely identifies the row, even when a primary key doesn't exist on the table. For example:

```
// insert row AND retrieve key
int rowcount = stmt.executeUpdate (
   "INSERT INTO LocalGeniusList (name) VALUES ('Karen')",
      Statement.RETURN_GENERATED_KEYS);
ResultSet rs = stmt.getGeneratedKeys();
// key is available for future queries
```

The application now has a value that it can use in the search condition of any subsequent queries to provide the fastest access to the row.

Retrieving Data

Retrieve only the data you need, and choose the most efficient method to retrieve that data. Use the guidelines in this section to help optimize your performance when retrieving data.

Retrieving Long Data

Retrieving long data—such as large XML files, long varchar/text, long varbinary, Clobs, and Blobs—across a network is slow and resource intensive. Most users really don't want to see long data. For example, imagine the user interface of an employee directory application that allows the user to look up an employee's phone extension and department, and optionally, view an employee's photograph by clicking the name of the employee.

Employee	Phone	Dept
Harding	X4568	Manager
Hoover	X4324	Sales
Lincoln	X4329	Tech
Taft	X4569	Sales

Retrieving each employee's photograph would slow performance unnecessarily. If the user does want to see the photograph, he can click the employee name and the application can query the database again, specifying only the long columns in the Select list. This method allows users to retrieve result sets without paying a high performance penalty for network traffic.

Although excluding long data from the Select list is the best approach, some applications do not formulate the Select list before sending the query to the driver (that is, some applications use SELECT * FROM table ...). If the Select list contains long data, the driver is forced to retrieve that long data, even if the application never requests the long data from the result set. For example, consider the following code:

```
ResultSet rs = stmt.executeQuery (
    "SELECT * FROM employees WHERE SSID = '999-99-2222'");
rs.next();
string name = rs.getString(1);
```

When a query is executed, the driver has no way to determine which result columns the application will use; an application may fetch any result column that is retrieved. When the driver processes a ResultSet.next() request, it retrieves at least one, and often multiple, result rows from the database across the network. A result row contains all the column values for each row. What if one of the columns includes long data such as an employee photograph? Performance would slow considerably.

> **Performance Tip**
>
> Because retrieving long data across the network negatively affects per-formance, design your application to exclude long data from the Select list.

Limiting the Select list to contain only the name column results in a faster performing query at runtime. For example:

```
ResultSet rs = stmt.executeQuery (
    "SELECT name FROM employees" +
    "WHERE SSID = '999-99-2222'");
rs.next();
string name = rs.getString(1);
```

Although the methods of the Blob and Clob interfaces allow an application to control how long data is retrieved, it's important to understand that drivers often emulate the getBlob() and getClob() methods because many databases do not support true Large Object (LOB) locators or because of the complexity of mapping LOBs to the JDBC model. For example, an application may execute

`Blob.getBytes(1,1000)` to retrieve only the first 1000 bytes of a 3MB Blob value. You may assume that only 1000 bytes are retrieved from the database. If the driver emulates this functionality, the reality is that the entire 3MB Blob value is retrieved across the network and cached, which slows performance.

Limiting the Amount of Data Retrieved

If your application executes a query that retrieves five rows when it needs only two, application performance suffers, especially if the unnecessary rows include long data.

> ### Performance Tip
>
> One of the easiest ways to improve performance is to limit the amount of network traffic between the driver and the database server—optimally by writing SQL queries that instruct the driver to retrieve from the database only the data that the application requires.

Make sure that your `Select` statements use a `Where` clause to limit the amount of data that is retrieved. Even when using a `Where` clause, a `Select` statement that does not adequately restrict its request could retrieve hundreds of rows of data. For example, if you want data from the employees table for each manager hired in recent years, your application could execute the following statement, and subsequently, filter out the rows of employees who are not managers:

```
SELECT * FROM employees
WHERE hiredate > 2000
```

However, suppose the employees table contains a column that stores photographs of each employee. In this case, retrieving extra rows is extremely expensive to your application performance. Let the database filter the request for you and avoid sending extra data that you don't need across the network. The following query uses a better approach, limiting the data retrieved and improving performance:

```
SELECT * FROM employees
WHERE hiredate > 2003 and job_title='Manager'
```

Sometimes applications need to use SQL queries that generate a large amount of network traffic. For example, consider an application that displays information from support case histories, which each contain a 10MB log file. Does the user really need to see the entire contents of the log file? If not, performance would improve if the application displayed only the first 1MB of the log file.

> **Performance Tip**
>
> When you cannot avoid retrieving data that generates a large amount of network traffic, your application can still control the amount of data being sent from the database to the driver by limiting the number of rows sent across the network and reducing the size of each row sent across the network.

Suppose you have a GUI-based application, and each screen can display no more than 20 rows of data. It's easy to construct a query that may retrieve a million rows, such as SELECT * FROM employees, but it's hard to imagine a scenario where a query that retrieves a million rows would be useful. When designing applications, it's a good practice to call the setMaxRows() method of the ResultSet interface as a fail-safe to limit the number of rows that a query can retrieve. For example, if an application calls rs.setMaxRows(10000), no query will retrieve more than 10,000 rows.

In addition, calling the setMaxFieldSize() method of the ResultSet interface limits the number of bytes of data that can be retrieved for a column value with the following data types:

- Binary
- Varbinary
- Longvarbinary
- Char
- Varchar
- Longvarchar

For example, consider an application that allows users to select from a repository of technical articles. Rather than retrieve and display the entire article, the application can call rs.setMaxFieldSize(153600) to retrieve only the first 150KB of text—enough to give users a reasonable preview of the article.

Determining the Number of Rows in a Result Set

Scrollable cursors let you go both forward and backward through a result set. However, because of limited support for server-side scrollable cursors in many database systems, JDBC drivers often emulate scrollable cursors, storing rows from a scrollable result set in a cache on the machine where the driver resides (client or application server).

Unless you are certain that the database natively supports using a scrollable result set, such as rs, do not call the rs.last() and rs.getRow() methods to find out how many rows the result set contains. For drivers that emulate scrollable cursors, calling rs.last() results in the driver retrieving all results across the network to reach the last row. This emulated model of scrollable cursors provides flexibility for the developer but comes with a performance penalty until the client cache of rows is fully populated. Instead of calling rs.last() to determine the number of rows, count the rows by iterating through the result set or obtain the number of rows by submitting a Select statement with the Count function. For example:

```
SELECT COUNT(*) FROM employees
```

Unfortunately, there's no easy way to tell if a database driver uses native server-side scrollable cursors or emulates this functionality. For Oracle or MySQL, you know the driver emulates scrollable cursors, but for other databases, it's more complicated. See "Using Scrollable Cursors," page 36, for details about which common databases support server-side scrollable cursors and how database drivers emulate scrollable cursors.

Performance Tip

In general, do not write code that relies on the number of result rows from a query because database drivers often must retrieve all rows in a result set to determine how many rows the query will return.

Choosing the Right Data Type

When designing your database schema, it's obvious that you need to think about the impact of storage requirements on the database server. Less obvious, but just as important, you need to think about the network traffic required to move data in its native format to and from the JDBC driver. Retrieving and sending certain data types across the network can increase or decrease network traffic.

> ### Performance Tip
>
> For multiuser, multivolume applications, billions, or even trillions, of network packets can move between the driver and the database server over the course of a day. Choosing data types that are processed efficiently can incrementally provide a measurable gain in performance.

See "Choosing the Right Data Type," page 34, for information about which data types are processed faster than others.

Choosing the Right Cursor

JDBC defines three cursor types:

- Forward-only
- Insensitive
- Sensitive

This section explains how to choose a cursor type for the best performance.

Forward-Only

A **forward-only** (or nonscrollable) cursor provides excellent performance for sequential reads of rows in a result set retrieved by a query. Using a forward-only cursor is the fastest method for retrieving table data in a result set. Because this cursor type is nonscrollable, you can't use it when the application needs to process rows in a nonsequential manner. For example, you can't use a forward-only cursor if you need to process the eighth row in a result set, followed by the first row, followed by the fourth row, and so on.

Insensitive

An **insensitive** cursor is ideal for applications that require high levels of concurrency on the database server and require the ability to scroll forward and backward through result sets. Most database systems do not support a native scrollable cursor type. However, most JDBC drivers support insensitive cursors by emulating this functionality in either of two ways:

- **Method 1**—At the first request of a row for an insensitive cursor, the driver retrieves all the result rows from the database and caches the entire contents of the result set on the driver machine in memory, on disk, or a combination of both. A severe performance hit occurs on the first request because the driver not only positions the cursor to the requested row, but also moves all the result rows across the network. Subsequent requests to position to the requested row do not affect performance because all the data has been cached locally; the driver simply positions the cursor to the row in the result set.

- **Method 2**—At the first request of a row for an insensitive cursor, the driver retrieves only as many result rows as necessary in as many network round trips to the database server as necessary and caches the result set on the driver machine. For example, suppose an application sends a `Select` statement that retrieves 10,000 rows and requests an insensitive cursor to position to row 40. If only 20 rows can be retrieved in one network round trip, the driver makes 2 network round trips to retrieve 40 rows on the first request. If the next request for a row is not in the cached result set, the driver makes the necessary number of round trips to retrieve more rows.

This method is known as **lazy fetching** and typically provides better performance for applications driven by a user interface.

For example, consider a GUI application that can't display more than 20 rows of data on a single screen. What happens when the application requests an insensitive scrollable cursor for a `Select` statement that retrieves 20,000 rows? If the application uses a driver that emulates insensitive cursors using Method 1, the user would experience a long wait for the first screen to display because the driver retrieves all 20,000 rows on the first request.

However, if the driver emulates insensitive cursors using Method 2, he can retrieve at least one screen of data using one network round trip on the first request. Users don't have to wait long for the first screen to display because the driver retrieves only 20 rows.

Suppose the user wants to see the last screen of data, and the application's first request is to position to row 20,000. In this case, the performance penalty is the same regardless of which method of emulation is used because all result rows have to be retrieved and cached to satisfy the request.

You also need to be aware of the amount of memory that the driver consumes when emulating insensitive cursors, especially when long data may be retrieved. For example, using either emulation method, what if our application retrieved 20,000 rows on the first request and each result row contained a 10MB

Clob value? All result rows, including the long data, would be retrieved and cached. This operation could quickly consume available memory on the driver machine. In this case, it's best to use a forward-only or sensitive cursor.

Sensitive

A **sensitive** cursor picks up data modifications in the database that affect the result set and is useful for applications that have the following characteristics:

- Provide forward and backward access to data
- Access data that changes frequently
- Retrieve a large number of rows and can't afford to pay the performance penalty associated with emulated insensitive cursors

Sometimes known as keyset-driven cursors, sensitive cursors, similar to insensitive cursors, often are emulated by JDBC drivers because they're not supported natively by the database.

Because sensitive cursors provide access to up-to-date data, the JDBC driver can't retrieve result rows and cache them on the driver machine because the values of the data stored in the database may change after they are cached. Instead, most drivers emulate sensitive cursors by modifying the query before it's sent to the database to include a key or a pseudo-column that serves as a key. When a sensitive cursor is requested, the driver retrieves the keys for every result row and caches those keys on the driver machine. When the application positions to a row, the driver looks up the value of the key associated with the requested row and executes a SQL statement using the key in the Where clause to ensure that only one result row, the one requested by the application, is retrieved.

For example, an Oracle JDBC driver may emulate a sensitive scrollable cursor in the following way:

Application Request	Driver Actions
executeQuery ("SELECT name, addr, picture FROM employees WHERE location = 'Raleigh'")	1. The driver sends the following statement to the Oracle database: `SELECT rowid FROM employees WHERE location = 'Raleigh'`
	2. The driver retrieves all result ROWIDs and caches them locally.

	3. The driver prepares the following statement to the Oracle database for future use:
	`SELECT name, addr, picture FROM employees`
	`WHERE ROWID = ?`

Application Request	**Driver Actions**

`next()` // position to row 1	1. The driver looks up the ROWID for row 1 in the cache.
	2. The driver executes the prepared statement, sending as a parameter the ROWID value from the lookup process:
	
	`SELECT name, addr, picture FROM employees`
	`WHERE ROWID = ?`
	
	3. The driver retrieves row 1 from the database and then returns success to the application indicating that the row is now positioned to row 1.

`next()`	1. The driver looks up the ROWID for row 2 in the cache.
	2. The driver executes the prepared statement, sending as a parameter the ROWID value from the lookup process:
	
	`SELECT name, addr, picture FROM employees`
	`WHERE ROWID = ?`
	
	3. The driver retrieves row 2 from the database and then returns success to the application indicating that the row is now positioned to row 2.

`last()`	1. The driver looks up the ROWID for the last row in the cache.
	2. The driver executes the prepared statement, sending as a parameter the ROWID value from the lookup process:
	
	`SELECT name, addr, picture FROM employees`
	`WHERE ROWID = ?`
	
	3. The driver retrieves the last row from the database and then returns success to the application indicating that the row is now positioned to the last row in the result set.

Unfortunately, this emulation technique isn't foolproof. If the SQL statement performs an outer join of multiple tables or uses a Group By clause, the emulation fails because a single key can't be used to obtain a result row. Typically, the cursor is automatically downgraded to an insensitive scrollable cursor.

Updating Data

Use the guidelines in this section to manage your updates more efficiently.

Using Positioned Updates, Inserts, and Deletes (**updateXXX** Methods)

Positioned Updates, Inserts, and Deletes, which are implemented using the updateXXX methods of the ResultSet object, are useful for GUI applications that allow application users to scroll through a result set, updating and deleting rows as they go. The application simply supplies the column in the result set to be updated and the data to be changed. Then, before moving the cursor from the row in the result set, the updateRow() method is called to update the database.

For example, in the following code, the value of the Age column of the ResultSet object rs is fetched using the getInt() method, and the updateInt() method is used to update the column with an int value of 25. The updateRow() method is called to update the row in the database with the modified value.

```
int n = rs.getInt("Age");
// n contains value of Age column in the resultset rs
...
rs.updateInt("Age", 25);
rs.updateRow();
```

Positioned updates typically are faster than updates using SQL commands because the cursor is already positioned on the row for the Select statement in process. If the row must be located, the database usually can use a key (for example, a ROWID for Oracle) that serves as an internal pointer to the row. In addition, positioned updates reduce the need to write complex SQL statements to update data, making the application easier to maintain.

Using **getBestRowIdentifier()** to Optimize Updates and Deletes

Some applications cannot be designed to take advantage of positioned Updates and Deletes. These applications typically formulate the Where clause by calling getPrimaryKeys() to use all searchable result columns or by calling getIndexInfo() to find columns that may be part of a unique index. These methods usually work but can result in fairly complex queries. For example:

```
ResultSet WSrs = WSs.executeQuery
    ("SELECT first_name, last_name, ssn, address, city,
    state, zip FROM employees");
```

```
// fetch data using complex query
...
WSs.executeQuery ("UPDATE employees SET address = ?
    WHERE first_name = ? and last_name = ? and ssn = ?
    and address = ? and city = ? and state = ?
    and zip = ?");
```

Many databases support pseudo-columns that are not explicitly defined by the user in the table definition but are hidden columns in every table (for example, ROWID for Oracle). Pseudo-columns often provide the fastest access to the data. Because pseudo-columns aren't part of the explicit table definition, they're not retrieved when getColumns() is called.

Performance Tip

Use the getBestRowIdentifier() method to determine the optimal set of columns that uniquely identify a row to use in the WHERE clause for updating data.

For example, to determine whether pseudo columns exist, use the following code:

```
...
ResultSet WSrowid = WSdbmd.getBestRowIdentifier()
    (... "employees", ...);
...
WSs.executeUpdate ("UPDATE employees SET ADDRESS = ?
    WHERE ROWID = ?";
// fastest access to the data!
```

If your database doesn't contain pseudo-columns, the result set of getBestRowIdentifier() consists of columns of the optimal unique index on the specified table (if a unique index exists). Therefore, your application doesn't need to call getIndexInfo() to find the smallest unique index.

Using Database Metadata Methods

Database metadata methods retrieve information about a result set, such as the number and type of columns. Because database metadata methods that generate ResultSet objects are slow compared to other JDBC methods, using them frequently can impair performance. Use the guidelines in this section to optimize performance when selecting and using database metadata.

Minimizing the Use of Database Metadata Methods

Compared to other JDBC methods, database metadata methods that generate result sets are slow. To retrieve all result column information mandated by the JDBC specification, a JDBC driver often must perform multiple or complex queries to retrieve the result set for a single call to a database metadata method.

> **Performance Tip**
>
> Although it's almost impossible to write a JDBC application without using a database metadata method, you can improve performance by minimizing their use.

In addition, to avoid executing database metadata methods multiple times, you should cache information retrieved from result sets generated by database metadata methods. For example, call getTypeInfo() once, and cache the elements of the result set that your application depends on. It's unlikely that any application will use all elements of the result set generated by a database metadata method, so the cache of information shouldn't be difficult to maintain.

Avoiding Search Patterns

Database metadata methods support arguments that can limit the amount of data retrieved. Using null values or search patterns, such as %A%, for these arguments often generates time-consuming queries. In addition, network traffic can increase because of unnecessary results.

> **Performance Tip**
>
> Always supply as many non-null arguments as possible to result sets that generate database metadata methods.

In the following example, an application uses the getTables() method to determine if the table named WSTable exists and provides null values for most of the arguments:

```
ResultSet WSrs = WSdbmd.getTables(null, null, "WSTable",
    null);
```

The driver interprets the request as follows: Retrieve all tables, views, system tables, synonyms, temporary tables, and aliases named WSTable that exist in any database schema in the database catalog.

In contrast, the following request provides non-null values for all arguments, allowing the driver to process the request more efficiently:

```
String[] tableTypes = {"TABLE"}; WSdbmd.getTables ("cat1",
    "johng", "WSTable", tableTypes);
```

The driver interprets the request as follows. Retrieve all tables in catalog "cat1" that are named "WSTable" and owned by "johng". No synonyms, views, system tables, aliases, or temporary tables are retrieved.

Sometimes little is known about the object that you are requesting information for. Any information that the application can provide the driver when calling database metadata methods can result in improved performance and reliability.

Using a Dummy Query to Determine Table Characteristics

Sometimes you need information about columns in the database table, such as column names, column data types, and column precision and scale. For example, an application that allows users to choose which columns to select may need to request the names of each column in the database table.

Performance Tip

To determine characteristics about a database table, avoid using the getColumns() method. Instead, use a dummy query inside a prepared statement that executes the getMetaData() method. Only use the getColumns() method when you can't obtain the requested information from result set metadata (for example, using the table column default values).

The following examples show the benefit of using the `getMetadata()` method over using the `getColumns()` method.

Example A: Using the `getColumns()` Method

A potentially complex query is prepared and executed, result description information is formulated, the driver retrieves the result rows, and the application fetches the result. This method results in increased CPU use and network communication.

```
ResultSet WSrc = WSc.getColumns (... "UnknownTable" ...);
// getColumns() will generate a query to
// the system catalogs and possibly a join
// that must be prepared, executed, and produce
// a result set
...
WSrc.next();
string Cname = getString(4);
...
// user must retrieve N rows from the database
// N = # result columns of UnknownTable
// result column information has now been obtained
```

Example B: Using the `getMetadata()` Method

A simple query that retrieves result set information is prepared, but the query is not executed and the driver does not retrieve result rows. Only information about the result set is retrieved (the same information retrieved by `getColumns()` in Example A).

```
// prepare dummy query
PreparedStatement WSps = WSc.prepareStatement
    ("SELECT * FROM UnknownTable WHERE 1 = 0");

// query is not executed on the database - only prepared
ResultSetMetaData WSsmd=WSps.getMetaData();
```

```
int numcols = WSrsmd.getColumnCount();
...
int ctype = WSrsmd.getColumnType(n)
...
// Result column information has now been obtained
// Note we also know the column ordering within the
// table!
```

What if the database system, such as Microsoft SQL Server, doesn't support prepared statements by default? The performance of Example A wouldn't change, but the performance of Example B would decrease slightly because the dummy query is evaluated in addition to being prepared. Because the Where clause of the query always evaluates to FALSE, the statement executes without retrieving result rows. So, even with a slight decrease in performance, Example B still outperforms Example A.

Summary

The performance of JDBC applications can suffer if they fail to reduce network traffic, limit disk I/O, simplify queries, and optimize the interaction between the application and driver. Reducing network communication probably is the most important technique for improving performance. For example, when you need to update large amounts of data, using batches rather than executing an Insert statement multiple times reduces the number of network round trips required by the driver to complete the operation.

Typically, creating a connection is the most performance-expensive task your application performs. Connection pooling can help you manage connections efficiently, particularly if your application has numerous users. Regardless of whether your application uses connection pooling, make sure that you close connections immediately after your application is finished with them.

Making smart choices about how to handle transactions can also improve performance. For example, using manual commits instead of auto-commit mode provides better control over when work is committed. Similarly, if you don't need the protection of distributed transactions, using local transactions can improve performance.

Inefficient SQL queries slow the performance of JDBC applications. Some SQL queries don't filter data, causing the driver to retrieve unnecessary data. Your application pays a huge penalty in performance when that unnecessary data is long data such as data stored as a Blob or Clob. Other queries can be overly complex, causing additional processing at runtime.

CHAPTER SEVEN

.NET Applications: Writing Good Code

Developing performance-optimized ADO.NET applications is not easy. Data providers don't throw exceptions to tell you when your code is running slow. Because programming concepts vary between different data providers, coding a .NET application can be more complex than coding an ODBC or JDBC application. In addition, designing a .NET application requires more knowledge about the database your application accesses.

This chapter describes some general guidelines for coding practices that improve ADO.NET application performance. These guidelines have been compiled by examining the ADO.NET implementations of numerous shipping ADO.NET applications. In general, the guidelines described in this chapter improve performance because they accomplish one or more of the following goals:

- Reduce network traffic
- Limit disk I/O
- Optimize application-to-data provider interaction
- Simplify queries

If you've read the other coding chapters (Chapters 5 and 6), you'll notice that some of the information here resembles those chapters. While there are some similarities, this chapter focuses on specific information about coding for ADO.NET.

Managing Connections

Typically, creating a connection is one of the most performance-expensive operations that an application performs. Developers often assume that establishing a connection is a simple request that results in the data provider making a single network round trip to the database server to validate the user's credentials. In reality, a connection involves many network round trips between the data provider and the database server. For example, when a data provider connects to Oracle or Sybase ASE, that connection may require seven to ten network round trips. In addition, the database establishes resources on behalf of the connection, which involves performance-expensive disk I/O and memory allocation.

Your time will be well spent if you sit down and design how to handle connections before implementing them in your application. Use the guidelines in this section to manage your connections more efficiently.

Connecting Efficiently

Database applications use either of the following methods to manage connections:

- Obtain a connection from a connection pool.
- Create a new connection one at a time as needed.

When choosing a method to manage connections, keep in mind the following facts about connections and performance:

- Creating a connection is performance-expensive.
- Open connections use a substantial amount of memory on both the database server and the database client.
- Opening numerous connections can contribute to an out-of-memory condition, which causes paging of memory to disk and, thus, overall performance degradation.

Using Connection Pooling

If your application has multiple users and your database server provides sufficient database resources, such as memory and CPU, using connection pooling can provide significant performance gains. Reusing a connection reduces the number of network round trips needed to establish a physical connection between the provider and the database. The performance penalty is paid up front at the time the connection pool is populated with connections. Because the connections in the pool are actually used by the application, performance improves significantly. Obtaining a connection becomes one of the fastest operations an application performs instead of one of the slowest.

Connection pooling for ADO.NET is not part of the .NET Framework. To use connection pooling, the data provider or your application must implement it. As of the publishing date of this book, most commercial ADO.NET data providers provide connection pooling. Check your own data provider to verify that it provides this functionality. For all commercial ADO.NET providers that offer connection pooling, connections are pooled by default.

Although obtaining connections from a pool is efficient, when your application opens and closes connections impacts the scalability of your application. When opened, connections are marked as "in use" by the pool manager. When closed, connections are marked as "not in use" and are made available for other users. Open connections just before the user needs them, not sooner, to minimize the time that the physical connection is marked "in use." Similarly, close connections as soon as the user no longer needs them so that they are available for other users.

For ADO.NET, each unique connection string creates a connection pool (except in the case of reauthentication). Once created, connection pools are not closed until the data provider is unloaded. Typically, more memory is required to manage multiple connection pools. However, it's important to understand that it's the number of connections, not the number of connection pools, that consumes significant memory. In a well-designed connection pooling implementation, the maintenance of inactive or empty connection pools involves minimal system overhead.

To minimize the number of connections required in a connection pool to service users, you can switch a user associated with a connection to another user if your data provider supports a feature known as reauthentication. Minimizing the number of connections conserves memory and can improve performance. See "Using Reauthentication with Connection Pooling," page 232.

See Chapter 8, "Connection Pooling and Statement Pooling," for details about connection pooling.

Establishing Connections One at a Time

Some applications are not good candidates for using connection pooling. See "When Not to Use Connection Pooling," page 15, for examples.

> **Performance Tip**
>
> If your application does not use connection pooling, avoid connecting and disconnecting multiple times throughout your application to execute SQL statements because of the performance hit your application pays for opening connections. You don't need to open a new connection for each SQL statement your application executes.

Disconnecting Efficiently

Each physical connection to the database consumes a substantial amount of memory on both the client and database server.

> **Performance Tip**
>
> Remember to close connections immediately after your application is finished with them—don't wait for the garbage collector to close them for you. This is particularly important if your application uses connection pooling so that connections are returned to the connection pool immediately for other users to use. However, remember that closing a connection automatically closes all `DataReader` objects associated with the connection and the ability to fetch results using those objects.

For ADO.NET applications, the .NET **Common Language Runtime (CLR)** uses garbage collection to automatically identify and reclaim memory allocated to objects that are no longer in use. If you wait for the garbage collector to clean up connections that are no longer being used, memory is tied up for longer than necessary. The garbage collector in the CLR typically runs only when there are sufficient CPU resources to accommodate it. If your application runs on a busy computer, the garbage collector may run infrequently, leaving connections that are no longer being used in an open or "in use" state for extended periods of time.

Even when connection pooling is used, relying on the garbage collector to clean up connections that are no longer being used impairs performance. When a user requests a connection and one is unavailable, the data provider waits for a specified period for a connection to be marked "not in use." Therefore, connections waiting for the garbage collector can cause significant delays to other users. Instead, always remember to explicitly close connections as soon as the user no longer needs them.

As a fail-safe for closing open connections, not as a substitute, you can close connections inside a finally block, as shown in the following example. Code in the finally block always runs, even if an exception occurs. This code guarantees that any connections you may not have explicitly closed are closed without waiting for the garbage collector.

```
try
{
    DBConn.Open();

    // Do some other interesting work
}
catch (Exception ex)
{

    // Handle exceptions
}
finally
{

// Close the connection
        if (DBConn != null)
            DBConn.Close();
}
```

Another way you can guarantee that your connections are explicitly closed is to use a using block, as shown in the following example:

```
Using DBConn As New DDTek.Oracle.OracleConnection
    DBConn.Open();
    MsgBox("Connected.")
End Using
```

For more information about how garbage collection works in the Common Language Runtime (CLR), see ".NET CLR," page 82.

Obtaining Database and Data Provider Information Efficiently

Remember that creating a connection is one of the most performance-expensive operations that an application performs.

Performance Tip

Because of the performance hit your application pays for opening connections, avoid establishing additional connections to gather information about the data provider and the database, such as supported data types or database versions. For example, some applications establish a connection and then call a method in a separate component that reconnects and gathers information about the data provider and the database. Use the `DbMetaDataCollectionNames.DataSourceInformation` field of the `GetSchema` method to share metadata.

How often do databases change their supported data types or database versions between connections? Because this type of information typically doesn't change between connections and isn't a large amount of information to store, you may want to retrieve and cache the information so the application can access it later.

Managing Transactions

To ensure data integrity, all statements in a transaction are committed or rolled back as a unit. For example, when you use a computer to transfer money from one bank account to another, the request involves a transaction—updating values stored in the database for both accounts. If all parts of that unit of work succeed, the transaction is committed. If any part of that unit of work fails, the transaction is rolled back.

Use the guidelines in this section to manage transactions more efficiently.

Managing Commits in Transactions

Committing (and rolling back) transactions is slow because of the disk I/O and, potentially, the number of network round trips required. What does a commit actually involve? The database must write to disk every modification made by a transaction to the database. This is usually a sequential write to a journal file (or log); nevertheless, it involves expensive disk I/O.

In ADO.NET, the default transaction commit mode is auto-commit. In auto-commit mode, a commit is performed for every SQL statement that requires a request to the database (Insert, Update, Delete, and Select statements). When auto-commit mode is used, your application doesn't control when database work is committed. In fact, commits commonly occur when there's actually no real work to commit.

Some databases, such as DB2, don't support auto-commit mode. For these databases, the data provider sends a commit request after every successful operation (SQL statement). The commit request equates to a network round trip between the provider and the database. The round trip to the database occurs even though the application didn't request the commit and even if the operation made no changes to the database. For example, the data provider makes a network round trip even when a Select statement is executed.

Let's look at the following code, which doesn't turn off auto-commit mode. Comments in the code show when commits occur if the data provider or the database performs commits automatically.

```
// For conciseness, this code omits error checking

// Allocate a Command object
cmd = conn.CreateCommand();

// Bind parameters
cmd.Parameters.Add("id", DB2DbType.Integer);
cmd.Parameters.Add("name", DB2DbType.VarChar);
cmd.Parameters.Add("name", DB2DbType.Integer);

// Prepare an INSERT statement for multiple executions
sql = "INSERT INTO employees VALUES(?, ?, ?)";
cmd.CommandText = sql;
cmd.Prepare();

// Set parameter values before execution
cmd.Parameters[0].Value=20;
cmd.Parameters[1].Value="Employee20";
cmd.Parameters[2].Value=100000;
```

```
cmd.ExecuteNonQuery();

// A commit occurs because auto-commit is on

// Change parameter values for the next execution
cmd.Parameters[0].Value = 21;
cmd.Parameters[1].Value = "Employee21";
cmd.Parameters[2].Value = 150000;

cmd.ExecuteNonQuery();

// A commit occurs because auto-commit is on

// Execute a SELECT statement. A prepare is unnecessary
// because it's executed only once.
sql = "SELECT id, name, salary FROM employees";
cmd.CommandText = sql;

// Fetch the data
dataReader = cmd.ExecuteReader();
while (dataReader.Read()) {
   System.Console.WriteLine("Id: " + dataReader.GetInt32(0) +
                   " Name: " + dataReader.GetString(1) +
                   " Salary: " + dataReader.GetInt32(2));
}

// Close the DataReader
System.Console.WriteLine();
dataReader.Close();

// Whether a commit occurs after a SELECT statement
// because auto-commit is on depends on the provider.
// It's safest to assume a commit occurs here.
```

```
// Prepare the UPDATE statement for multiple executions
sql="UPDATE employees SET salary = salary * 1.05 WHERE id=?";
cmd.CommandText = sql;
cmd.Prepare();

// Execute the UPDATE statement for each
// value of index between 0 and 9
for (int index = 0; index < 10; index++) {
   cmd.Parameters[0].Value = index;
   cmd.ExecuteNonQuery();

// Because auto-commit is on, a commit occurs each time
// through loop for total of 10 commits.

}

// Execute a SELECT statement. A prepare is unnecessary
// because it's only executed once.
sql = "SELECT id, name, salary FROM employees";
cmd.CommandText = sql;

// Fetch the data
dataReader = cmd.ExecuteReader();
while (dataReader.Read()) {
   System.Console.WriteLine("Id: " + dataReader.GetInt32(0) +
                     " Name: " + dataReader.GetString(1) +
                     " Salary: " + dataReader.GetInt32(2));
}

System.Console.WriteLine();

// Whether a commit occurs after a SELECT statement
// because auto-commit is on depends on the provider.
// It's safest to assume a commit occurs here.
```

```
// Close the DataReader
dataReader.Close();
}
finally {
   dataReader.Close();

   cmd.Dispose();
}
```

Performance Tip

Because of the significant amount of disk I/O on the database server required to commit every operation and the extra network round trips that occur between the data provider and the database server, it's a good idea to turn off auto-commit mode in your application and use manual commits instead. Using manual commits allows your application to control when database work is committed, which provides dramatically better performance. Auto-commit mode is automatically turned off when a transaction is explicitly requested.

For example, let's look at the following code. It's identical to the previous code except that it turns off auto-commit mode by starting a transaction and uses manual commits.

```
// For conciseness, this code omits error checking

// Start the transaction. This turns auto-commit off.
transaction = conn.BeginTransaction();

// Allocate a Command object
cmd = conn.CreateCommand();
cmd.Transaction = transaction;

// Bind parameters
cmd.Parameters.Add("id", DB2DbType.Integer);
```

```
cmd.Parameters.Add("name", DB2DbType.VarChar);
cmd.Parameters.Add("name", DB2DbType.Integer);

// Prepare an INSERT statement for multiple executions
sql = "INSERT INTO employees VALUES(?, ?, ?)";
cmd.CommandText = sql;
cmd.Prepare();

// Set parameter values before execution
cmd.Parameters[0].Value = 20;
cmd.Parameters[1].Value = "Employee20";
cmd.Parameters[2].Value = 100000;

cmd.ExecuteNonQuery();

// Change parameter values for the next execution
cmd.Parameters[0].Value = 21;
cmd.Parameters[1].Value = "Employee21";
cmd.Parameters[2].Value = 150000;

cmd.ExecuteNonQuery();

// Manual commit
transaction.Commit();

// Execute a SELECT statement. A prepare is unnecessary
// because it's only executed once.
sql = "SELECT id, name, salary FROM employees";
cmd.CommandText = sql;

// Fetch the data
dataReader = cmd.ExecuteReader();
while (dataReader.Read()) {
   System.Console.WriteLine("Id: " + dataReader.GetInt32(0) +
                     " Name: " + dataReader.GetString(1) +
```

```
                              " Salary: " + dataReader.GetInt32(2));
}

System.Console.WriteLine();

// Close the DataReader
dataReader.Close();

// Prepare the UPDATE statement for multiple executions
transaction = conn.BeginTransaction();
sql = "UPDATE employees SET salary = salary * 1.05" +
   "WHERE id=?";
cmd.CommandText = sql;
cmd.Prepare();

// Execute the UPDATE statement for each
// value of index between 0 and 9
for (int index = 0; index < 10; index++) {
   cmd.Parameters[0].Value = index;
   cmd.ExecuteNonQuery();
}

// Manual commit
transaction.Commit();

// Execute a SELECT statement. A prepare is unnecessary
// because it's only executed once.
sql = "SELECT id, name, salary FROM employees";
cmd.CommandText = sql;

// Fetch the data
dataReader = cmd.ExecuteReader();
while (dataReader.Read()) {
   System.Console.WriteLine("Id: " + dataReader.GetInt32(0) +
                    " Name: " + dataReader.GetString(1) +
```

```
                    " Salary: " + dataReader.GetInt32(2));
   }

   System.Console.WriteLine();

   // Close the DataReader
   dataReader.Close();
   }
   finally {
      dataReader.Close();
      cmd.Dispose();
   }
```

See "Managing Commits in Transactions," page 22, for information on when to commit work if you've turned off auto-commit mode.

Choosing the Right Transaction Model

Which type of transaction should you use: local or distributed? A local transaction accesses and updates data on a single database. A distributed transaction accesses and updates data on multiple databases; therefore, it must be coordinated among those databases.

> **Performance Tip**
>
> Distributed transactions are substantially slower than local transactions because of the logging and network round trips needed to communicate between all the components involved in the distributed transaction. Unless distributed transactions are required, you should use local transactions.

In .NET Framework 2.0, the System.Transactions namespace manages transactions. The best way to determine if your application is using distributed transactions is to look for the following line of code and examine the code that follows:

```
using System.Transactions;
```

See "Transaction Management," page 21, for more information about performance and transactions.

Executing SQL Statements

Use the guidelines in this section to help you select which ADO.NET objects and methods will give you the best performance when executing SQL statements.

Executing SQL Statements that Retrieve Little or No Data

In .NET applications, you can execute SQL statements using the following methods of the Command object:

- The ExecuteNonQuery method returns the number of rows affected, but does not return actual rows.
- The ExecuteReader method returns a DataReader object containing one or multiple rows of data.
- The ExecuteScalar method returns the first column of the first row of the result set.

Performance Tip

Execute SQL statements that don't retrieve data, such as Update, Insert, and Delete statements, using the ExecuteNonQuery method of the Command object. Although you can execute these statements using the ExecuteReader method, using ExecuteNonQuery improves performance because it allows the data provider to optimize the statement in the following ways: It reduces the number of network round trips to the database server because it doesn't request a description of the result set and it eliminates the need to allocate and deallocate buffers to hold the result set description on the client or application server.

The following example shows how to insert a row into the employees table using ExecuteNonQuery:

```
DBConn.Open();
DBTxn = DBConn.BeginTransaction();
```

```
// Set the Connection property of the Command object
DBCmd.Connection = DBConn;

// Set the text of the Command to the INSERT statement
DBCmd.CommandText = "INSERT into employees" +
   "VALUES (15, 'HAYES', 'ADMIN', 6, " +
   "'17-APR-2002', 18000, NULL, 4)";

// Set the transaction property of the Command object
DBCmd.Transaction = DBTxn;

// Execute using ExecuteNonQuery because we do not
// retrieve a result set
DBCmd.ExecuteNonQuery();

// Commit the transaction
DBTxn.Commit();

// Close the connection
DBConn.Close();
```

Performance Tip

If your SQL statement retrieves a single value, such as a sum or count, execute that statement using the ExecuteScalar method of the Command object. Again, you can use the ExecuteReader method to execute statements that retrieve a single value, but using the ExecuteScalar method allows the data provider to optimize for a result set that consists of a single row and column. The data provider improves performance by avoiding much of the same overhead described previously for ExecuteReader versus ExecuteNonQuery.

The following example shows how to retrieve the count of all employees with a yearly salary of more than $50,000 from the employees table using ExecuteScalar:

```
// Open a connection to the database
SybaseConnection Conn;
```

```
Conn = new SybaseConnection(
    "host=server1;port=4100;User ID=test;Password=test;
    Database Name=Accounting");
Conn.Open();

// Open a command object
SybaseCommand  salCmd = new SybaseCommand(
    "SELECT count(sal) FROM employees" +
    "WHERE sal>'50000'", Conn);

try
{
    int count = (int)salCmd.ExecuteScalar();
}
catch (Exception ex)
{

    // Display exceptions in a message box
    MessageBox.Show (ex.Message);
}

// Close the connection
Conn.Close();
```

Using the **Command.Prepare** Method

Most applications have a certain set of SQL statements that are executed multiple times and a few SQL statements that are executed only once or twice during the life of the application. You may want to use a prepared Command object depending on how frequently you plan to execute a SQL statement.

Some data providers don't perform an operation with the database when an application calls Command.Prepare(). These data providers still optimize objects associated with the Command object on the database client.

A nonprepared Command object is optimized for a SQL statement that is only executed once. In contrast, a prepared Command object is optimized for SQL statements that are executed multiple times. Although the overhead for the initial execution of a prepared Command object is high, the advantage is realized with subsequent executions of the prepared Command object.

Using a prepared Command object typically results in at least two network round trips to the database server:

- One network round trip to parse and optimize the statement
- One or more network round trips to execute the statement and retrieve results

---

Performance Tip

If the application makes a request only once during its life span, using a nonprepared Command object instead of a prepared Command object is a better choice because it results in only a single network round trip. Remember, reducing network communication typically provides the most performance gain.

See "SQL Statements," page 27, for more information about using statements versus prepared statements. See "Using Statement Pooling with Connection Pooling," page 238, for information about performance and using statement pooling with connection pooling.

Using Arrays of Parameters/Batches Versus Prepared Statements

Updating large amounts of data typically is done by preparing an Insert statement and executing that statement multiple times, resulting in numerous network round trips.

Performance Tip

To reduce the number of network round trips when updating large amounts of data, you can use arrays of parameters or batches of SQL statements.

Let's compare the following examples.

Example A: Executing a Prepared Command Object Multiple Times

A prepared Command object is used to execute an Insert statement multiple times. In this case, 101 network round trips are required to perform 100 Insert operations: 1 round trip to prepare the statement and 100 additional round trips to execute its iterations.

```
sql = "INSERT INTO employees VALUES (?, ?, ?)";
cmd.CommandText = sql;
cmd.Prepare();
for (n = 0; n < 100; n++) {
   cmd.Parameters[0].Value = id[n];
   cmd.Parameters[1].Value = name[n];
   cmd.Parameters[2].Value = salary[n];
   cmd.ExecuteNonQuery();
}
```

Example B: Using Arrays of Parameters and Batches

Command.CommandText is set to a string containing a single Insert statement and an array of parameters. Only two network round trips are required: one to prepare the statement and another to execute the array. Although arrays use more CPU cycles, performance is gained by reducing the number of network round trips.

```
sql = "INSERT INTO employees VALUES (?, ?, ?)";
cmd.CommandText = sql;
cmd.ArrayBindCount = 10;
cmd.Prepare();
cmd.Parameters[0].Value = idArray;
cmd.Parameters[1].Value = nameArray;
cmd.Parameters[2].Value = salaryArray;
cmd.ExecuteNonQuery();
```

Some data providers don't support arrays of parameters but do support batches of SQL. In this case, you can set `Command.CommandText` to a string that contains 100 `Insert` statements and execute those statements as a batch.

```
sql = "INSERT INTO employees VALUES (?, ?, ?)" +
  ";INSERT INTO employees VALUES (?, ?, ?)" +
  ...
  ";INSERT INTO employees VALUES (?, ?, ?)";
cmd.CommandText = sql;
cmd.Prepare();
cmd.Parameters[0].Value = id[0];
cmd.Parameters[1].Value = name[0];
cmd.Parameters[2].Value = salary[0];
...
cmd.Parameters[27].Value = id[9];
cmd.Parameters[28].Value = name[9];
cmd.Parameters[29].Value = salary[9];
cmd.ExecuteNonQuery();
```

If your application updates disconnected `DataSets` and your data provider supports batch processing, you can improve performance by setting the `UpdateBatchSize` property of the `DataAdapter` object. Setting this property improves performance by specifying the number of network round trips that are made to the database server. For example, the following code tells the data provider to group five commands and send them to the database in a single network round trip.

```
SqlDataAdapter adpt = new SqlDataAdapter();
adpt.InsertCommand = command;

// Specify the number of rows
adpt.UpdateBatchSize = 5;
```

Using Bulk Load

If you have a large amount of data to insert into a database table and your data provider supports bulk load, also known as bulk copy, using bulk load can be even faster than using arrays of parameters. You use bulk load functionality through the *xxx*BulkCopy class (for example, SqlBulkCopy or OracleBulkCopy), which many data providers support.

Using bulk load, rows are sent from the database client to the database in a continuous stream, without making extra network round trips. In addition, when a bulk load operation is performed, the database can optimize the way rows are inserted.

However, you should be aware that using bulk load can have negative side effects. For example, data inserted with bulk load may ignore referential integrity, causing consistency problems with data in the database.

Using Pure Managed Providers

Using 100% **managed code** allows your .NET assemblies to run inside the CLR. When the data provider bridges into **unmanaged code**, or code that is outside the .NET CLR, it adversely affects performance. The overhead associated with each call made outside the CLR is a subject that is highly debated, with various sources claiming that performance can degrade anywhere from 5% to 100% when compared to calls into managed code. In general, the performance hit is greater if the machine running the application is busy.

Be wary when choosing a data provider that advertises itself as a 100% or a pure managed code data provider. Many ADO.NET data providers make this claim yet use an architecture that bridges into native Windows code, as shown in Figure 7-1. For example, these data providers may call into the DB2 Call Level Interface (CLI) or Oracle SQL*Net.

Performance Tip

Using unmanaged code can significantly impact performance depending on how busy the machine running your application is. The bottom line is this: If a "managed" data provider requires unmanaged database clients or other unmanaged pieces, it's not a true managed data provider. Only a few vendors produce true managed data providers that work as a 100% managed component.

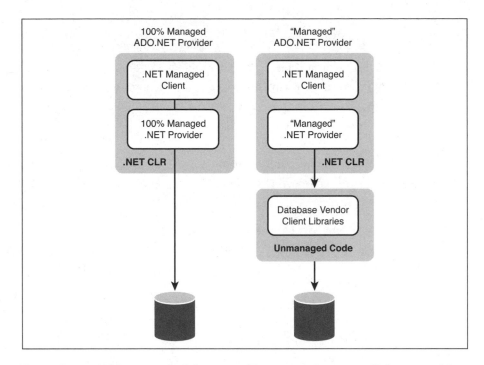

Figure 7-1   100% managed data provider versus "managed" data provider

Selecting .NET Objects and Methods

The guidelines in this section will help you to optimize system performance when selecting and using ADO.NET objects and methods.

Avoiding the CommandBuilder Object

Because of concurrency restrictions, the CommandBuilder often generates inefficient SQL statements. In most cases, you can code statements yourself that are more efficient than those the CommandBuilder generates. In addition, the CommandBuilder object generates statements at runtime. Each time the DataAdapter.Update method is called, the CommandBuilder analyzes the contents of the result set and generates Insert/Update/Delete statements for the DataAdapter. When you explicitly specify Insert/Update/Delete statements, this extra processing step is eliminated.

> ### Performance Tip
>
> Although using a `CommandBuilder` object to generate SQL statements is tempting because it can save you time when coding an application that uses `DataSets`, this shortcut can impair performance.

Suppose you have an 8-column database table named employees that contains employee records. A `CommandBuilder` object would generate the following `Update` statement:

```
"UPDATE employees SET empno = ?, ename = ?,
    job = ?, mgr = ?, hiredate = ?, sal = ?, comm = ?,
    dept = ?
    WHERE (
        (empno = ?) AND (ename = ?) AND
        (job = ?) AND ((mgr IS NULL and ? IS NULL) OR (mgr = ?))
        AND (hiredate = ?) AND (sal = ?) AND (
            (comm IS NULL AND
            ? IS NULL) OR (comm = ?)) AND (dept = ?))
```

If you know the underlying database schema and know that the empno column of the employees table is the primary key for the table, you can code the following `Update` statement, which is more efficient than the previous `Update` statement generated by the `CommandBuilder`:

```
UPDATE employees SET empno = ?, ename = ?, job = ?,
    mgr = ?, hiredate = ?, sal = ?, comm = ?, dept = ?
    WHERE empno = ?
```

In this example, although we've lost some concurrency control, we've improved performance. Notice that in the first example, the `Where` clause compares every column value, which ensures the value hasn't changed since the data was retrieved. In the second example, the `Update` statement compares only the value of the empno column. So before you implement this performance tip, you must decide how tolerant your database is to a lower level of concurrency.

Choosing Between a **DataReader** and **DataSet** Object

Which ADO.NET object should you use to retrieve the results of a SQL statement?

- The DataReader object is optimized for retrieving large amounts of data at a fast speed. Data is read-only and can only be fetched in a forward-only order. Memory usage is minimal.
- The DataSet object is a cache of data that represents the complete set of data results, including related tables, constraints, and relationships among the tables. It is, in effect, a locally cached database. You can modify the data in the DataSet and fetch data in any order. Because the DataSet is disconnected from the database, any changes you make to the data in the DataSet must be explicitly synchronized with the data in the database. You also can create a DataSet from an XML stream or document, or you can serialize a DataSet to XML. Memory usage is high.

Performance Tip

If you need to retrieve large amounts of read-only data, a DataReader object always provides the best performance. Only use a DataSet object if you need to insert, update, or delete data, fetch data in any order, or work with XML. Although the flexibility of a DataSet can benefit your application, it comes with the high cost in memory consumption.

Using **GetXXX** Methods to Fetch Data from a **DataReader**

The .NET API provides the following methods of fetching data from a DataReader:

- Generic data type methods, such as GetValue() and GetValues()
- Specific data type methods, such as GetDateTime(), GetDecimal(), and GetInt32()

When using a generic method such as GetValue() to fetch data from the DataReader, extra processing is required to convert the value data type to a reference data type, essentially wrapping the value data type with an object. This process is called **boxing**. When boxing occurs, memory is allocated from the managed heap on the database client to create an object for the reference data type, which can force a garbage collection to occur. See ".NET CLR," page 82, for more information about the impact garbage collection has on performance.

> **Performance Tip**
>
> To avoid boxing, use a specific method of fetching data for the data type instead of a generic method. For example, use the `GetInt32()` method to fetch a 32-bit signed `Integer` value instead of the `GetValue()` method.

Retrieving Data

Retrieve only the data you need, and choose the most efficient method to retrieve that data. Use the guidelines in this section to optimize your performance when retrieving data.

Retrieving Long Data

Retrieving long data—such as large XML data, long varchar/text, long varbinary, Clobs, and Blobs—across a network is slow and resource intensive. Most users really don't want to see long data. For example, consider the user interface of an employee directory application that allows the user to look up an employee's phone extension and department, and optionally, view an employee's photograph by clicking the name of the employee.

Employee	Phone	Dept
Harding	X4568	Manager
Hoover	X4324	Sales
Taft	X4569	Sales
Lincoln	X4329	Tech

In this case, retrieving each employee's photograph would slow performance unnecessarily. If the user does want to see the photograph, he can click the employee name and the application can query the database again, specifying only the long columns in the `Select` list. This method allows users to retrieve result sets without paying a high performance penalty for network traffic.

Although excluding long data from the `Select` list is the best approach, some applications do not formulate the `Select` list before sending the query to the data provider (that is, some applications use SELECT * FROM table ...). If the `Select` list contains long data, the data provider is forced to retrieve that long data, even if the application never requests the long data from the result set. For example, consider the following code:

```
sql = "SELECT * FROM employees
        WHERE SSID = '999-99-2222'";
cmd.CommandText = sql;
dataReader = cmd.ExecuteReader();
dataReader.Read();
string name = dataReader.GetString(0);
```

When a query is executed, the data provider has no way to determine which result columns the application will use; an application may fetch any of the result columns that are retrieved. When the data provider processes the fetch request, it retrieves at least one, and often multiple, result rows from the database across the network. In this case, a result row contains all the column values for each row. If one of the columns includes long data such as an employee photograph, performance slows considerably.

> **Performance Tip**
>
> Because retrieving long data across the network negatively affects performance, design your application to exclude long data from the Select list.

Limiting the Select list to contain only the name column results in a faster performing query at runtime. For example:

```
sql = "SELECT name FROM employees" +
        "WHERE SSID = '999-99-2222'";
cmd.CommandText = sql;
dataReader = cmd.ExecuteReader();
dataReader.Read();
string name = dataReader.GetString(0);
```

Limiting the Amount of Data Retrieved

If your application executes a query that retrieves five rows when it needs only two, application performance suffers, especially if the unnecessary rows include long data.

> **Performance Tip**
>
> One of the easiest ways to improve performance is to limit the amount of network traffic between the data provider and the database server—optimally by writing SQL queries that instruct the data provider to retrieve from the database only the data that the application requires.

Particularly when using a DataSet, make sure that your Select statements limit the data that is retrieved by using a Where clause. Even when using a Where clause, a Select statement that does not adequately restrict its request could retrieve hundreds of rows of data. For example, if you want data from the employees table for each manager hired in recent years, your application could execute the following statement, and subsequently, filter out the rows of employees who are not managers:

```
SELECT * FROM employees
WHERE hiredate > 2000
```

However, suppose the employees table contains a column that stores photographs of each employee. In this case, retrieving extra rows is extremely expensive to your application performance. Let the database filter the request for you and avoid sending extra data that you don't need across the network. The following query uses a better approach, limiting the data retrieved and improving performance:

```
SELECT * FROM employees
WHERE hiredate > 2003 and job_title='Manager'
```

Sometimes applications need to use SQL queries that generate a large amount of network traffic. For example, consider an application that needs to display information from support case histories, which each contain a 10MB log file. Does the user really need to see the entire contents of the file? If not, performance would improve if the application displayed only the first 1MB of the log file.

> **Performance Tip**
>
> When you cannot avoid retrieving data that generates a large amount of network traffic, your application can still control the amount of data being sent from the database to the data provider by limiting the number of rows sent across the network and reducing the size of each row sent across the network.

Suppose that you have a GUI-based application, and each screen can display only 20 rows of data. It's easy to construct a query that may retrieve a million rows, such as SELECT * FROM employees, but it's hard to imagine a scenario where a query that retrieves a million rows would be useful. Some data providers allow you to use a MaxRows property on the Command object. For example, if an application calls the following command, no query to the Oracle database will retrieve more than 10,000 rows to the application:

```
OracleCommand.MaxRows=10000;
```

Some data providers allow you to limit the bytes of data a connection uses to retrieve multiple rows. Similarly, some data providers allow you to limit the bytes of data that can be retrieved from TEXT or IMAGE columns. For example, with Microsoft SQL Server and Sybase ASE, you can execute Set TEXTSIZE n on any connection, where n is the maximum number of bytes that will be retrieved from any TEXT or IMAGE column.

Choosing the Right Data Type

Advances in processor technology have brought significant improvements to the way that operations such as floating-point math are handled. However, when the active portion of your application will not fit into the on-chip cache, sending and retrieving certain data types is still expensive. When you are working with data on a large scale, it's important to select the data type that can be processed most efficiently. Sending and retrieving certain data types across the network can increase or decrease network traffic.

> ### Performance Tip
>
> For multiuser, multivolume applications, billions, or even trillions, of network packets can move between the provider and the database server over the course of a day. Choosing data types that are processed efficiently can incrementally create a measurable gain in performance.

See "Choosing the Right Data Type," page 34, for information about which data types are processed faster than others.

Updating Data

Because data in a DataSet is disconnected from the database, you must explicitly synchronize any changes you make to the data in the DataSet with the data stored in the database.

> ### Performance Tip
>
> When you're updating data in the database from a DataSet, make sure to uniquely identify rows to be changed using a Where clause so that updates are processed faster. For example, you can use a column with a unique index or a primary key, or a pseudo-column. A **pseudo-column** is a hidden column that represents a unique key associated with every row in a table. Typically, using pseudo-columns in a SQL statement is the fastest way to access a row because they usually point to the exact location of the physical record.

The following example shows the application flow for updating the database with a DataSet using the Oracle ROWID pseudo-column as a search condition:

```
// Create the DataAdapter and DataSets
OracleCommand DbCmd = new OracleCommand (
    "SELECT rowid, deptid, deptname FROM department", DBConn);

myDataAdapter = new OracleDataAdapter();
myDataAdapter.SelectCommand = DBCmd;
myDataAdapter.Fill(myDataSet, "Departments");
```

```
// Build the Update rules
// Specify how to update data in the data set
myDataAdapter.UpdateCommand = new
OracleCommand(
    "UPDATE department SET deptname = ? ", deptid = ? " +
    "WHERE rowid =?", DBConn);

// Bind parameters
myDataAdapter.UpdateCommand.Parameters.Add(
    "param1", OracleDbType.VarChar, 100, "deptname");
myDataAdapter.UpdateCommand.Parameters.Add(
    "param2", OracleDbType.Number, 4, "deptid";
myDataAdapter.UpdateCommand.Parameters.Add(
    "param3", OracleDbType.Number, 4, "rowid");
```

Summary

The performance of .NET applications can suffer if they fail to reduce network traffic, limit disk I/O, simplify queries, and optimize the interaction between the application and data provider. Reducing network communication probably is the most important technique for improving performance. For example, when you need to update large amounts of data, using arrays of parameters rather than executing an Insert statement multiple times reduces the number of network round trips required by the data provider to complete the operation. In addition, using a 100% managed data provider, which eliminates calls outside the CLR to client libraries or code written before the .NET Framework was developed, can improve performance, especially when the application is running on a busy machine.

Typically, creating a connection is the most performance-expensive task your application performs. Connection pooling can help you manage connections efficiently, particularly if your application has numerous users. Regardless of whether your application uses connection pooling, make sure that you close connections immediately after your application is finished with them.

Making smart choices about how to handle transactions can also improve performance. For example, using manual commits instead of auto-commit mode provides better control over when work is committed. Similarly, if you don't need the protection of distributed transactions, using local transactions can improve performance.

Inefficient SQL queries slow the performance of .NET applications. Some SQL queries don't filter data, causing the provider to retrieve unnecessary data. Your application pays a huge penalty in performance when that unnecessary data is long data, such as data stored as a Blob or Clob. Other queries, such as those the `CommandBuilder` object generates, can be overly complex, causing additional processing at runtime. Even well-formed SQL queries can be more or less effective depending on how they are executed. For example, using the `ExecuteNonQuery()` method of the `Command` object for queries that don't retrieve data reduces the number of network round trips to the database server and improves performance.

CHAPTER EIGHT

Connection Pooling and Statement Pooling

In Chapter 2, "Designing for Performance: What's Your Strategy?," we defined connection pooling and statement pooling and discussed the performance implications of using these features. But we didn't go into specifics, such as the different connection pool models, how reauthentication works with connection pooling, and how using statement pooling with connection pooling might consume more memory on the database server than you realize. If you are interested in these details and more, read this chapter. If you haven't already read the section about these features in Chapter 2, you may want to do that first.

Connection Pool Model for JDBC

A JDBC application can use connection pooling through a Connection Pool Manager provided by an application server vendor or a database driver vendor. A **Connection Pool Manager** is the utility that manages the connections in the pool and defines the attributes of the connection pool, such as the initial number of connections placed in the pool, when an application server is started. We discuss the attributes of connection pools in a JDBC environment later in this section.

Connection pooling doesn't affect application code. If you turn on connection pooling and use a `DataSource` object (an object implementing the `DataSource` interface) to obtain a connection instead of using the `DriverManager` class, when the connection is closed, it is placed in the connection pool for reuse instead of being physically closed.

The number of connection pools that an application uses depends on the number of data sources used in the application. Typically, the number is only one. There is a one-to-one relationship between a pool and a data source. Therefore, the number of connection pools on an application server depends on the number of data sources configured to use connection pooling. If multiple applications are configured to use the same data source, those applications share the same connection pool, as shown in Figure 8-1.

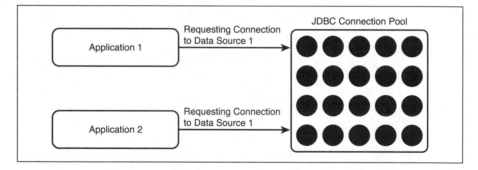

Figure 8-1   JDBC connection pool

But let's not stop there. An application can have one data source and allow multiple users, each with his own set of login credentials, to get a connection from the same pool. This is unlike some ADO.NET and ODBC implementations, where a connection pool is associated with a specific connection string, which means connections for only one set of user login credentials are in the pool. In the JDBC case, the connection pool contains connections for all unique users using the same data source, as shown in Figure 8-2.

This information is important because it affects the way you configure the attributes of your connection pool, as we discuss next.

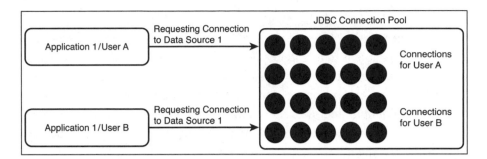

Figure 8-2   JDBC connection pool: one pool for multiple unique users

Configuring Connection Pools

Typically, you can define the following attributes of a connection pool, which enables you to configure a pool for optimal performance:

- **Minimum pool size** is the minimum number of connections that will be kept in the pool for each user. Depending on the implementation, the minimum number means either the total number of both active and idle connections or the total number of idle connections only. Because this is an important difference, check your implementation so that you can tune your pool correctly. **Active connections** are the connections that are currently in use by the application, and **idle connections** are the connections that are available for use in the pool.

- **Maximum pool size** is the maximum number of connections in the pool for each user. Depending on the implementation, the maximum number means either the total number of both active and idle connections or the total number of idle connections only. Again, because this is an important difference, check your implementation so that you can tune your pool correctly.

- **Initial pool size** is the number of connections created for each user when the connection pool is initialized. For most application servers, connections are created when the application server is initialized.

- **Maximum idle time** is the amount of time a pooled connection remains idle before it is removed from the connection pool.

Performance Tip
The goal is to maintain a reasonable connection pool size while ensuring that each user who needs a connection has one available within an acceptable response time. To achieve this goal, you can configure the minimum and maximum number of connections that are in the pool at any given time and how long idle connections stay in the pool, as we discuss next.

Guidelines

Here are some guidelines for setting connection pool attributes:

- To determine the optimal setting for the maximum number of connections for a pool, plan for the typical number of concurrent connections that your application or applications uses, not the number at the busiest time of day or the number at the slowest time of day. For example, suppose you have two applications that use the same data source and the same user login credentials and these applications consistently have about 16 users combined. In this case, you would want to set the maximum number of connections for the pool to 16 so that the pool is not maintaining more connections than are needed for typical application usage. Remember, more connections means more database memory and CPU use.

  Let's contrast this to two applications that use the same data source but different user login credentials. Also, the applications consistently have about 16 users combined. If each application has about the same number of users—about 8—you would want to set the maximum number of connections for the pool to 8. With this configuration, the pool would have 8 connections for each application, or a maximum of 16 connections in the pool at any one time.

Note
The maximum number of connections is calculated differently if you are using reauthentication with connection pooling. See the section, "Using Reauthentication with Connection Pooling," page 232.

Also, you can use the maximum pool size attribute to limit the number of database server licenses in use by your applications.

- To determine the optimal setting for the minimum number of connections for a pool, calculate the number of concurrent connections used by your application or applications at the slowest time of day. Use this number for the minimum number of connections for your pool. Just like configuring the maximum number, the way you set the minimum number of connections depends on whether your applications are configured to allow use of multiple sets of user login credentials for a single data source.

Note

The minimum number of connections is calculated differently if you are using reauthentication with connection pooling. See the section, "Using Reauthentication with Connection Pooling," page 232.

- To determine the optimal setting for the initial pool size, think about the usage of your application server or application, if it doesn't reside on an application server. If the application server that contains your application(s) starts at the beginning of the business day, which typically is the slowest time of day, you may want to consider initializing your pool with the minimum number of connections allowed in your pool. If, on the other hand, the application server runs 24 hours a day and is only restarted when absolutely necessary, you may want to consider initializing your pool with the typical number of concurrent connections used by your application(s).

Note

The initial pool size is calculated differently if you are using reauthentication with connection pooling. See the section, "Using Reauthentication with Connection Pooling," page 232.

- To determine the optimal setting for the maximum idle time, think about the slowest time of day for your applications and set this option accordingly. For example, if in the evening you know that only one or two users are logging into applications every hour or so, you would want to configure this setting to at least 60 minutes. That way, a connection will be waiting in the pool for your users; a connection will not have to be reestablished, which we know is performance expensive.

Connection Pool Model for ODBC

Connection pooling in ODBC is provided by the Microsoft ODBC Driver Manager on Windows platforms, application providers, some database driver vendors, or not at all. At the time of the publishing of this book, we know of only one UNIX implementation of connection pooling for ODBC, and its implementation is similar to the ADO.NET connection pool model (see "Connection Pool Model for ADO.NET," page 230). Also, the implementations of connection pooling available on Windows platforms differ. Some are similar to the ADO.NET connection pool model.

In this section, we discuss only the model as defined in the ODBC specification.

Connection Pooling as Defined in the ODBC Specification

We want to start by saying that the connection pool model in ODBC was defined before application servers were widely adopted. Application servers allow multiple applications to run in the same process, which makes sharing connection pools across applications possible. However, the scenario of an application server for ODBC applications (C/C++ applications) is unlikely.

As stated in the ODBC specification, "The connection pooling architecture enables an environment and its associated connection to be used by multiple components in a single process."[1] An **environment** is a global context that is used to access data from an application. In association with connection pooling, an environment "owns" the connections inside an application. Typically, there is only one environment within an application, which means that there is usually one connection pool for one application.

---

1 *Microsoft ODBC 3.0 Programmer's Reference and SDK Guide*, Volume I. Redmond: Microsoft Press, 1997.

Here are some facts about the ODBC connection pool model as defined in the ODBC specification:

- The Driver Manager maintains the connection pool.
- Connection pooling is enabled by calling `SQLSetEnvAttr` to set the `SQL_ATTR_CONNECTION_POOLING` environment attribute. This environment attribute can be set to associate a single pool either with each driver used by an application or with each environment configured for an application (which is typically only one).
- When the application calls either `SQLConnect` or `SQLDriverConnect`, a connection is used from the pool *if* a connection with the arguments passed by the ODBC call can be matched with a connection in the pool. If not, a new connection is established and placed in the pool when physically closed.
- When the application calls `SQLDisconnect`, the connection is returned to the pool.
- The pool grows dynamically as applications use it; it is limited only by memory constraints and licensing limits on the server.
- If a connection is inactive for a specified period, it is removed from the pool.

Configuring Connection Pools

You can define the following attributes of a connection pool, which helps you configure a pool for optimal performance:

- Connection pooling timeout, which is set in the ODBC Administrator, is the amount of time that connections remain in the pool before being removed.
- Connection pool one per driver, which is set in your application. If your application works with many drivers and few environments, using this configuration may be optimal because fewer comparisons may be required to find the correct connection. For example, the application creates one environment handle (`henv`). On `henv`, the application connects to a Sybase driver and to an Oracle driver. With this configuration, a pool will exist for connections to the Sybase driver, and a second pool will exist for connections to the Oracle driver.
- Connection pool one per environment, which is set in your application. If your application works with many environments and a few drivers, using this configuration may be optimal because fewer comparisons may be required. For example, the application creates two environment handles (`henv1` and `henv2`). On `henv1`, the application connects to a Sybase driver and a Microsoft SQL Server driver. On `henv2`, it connects to an Oracle driver and a DB2 driver. With this configuration, a pool will exist for `henv1` that has

connections to Sybase and Microsoft SQL Server, and a pool will exist for henv2 that has connections to Oracle and DB2.

We have included this configuration option here for completeness; however, it would be unusual to configure your application to use many environments.

Guidelines

In the ODBC model as defined in the ODBC specification, you can't define a minimum and a maximum pool size, which can cause resource issues because the connections, even when not in use, hold onto resources. Holding these resources can affect performance by limiting their availability to other threads or processes. The size of the pool is limited only by memory or licensing constraints on the server.

Even with this limitation in the ODBC connection pool model, you will want to use connection pooling when you have the following:

- A middle-tier application that connects over a network
- An application that repeatedly connects and disconnects, such as an Internet application

Connection Pool Model for ADO.NET

Connection pooling in ADO.NET isn't provided by the core components of the .NET Framework. If present, it must be implemented in the ADO.NET data provider. The most popular and widely used implementation is discussed in this section.

In ADO.NET, a connection pool is associated with a specific connection string. A connection pool is created for each connection request that uses a unique connection string. For example, if an application requests two connections over its lifetime using the following two connection strings, two connection pools are created, one for each connection string:

```
Host=Accounting;Port=1521;User ID=scott;Password=tiger;
   Service Name=ORCL;
Host=Accounting;Port=1521;User ID=sam;Password=lion21;
   Service Name=ORCL;
```

The number of connection pools that an application uses depends on the number of unique connection strings that application uses. The more pools that an application maintains, the more memory usage on both the client machine and the database server.

Configuring Connection Pools

You can define the following attributes of a connection pool, which help you configure a pool for optimal performance:

- **Maximum pool size** is the maximum number of connections allowed in a pool, both active and idle. **Active connections** are the connections that are currently in use by the application, and **idle connections** are the connections that are available for use in the pool.
- **Minimum pool size** is the number of connections created when a connection pool is initialized and the minimum number of active and idle connections that will be kept in the pool. A connection pool is created when the first connection with a unique connection string connects to the database. The connection pool retains this number of connections, even when some connections exceed their load balance timeout value.
- **Load balance timeout** is the amount of time idle connections remain in the pool before being destroyed.

Performance Tip
The goal is to maintain a reasonable connection pool size while ensuring that each user who needs a connection has one available within an acceptable response time. To achieve this goal, you can configure the minimum and maximum number of connections that are in the pool at any given time and how long idle connections stay in the pool, as we discuss next.

Guidelines

Here are some guidelines for setting connection pool attributes:

- To determine the optimal setting for the maximum number of connections for a pool, plan for the typical number of concurrent connections used by your application, not the number at the busiest time of day or the number at the slowest time of day. For example, suppose you have an application that consistently has about 15 users. You would want to set the maximum number of connections for the pool to 15 so that the pool isn't maintaining more connections than are needed for typical application usage. Remember, more connections means more database memory and CPU usage.

Also, you can use the maximum pool size attribute to limit the number of database server licenses that your applications use.

- To determine the optimal setting for the minimum number of connections for a pool, calculate the number of concurrent connections used by your application at the slowest time of day. Use this number for the minimum number of connections for your pool. In ADO.NET, the minimum pool size is also the initial pool size, so you should consider the following information about initial pool size when making your decision about this setting.

- To determine the optimal setting for the initial pool size, think about the usage of your application. If your application starts at the beginning of the business day, which is the slowest time of day, you may want to consider initializing your pool with the minimum number of connections allowed in your pool. If, on the other hand, your application runs 24 hours a day and is only restarted when absolutely necessary, you may want to consider initializing your pool with the typical number of concurrent connections that your application uses.

- To determine the optimal setting for the maximum idle time (load balance timeout), think about the slowest time of day for your applications and set this option accordingly. For example, if in the evening you know that only one or two users are logging into applications every hour or so, you would want to configure this setting to at least 60 minutes. That way, a connection will be waiting in the pool for your users; a connection will not have to be reestablished, which we know is performance expensive.

Using Reauthentication with Connection Pooling

To minimize the number of connections required in a connection pool, the user associated with a connection can be switched to another user, a process known as **reauthentication**.[2] For example, suppose using the same set of login credentials

---

[2] Different databases refer to this functionality using different terminology. For example, Oracle uses *proxy authentication* and Microsoft SQL Server uses *impersonation*.

for all users isn't an option for security reasons; therefore, you are using Kerberos authentication to authenticate users using their operating system user name and password. To reduce the number of connections that must be created and managed, you can use reauthentication to switch the user associated with a connection to multiple users. For example, suppose your connection pool contains a connection, Conn, which was established using the user ALLUSERS. You can have that connection service multiple users—User A, B, C, and so on—by switching the user associated with the connection Conn to User A, B, C, and so on. Minimizing the number of connections conserves memory, which improves performance.

Not all database drivers support reauthentication. For those drivers that do, the user performing the switch must be granted specific database permissions.

In JDBC, reauthentication is implemented in both the driver and the Connection Pool Manager. In ODBC and ADO.NET (if reauthentication is implemented), it is implemented in the driver/provider.

Without reauthentication, the Connection Pool Manager or the driver/ provider maintains a different set of connections for each user logged on the database with different user credentials because the resulting connection strings are different. For example, depending on the implementation, one set of connections is maintained for User A and another set for User B, and still another set for User C, and so on, in the same connection pool or in different pools. For the purposes of this discussion, let's assume an ADO.NET implementation where the provider maintains connections for each user in different pools. If each connection pool has a minimum pool size set to a value of 10, the provider needs to maintain 10 connections for User A, another 10 connections for User B, and another 10 connections for User C, as shown in Figure 8-3.

What if User B and User C don't require as many connections as User A on a regular basis? You could reduce the minimum pool size of the connection pools that User B and User C use to five connections, but the provider still has to maintain different sets of connections. What if you could minimize the number of connections required and simplify your entire connection pooling environment?

Using reauthentication, any available connection in the pool can be assigned to a user if the user has the appropriate database permissions—the user associated with the connection is switched to the new user. For example, if the connection pool has a minimum pool size set to 15, the pool manager or driver/provider could maintain 15 connections that User A, User B, or User C can use, as shown in Figure 8-4. The pool manager or driver/provider only has to maintain one connection pool for all users, which reduces the number of total connections.

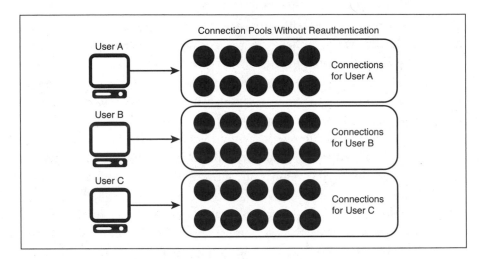

Figure 8-3   Connection pools without reauthentication

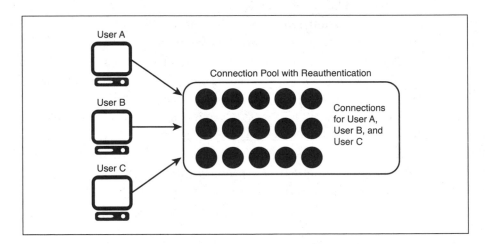

Figure 8-4   Connection pool with reauthentication

Depending on the driver, switching the user associated with a connection to a new user takes one or two network round trips to the server and a small amount of processing time on the server. The resources used for reauthentication are minimal compared to the resources used to establish and maintain the extra connections needed in the pool if reauthentication isn't used. Remember that establishing a connection can take from 7 to 10 network round trips, and pooled connections use memory and licenses on the server.

Configuring Connection Pooling with Reauthentication in a JDBC Environment

As we stated in "Connection Pool Model for JDBC," page 223, the way you configure the maximum and minimum number of connections in a connection pool, and the initial size of a connection pool is different when you are using reauthentication. Here's how.

Example A: JDBC Connection Pool Without Reauthentication

This example shows a connection pool that is configured to work without reauthentication. As you can see in Figure 8-5, two users share connections from the connection pool, but the connections are functionally separated into one group of connections for User A and another group of connections for User B. When User A requests a connection, the Connection Pool Manager assigns an available connection associated with User A. Similarly, if User B requests a connection, the Connection Pool Manager assigns an available connection associated with User B. If a connection is unavailable for a particular user, the Connection Pool Manager creates a new connection for that user, up to a maximum of 10 connections for each user. In this case, the maximum number of connections in the pool is 20 (10 connections for each user).

The Connection Pool Manager implements the minimum pool size and initial pool size in a similar way. It initially populates five connections for User A and five connections for User B and ensures that, at a minimum, five connections are maintained in the pool for each user.

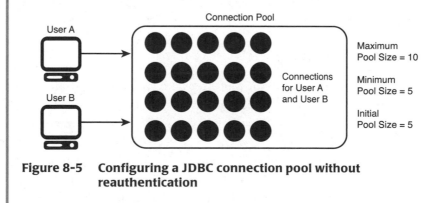

Figure 8-5 **Configuring a JDBC connection pool without reauthentication**

Example B: JDBC Connection Pool with Reauthentication

In contrast, this example shows a connection pool that is configured to work with reauthentication. As shown in Figure 8-6, the Connection Pool Manager treats all connections as one group of connections. When User A requests a connection, the pool manager assigns an available connection associated with User A. Similarly, when User B requests a connection, the Connection Pool Manager assigns an available connection associated with User B. If a connection is unavailable for a particular user, it assigns any available connection to that user, switching the user associated with the connection to the new user. In this case, the maximum number of connections in the pool is 10, regardless of how many users are using the connection pool.

The Connection Pool Manager initially populates the pool with five connections and ensures that, at a minimum, five connections are maintained in the pool for all users.

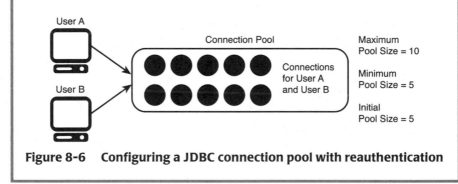

Figure 8-6   Configuring a JDBC connection pool with reauthentication

Using Statement Pooling

A **statement pool** is a group of prepared statements that an application can reuse. Statement pooling is not a feature of database systems; it is a feature of database drivers and application servers. A **prepared statement** is a SQL statement that has been compiled; the SQL processor parses and analyzes the statement and creates an execution plan for it. In a .NET environment, you may see this functionality referred to as **statement caching**.

If you have an application that repeatedly executes the same SQL statements, statement pooling can improve performance because it prevents the overhead of repeatedly parsing and creating cursors (server-side resource to manage the SQL request) for the same statement, along with the associated network round trips.

A statement pool is owned by a physical connection, and prepared statements are placed in the pool after their initial execution. Statements remain in the pool until the physical connection is closed or the maximum size is reached.

Statement pooling typically doesn't affect application code. If you use prepared statements and turn on statement pooling, when the prepared statement is closed, it is placed in the statement pool for reuse instead of actually being closed.

All implementations of statement pooling that we have seen have at least one attribute you can configure: maximum pool size, which defines the maximum number of prepared statements that can be associated with a connection. We provide guidelines for setting this attribute later in this section.

Some implementations of statement pooling have additional features that allow you to do the following:

- Import statements into a pool to preload the pool, which means the startup time for the statement pool is paid when the application or application server is started, not when the application is running.
- Clear the pool. This feature is mainly used for maintenance purposes. For example, if a change is made to an index on the database server and this index is part of an execution plan for a pooled statement, the statement will fail upon execution. In this case, you need a way to clear the pool so that a new execution plan can be created for the statement.

Note

JDBC 4.0 provides a more granular level of statement pooling by allowing applications to hint to the pool manager about whether or not a prepared statement should be pooled.

Performance Tip

Use parameters in your SQL statements to take full advantage of statement pooling. The parsed information from statements using parameters can be reused even if the parameter values change in subsequent executions. In contrast, if you use literals and the literal values change, the application cannot reuse the parsed information.

Using Statement Pooling with Connection Pooling

Statement pooling is often used with connection pooling. In fact, some implementations of statement pooling require that you also use connection pooling. Using statement pooling with connection pooling might consume more memory on the database server than you realize. Let's look at why.

All connections in a connection pool are maintained in the database's memory. If you implement statement pooling with connection pooling, each pooled connection has its own statement pool associated with it. On the database client, client resources that correlate to each pooled statement are stored in memory. On the database server, each pooled connection has a statement associated with it that's also maintained in memory. For example, if you have 5 pooled connections and 20 prepared statements, each statement pool associated with a connection may have all 20 prepared statements in it, which means that a total of 100 prepared statements could be maintained in the database's memory. All these connections and statements stay in memory even if no active users are on the system. Here is how this can happen.

The application connects, prepares statement1, closes statement1, and closes the connection. Then the application repeats this operation.

The first time the operation is executed, the application user receives connection1 and at that time statement1 (S1) is associated with connection1, as shown in Figure 8-7.

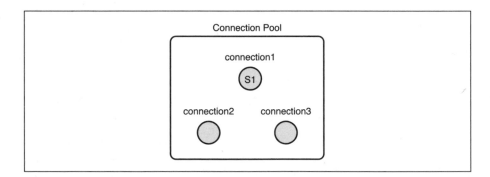

Figure 8-7   Part 1: Pooled statements associated with connections in the connection pool

The next time the operation is executed, connection1 is not available. The application user receives connection3, and statement1 (S1) is associated with connection3, as shown in Figure 8-8.

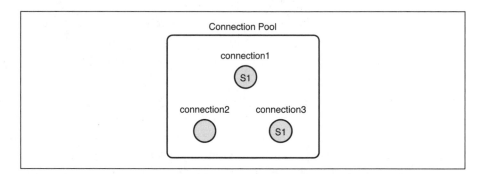

Figure 8-8   Part 2: Pooled statements associated with connections in the connection pool

Statement1 (S1) is now in two statement pools: the statement pool associated with connection1, and the one associated with connection3.

Even though the statements are the same, a statement cannot be shared across connections. Throughout the lifetime of the connection pool, each prepared statement may be associated with each pooled connection. This can equate to memory issues on the database server.

Guidelines

Here are some general guidelines for using statement pooling:

- Because all prepared statements go into the pool, do not use statement pooling unless at least 90% of your statements are executed multiple times.

Note

JDBC 4.0 provides a more granular level of statement pooling by allowing applications to hint to the pool manager about whether or not a prepared statement should be pooled.

- Most database servers impose a limit on the number of statements that can be active on a connection. Therefore, do not configure the maximum number of statements for a statement pool to be greater than the server's maximum limit. For example, if the maximum number of active statements per connection for the database server is 100, configure the maximum number of statements for a pool to be 100 or fewer. In this example, when statement 101 is executed, the database server will generate an error.

- Configure the maximum number of statements for a statement pool to be equal to or greater than the number of different SQL statements in your application. For example, suppose the maximum number of statements for the pool is 50 and the number of static SQL statements in your application is 55. When the application executes statement 51, the statement pool must close an existing pooled statement to add statement 51 because the pool cannot exceed 50 statements. In this scenario, the pool manager may have to switch statements in and out of the pool. This isn't an efficient way to configure statement pooling because the overhead of closing and opening statements causes unnecessary network round trips.

Note

Not all drivers/providers on the market support statement pooling. To use this feature, make sure you deploy a driver/provider with your database application that does.

Summary: The Big Picture

We discussed the performance benefits of connection pooling and statement pooling, and we talked about how multiple applications can use the same connection pool. As we previously explained, all connections in a connection pool are maintained in the database's memory. If you implement statement pooling with connection pooling, each pooled connection has its own statement pool associated with it. Each of these statement pools may contain the prepared statements that the application uses. All these pooled prepared statements are also maintained in the database's memory.

That isn't the whole picture. A typical application server environment has numerous connection pools and statement pools that use memory on the database server. Also, other application servers will likely be accessing that same database server, as shown in Figure 8-9. What this means is that your database server can potentially be a big bottleneck. You need to think about the big picture when you design your applications to use connection pooling and statement pooling.

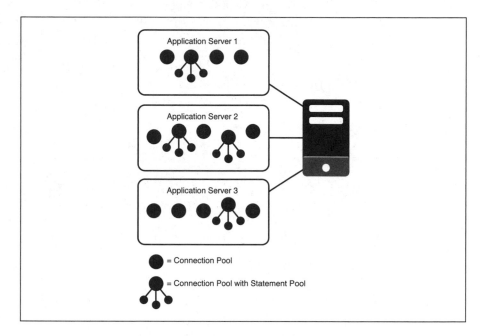

Figure 8-9   Connection pools and statement pools: the big picture

CHAPTER NINE

Developing Good Benchmarks

Benchmarks **measure the performance of an application or system on a well-defined task or set of tasks and are often designed to accomplish one or more of the following goals:**

- Predict the performance of a new application or system component
- Diagnose and pinpoint performance bottlenecks
- Plan for a system's future capacity
- Determine the impact of a change to an application, such as a change to application code or a change in a hardware or software component
- Ensure a minimum level of performance
- Compare components, such as different database drivers

Performance is typically measured by throughput, scalability, response time, or a combination.

In our line of work, we see a significant number of benchmarks. Because most of those we encounter don't do what they were intended to do, we felt compelled to include a chapter about developing good benchmarks.

Benchmarks can be a powerful tool to measure and predict performance, but there are some basic guidelines for writing benchmarks that many developers don't follow. As stated previously in this book, some factors that affect performance may be outside your realm of control to change. Therefore, we'll focus on those factors that typically *are* within your control, such as how efficiently your application is coded to access data and how efficiently your database middleware operates.

Developing the Benchmark

Standardized benchmarks are available for measuring the performance of databases (TPC, for example) and application servers (SPECjAppServer, for example), but standard industry benchmarks for measuring data access code and database middleware don't exist. To help you develop benchmarks that measure these important factors, follow these guidelines:

- Define benchmark goals.
- Reproduce the production environment.
- Isolate the test environment.
- Reproduce the workload.
- Measure the right tasks.
- Measure over a sufficient duration.
- Prepare the database.
- Make changes one at a time.
- Assess other factors.

Define Benchmark Goals

Before you design your benchmark, put some thought into defining what it is that you want the benchmark to measure and define what you consider good performance. Benchmark goals typically are driven by business needs. For example, here are some typical benchmark goals:

- The application must complete at least 10 transactions per second.
- The application must have a response time of no longer than 500ms when not executing transactions.

- The application must retrieve at least 100,000 rows in less than 10 seconds.
- The application must insert at least a million rows in less than 2 hours.

In addition to measuring throughput, such as how many rows are retrieved, updated, or inserted over a period of time, measuring CPU and memory use on the machine running your application can provide information about the scalability of that application or system. However, be careful to measure CPU and memory use in a way that provides useful results.

For example, suppose your benchmark executes the same set of SQL statements in a loop over a period of 100 seconds. Let's take a look at two different high-level approaches to measuring CPU use. We arrive at the total CPU time used by taking snapshots of the CPU time using standard operating system calls. The difference between those snapshots allows us to calculate the total time spent by process on the CPU.

Example A: Measuring Individual Operations

In this example, we take a CPU time snapshot within the loop, essentially measuring the elapsed CPU for each operation. To get the total CPU time, add each CPU time measurement. The problem with this approach is that the duration of the time that is measured for each operation is short. Benchmarks run over short durations provide results that often do not scale to real-world performance or results that may be inaccurate. See "Measure over a Sufficient Duration of Time," page 254, for an explanation.

1. Start the loop.
2. Save the CPU time.
3. Execute the SQL statements.
4. Save the CPU time.
5. End the loop.
6. Determine the difference between each CPU time snapshot, and add those times to arrive at the sum of CPU time.

Example B: Measuring the Overall Operation

In contrast, this example takes a better approach because it samples the CPU time at the start and end of the loop so the duration of the benchmark is measured over an entire period of 100 seconds—a sufficient duration.

1. Save the CPU time.
2. Start the loop.
3. Execute the SQL statements.
4. End the loop.
5. Save the CPU time.
6. Determine the difference between the CPU time snapshots to arrive at the CPU time.

Reproduce the Production Environment

It can be difficult and costly to reproduce your production environment, but to provide useful and reliable benchmark results, your test environment should resemble your production environment as closely as possible.

Design Your Test Environment

Before you design your test environment, you need to gather information about the essential characteristics of your production environment so that you can duplicate them in your test environment. See Table 9-1 for a list of important questions you should ask before defining your test environment.

Table 9-1   Questions to Ask Before Defining Your Test Environment

Question	Explanation
What is the version of your database?	Database vendors can make changes between releases of database versions that cause SQL statements to be evaluated differently. Similarly, database drivers may act differently when accessing different database versions.

Table 9-1   Continued

Question	Explanation
Is the database installed on the same machine running the application, or is it installed on a different machine?	When an application runs on the same machine as the database, the database driver uses the network in a loop-back mode, or it doesn't use the network at all and communicates directly with the database using shared memory. If your application makes data requests over the network in your production environment, you need to gauge what effect the network will have on performance in your test environment. See "Network," page 86, for more information.
What are the model, speed, cache, and number of CPUs and cores of the processor hardware on your database server and application server?	The processing speed and capacity of the CPU on the database server or application server affect performance. See "CPU (Processor)," page 112, for more information.
How much physical memory (RAM) is available on your database server and clients?	The memory on your client, application server, and database server affects performance. For example, large result sets can cause paging to disk if memory is insufficient, dramatically slowing performance. See "Memory," page 107, for more information.
What is the size and bus interface type of the hard disk on your database server and application server?	The capacity and bus interface type of the hard disk on your database server and application server affect performance. For example, SCSI is generally faster than Serial ATA (SATA). See "Disk," page 110, for more information.
What is the speed of the network adapter on your database server and clients?	The speed of the network adapter controls the amount of bandwidth a network link provides, which in turn affects performance. If the bandwidth constraints of the network in your test environment are significantly different from those of your production environment, your benchmark results may not be a reliable predictor of performance. See "Network Adapter," page 116, for more information.

Table 9-1   Continued

Question	Explanation
What is the version of the operating system on both the client and database server?	Seemingly minor operating system changes can affect performance. See "Operating System," page 83, for more information.
If your application uses a JVM, which JVM is it, and how is that JVM configured?	Your JVM choice and how the JVM is configured affect performance. See "JVM," page 77, for more information.
What compiler/loader options were used to build your application executable?	Some compiler options for creating application executables affect performance. Use the same options in your test environment that you use in your production environment.
Does your application run on an application server?	All application servers are not the same. For example, if you run your benchmark against a JBoss application server and deploy your application on a WebSphere application server, the performance may vary.
At peak times, how many users run your application?	Performance can vary dramatically with 100 users versus 10 users. If your application accommodates multiple users, duplicate the same workload in your test environment. See "Reproduce the Workload," page 252, for more information.
Do network requests travel over a LAN or a WAN? Do network requests travel over a VPN?	Because communication across a WAN typically requires more network hops than communication across a LAN, your application is more likely to encounter varying MTU sizes, resulting in packet fragmentation. If the network characteristics in your test environment are significantly different from those used in your production environment, your benchmark results may not be a reliable predictor of performance. See "LAN versus WAN," page 103, and "VPNs Magnify Packet Fragmentation," page 102, for more information.

Table 9-1   Continued

Question	Explanation
What tuning options are set for your database driver?	Many database drivers allow you to tune certain options that affect performance. Just as you tune your database for the best performance, you should tune your database driver. If your production environment is tuned for performance and your test environment is not, your benchmark results may not be a reliable predictor of performance.

Make Your Test Data Realistic

Using a copy of your production data is a good idea, but that may not be possible in all cases. At a minimum, model your test data after real data, as shown in the following examples.

Example A: Design Test Data to Match Production Data

If your application retrieves data from a database table with 40 columns and 1,000 rows, design the test database table to have 40 columns with 1,000 rows.

Example B: Retrieve the Same Type of Data That Your Application Retrieves in Production–Long Data

If your application retrieves long data, such as Blobs and Clobs, in addition to numeric and character data, make sure your benchmark retrieves long data. Many database drivers emulate retrieving LOBs. You need to gauge how efficient the database driver is at retrieving long data.

Example C: Retrieve the Same Type of Data That Your Application Retrieves in Production—Unicode

If your application retrieves Unicode data, make sure that your benchmark retrieves Unicode data. Unicode is a standard encoding that is used to support multilingual character sets. If your application, database driver, and database do not fully support Unicode, more data conversion is required, which affects performance. You need to gauge how efficiently Unicode data can be retrieved.

Example D: Avoid Using Duplicate Values in Your Test Data

As a shortcut to creating test data, some benchmark developers populate test tables with duplicate values. For example, the following table contains a high percentage of duplicate values.

first_name	last_name	SSN
Grover	Cleveland	246-82-9856
Grover	Cleveland	246-82-9856
Abraham	Lincoln	684-12-0325
Grover	Cleveland	246-82-9856
Grover	Cleveland	246-82-9856
Grover	Cleveland	246-82-9856
Grover	Cleveland	246-82-9856
Abraham	Lincoln	684-12-0325
Abraham	Lincoln	684-12-0325
Ulysses	Grant	772-13-1127
...	...	...

Some database vendors have figured out that benchmark developers often take the easy way out. As a way to gain an advantage over other databases and database drivers in benchmark tests, they intentionally design their database clients and databases to perform an optimization when duplicate values in rows are encountered. Instead of returning all values in each row, the database only returns values that aren't duplicates of the values in the previous row. Each value that's deemed a duplicate returns a several-byte marker to represent that value in the row instead of the actual values.

For example, if we query the preceding table and request all rows in the table, the result set would look something like this. (The @ symbol represents a 4-byte marker.)

first_name	last_name	SSN
Grover	Cleveland	246-82-9856
@	@	@
@	@	@
Abraham	Lincoln	684-12-0325
Grover	Cleveland	246-82-9856
@	@	@
@	@	@
@	@	@
Abraham	Lincoln	684-12-0325
@	@	@
Ulysses	Grant	772-13-1127
...	...	...

This type of optimization results in better performance because there are fewer bytes of data to transmit. However, real-world data is seldom as uniform as the examples shown here, and the benchmark results in this case can't be trusted to predict performance.

Isolate the Test Environment

Because you must be able to reproduce consistent results to know whether changes have a positive or negative effect, it's important to isolate the test environment from influences that can skew benchmarking results. For example, if your benchmark is influenced by the ebb and flow of corporate network traffic, how can you trust the benchmark results? Isolate the network traffic generated by your benchmark runs from corporate network traffic by connecting your test machines through a single router, which can then connect to the corporate network. In this way, all the network traffic of your test environment goes through the router and is not influenced by the rest of the corporate network.

Developing Good Benchmarks

For the same reason, make sure that your test machines are "clean." Only run software that your application requires. Other applications running at the same time or in the background can profoundly influence test results. For example, if a virus-checking routine kicks off during a benchmarking run, it can slow performance significantly.

Reproduce the Workload

To design a good benchmark, you must have a solid understanding of the workload your application will deal with in the production environment. Ask yourself the following questions:

- What tasks does my application commonly perform? Which tasks are significant enough to measure?
- How many users does my application accommodate during peak traffic times?

Duplicating your real-world workload to an exact degree can be impractical or impossible, but it's important to emulate the essential characteristics of your workload and represent them accurately. For example, if you have a customer service application that typically performs the following actions, your test application should perform the same type of actions using the same data characteristics:

- Retrieves the customer record (one large row) from a table
- Retrieves invoices (multiple small rows) from another table
- Updates an invoice (one small row) as part of a transaction

Emulate the peak traffic that your application encounters in the production environment. For example, suppose that you have an intranet application that has 500 users, many working in an office on the West Coast of the United States. At 8:00 a.m. PST on a typical workday, as few as 20 users are active, whereas at 3:00 p.m. PST, approximately 400 users are active. In this case, design the benchmark to emulate 400 (or more) users. Commercial load test tools such as HP's LoadRunner allow you to easily emulate many concurrent users.

Measure the Right Tasks

Not all tasks that a database application performs are equally important. For example, a mail-order company that accepts orders over the phone may require a quick response time when referencing inventory availability to minimize the wait for the customer on the phone. That same company may not care as much about the response time required for the actual order to be processed. Ask your user liaisons what tasks are most important to them, and make testing of those tasks a priority.

Make sure the benchmark application makes the same API calls your database application makes. For example, we often see benchmarks that execute a query and retrieve a result set but do nothing with the data. Of course, this would never happen in a real-world application. For example, suppose you are tasked to design a benchmark that measures the time it takes for a JDBC application to process 50,000 rows. Let's take a look at the following simple benchmark:

```
Statement stmt = con.createStatement();
\\ Get start time
resultSet = stmt.executeQuery(
   "SELECT acct.bal FROM table");
while (resultSet.next())
{}
\\ Get finish time
```

Notice that the statement is opened and executed but is never closed, so resources are not released. Also, notice that the application positions a cursor on a row in the result set, but it subsequently ignores the data in that row. Different database drivers optimize retrieving data from network buffers and convert data at different times. For example, some drivers retrieve all requested data when a query is executed; others don't. Other drivers leave some data in the network buffer on the database server until the application actually requests that data. If you don't realize that this type of optimization occurs, you wouldn't know that results generated by the previous benchmark code would be greatly influenced by which driver you use.

Although these lapses in real-world modeling may not seem like a big deal, they can add up to make a big difference in performance. For most applications, 75% to 95% of the time it takes to process data is spent in the database driver and on the network. The difference between 75% and 95% can represent a big disparity in your application's performance.

So, let's rewrite the benchmark to reflect how the application would work in the real world:

```
Statement stmt = con.createStatement();
\\ Get start time
resultSet = stmt.executeQuery(
   "SELECT acct.bal FROM table");
while (resultSet.next()) {
```

```
    int id = resultSet.getInt(1);
  }
resultSet.close();
\\Get finish time
```

Also, exclude writing output from your benchmark timings. For example, suppose that your benchmark writes data to a console so that you can verify the results of each Select statement. For example, what if your benchmark includes the following line of code:

```
System.Console.WriteLine("Value of Column 2: " +
    dataReader.GetInt32(2));
```

If done once, it may add only a second or two to your benchmark results, but if done repeatedly, that time can add up, skewing your true results. Make sure that the console output occurs outside your timing loop.

Measure over a Sufficient Duration of Time

Design benchmarks so that they measure tasks over a sufficient duration. Benchmarks that are run over short durations make it difficult to reproduce meaningful and reliable results for the following reasons:

- They produce results that often do not scale. In most cases, you cannot extrapolate the results from a short duration and apply them to the larger context of your application.
- Computer system clocks, used to time benchmark runs, are notoriously imprecise because of design limitations, temperature changes, and diminished battery voltage over time. In fact, time kept by computer system clocks can fluctuate from the real time as much as several minutes a day. If a benchmark is run over a short duration, perhaps 10 seconds or less, the drift caused by a system clock can produce inconsistent results.
- Factors such as Java class loaders and the .NET Just-in-Time (JIT) compiler cause application start-up performance costs that skew performance results over short durations.

For example, suppose you want to measure the throughput of an application that retrieves 1,000-byte rows from a database table containing a million rows. First, the benchmark is run over 5 seconds, resulting in a throughput of 5 rows per second. What if another short-term process running in the background caused a "blip" in the system during that 5 seconds? You could run the same benchmark a second time for 5 seconds, and the outcome may result in a completely different metric—for example, 10 rows per second, which is a huge variance on this scale.

However, if you run the same benchmark again for 100 seconds, the throughput result is a more useful and reliable metric—for example, 30,000 rows per second—because any blips caused by another service running are averaged over a longer period.

Similarly, a system clock used to measure a benchmark can experience blips in its timekeeping that cause the clock to drift suddenly. For example, suppose that you run a benchmark over 5 seconds and a blip occurs causing the system clock to drift by 500ms. That's a significant difference that you may not even realize occurred. Running the benchmark for a sufficient duration—100 seconds, for example—ensures that any system clock blips are averaged over a longer period.

Other factors, such as Java class loaders and the .NET Just-in-Time (JIT) compiler, can skew results on short-running benchmarks. In Java, classes are loaded into the Java environment by class loaders when they are referenced by name, often at the start of an application. Similarly, in ADO.NET environments, the JIT compiler is invoked when a method is called the first time during an application's execution. These factors front-load some performance costs. For example, suppose we run a benchmark for only 10 seconds, as shown in Figure 9-1.

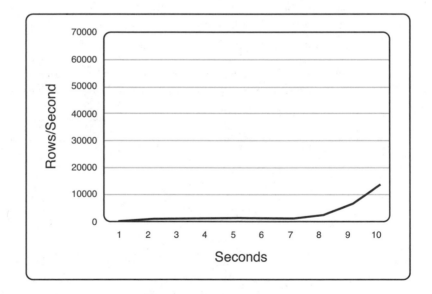

Figure 9-1   Benchmark run for 10 seconds

Now, let's look at different results of the same benchmark that is run over a longer duration—100 seconds—as shown in Figure 9-2. Notice how the performance impact is not as significant over time.

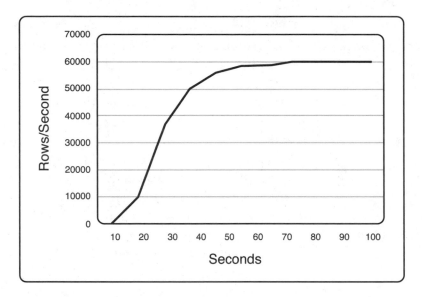

Figure 9-2   Benchmark run for 100 seconds

We can even take this improvement one step further, as shown in Figure 9-3, and run the benchmark twice without unloading the application, discarding the first run's results and the startup performance impact results.

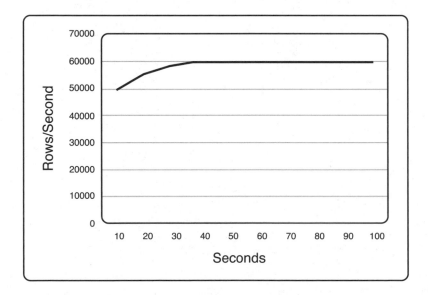

Figure 9-3   Benchmark run twice without unloading the application

Prepare the Database

Because disk I/O is much slower than memory I/O, any time the database retrieves data from or stores data to the disk on the database server, performance degrades significantly. The first time the application accesses a table row in a database, the database places a copy of the row on disk into a fixed-length block of memory known as a **page**. If the database can find the requested data on a page in memory when subsequent data requests are processed, the database optimizes its operation by avoiding disk I/O.

When the database fills up a page with data, it creates a new page. The pages in memory are ordered from MRU (Most Recently Used) to LRU (Least Recently Used). If the allocated memory buffer becomes full, the database makes room for a new page by discarding the LRU page. This method of memory management counts on the fact that the LRU page will probably not be needed any time soon.

When your application retrieves, inserts, or updates data in the real world, typically, the database has been running for some time, allowing your application to access data in memory. Running the benchmark at least once without timing it allows the database to place some, or possibly all, the data you will be working with in memory where it can be accessed on subsequent runs of the benchmark. This also helps model how your application will run in your production environment because applications typically access the same tables over and over.

Make Changes One at a Time

The most important guideline to remember when running a benchmark is that a seemingly insignificant change can have a dramatic effect on performance. It's crucial that you can demonstrate whether any change has a positive or negative impact; otherwise, your benchmark efforts are useless. With this in mind, make sure that you only change one variable at a time when you run the benchmark.

For example, suppose you want to explore the effect of setting two different connection options in your database driver. Instead of making both changes at once, make the changes one at a time and rerun the benchmark after each change. If you make both changes at once, how do you know if either change made a difference? Suppose one change has a positive effect on performance and a second change has a negative effect, cancelling any performance gain caused by the first change. How would you know if either change was good or bad?

Assess Other Factors

If your application does not perform in the real world as your benchmark predicted, what then? Look at external influences such as corporate traffic slowing down the network or excessive CPU and memory use on the client or database server.

In addition, be aware that some tasks such as stored procedures or application-side caching of a large amount of data can mask the performance of the network, database middleware, or application code. For example, if the execution of a stored procedure takes 50 times longer than retrieving the data, changing the application code or database driver so that it's 100% faster at data retrieval would not show a noticeable difference in the benchmark results because most of the time processing the data requests is spent on the database server. Using tools such as code profilers and network sniffers to create a log that times each operation can tell you where processing time is being spent and help you make educated guesses about where your efforts can improve performance.

Benchmark Example

The following example shows a benchmark that measures the response time of a typical reporting application to retrieve data. Although we don't show all the code involved, such as connecting to the database, we show the core parts of the benchmark that incorporate many of the principles discussed in this chapter, including these.

- Your test environment should resemble your production environment as closely as possible. Your test data should be realistic, and your benchmark should perform the types of tasks it will perform in the real world. Notice that the following benchmark retrieves different types of data, including long data.
- Your benchmark should measure the right tasks. Notice that the following benchmark records the CPU time at the start and end of a timing loop. In addition, it retrieves data from the result set, and it closes statements after they are executed to release resources.
- Your benchmark should measure over a sufficient duration. Notice that the following benchmark measures over a period of 100 seconds.

Creating the Test Data

First, let's create the test data. Notice the variety of data types, including BLOB and CLOB data types.

```
CREATE TABLE RetailTable (
    Name VARCHAR(128) Not null,
    ProductCategory VARCHAR(128) Not null,
    Manufacturer VARCHAR(64) Not null,
    MSRP Decimal(10,2) Not null,
    OurPrice Decimal(10,2) Not null,
    SalePrice Decimal(10,2),
    SaleStart Timestamp,
    SaleEnd Timestamp,
    SKU BigInt Not null,
    UPC Decimal(12) Not null,
    Quantity Integer Not null,
    Description VARCHAR(512) Not null,
    LongDescription Clob,
    ThumbnailPicture Blob Not null,
    Picture Blob,
    OtherOffers VARCHAR(4000),
    RebateInfo VARCHAR(1024),
    UserRating Decimal(4,1) Not null
)


CREATE INDEX Retail_Idx ON RetailTable (SKU)
```

Benchmark

Now let's create the benchmark. After initializing all the variables and the SQL we'll be using, we start the timer thread and sample the start time and the current CPU time. Next, we execute the query repeatedly until the specified time has elapsed. We stop the timer and again sample the elapsed time and the current CPU time. Finally, we close all open resources and report the benchmark's findings.

```java
public void run () {

   // Initialize variables
   ThreadInfo.numExecutes = 0;
   ThreadInfo.numRows = 0;
   ThreadInfo.actualTime = 0.;
   Connection conn = ThreadInfo.conn;
   int threadNumber = ThreadInfo.threadNumber;
   int totalExecutes = 0;
   int totalRows = 0;
   long start=0;
   long end=0;
   long cpuStart=0;
   long cpuEnd=0;
   PreparedStatement stmt = null;
   ResultSet rs = null;

   // Initialize fetch string
   String sqlStr = "SELECT Name, ProductCategory, " +
                   "Manufacturer, MSRP, OurPrice, " +
                   "SalePrice, SaleStart, SaleEnd, " +
                   "SKU, UPC, Quantity, Description, " +
                   "LongDescription, ThumbnailPicture, " +
                   "Picture, OtherOffers, RebateInfo, " +
                   "UserRating FROM RetailTable";

   // Start the timer
   start = System.currentTimeMillis();
   ThreadInfo.ready = true;

   while (Wait) {
      // Make an OS call.
      // This is to avoid a "tight" loop that may prevent
      // the timer thread from running.
      try {
         Thread.sleep(100);
      }
      catch (InterruptedException e) {
```

```
            System.out.println (e);
        }

    // Record the start time
    start = System.currentTimeMillis ();
    }

    // Record the current CPU time
    ThreadMXBean tb = ManagementFactory.getThreadMXBean();
    cpuStart = tb.getCurrentThreadCpuTime();

    // All work below is timed:
    // 1. Prepare the statement
    // 2. Execute the query
    // 3. Fetch data from all rows
    // 4. Repeat until time is up
    try {

        stmt = conn.prepareStatement (sqlStr);

        while (! Stop)
        {
            rs = stmt.executeQuery();
            totalExecutes++;

            while ((! Stop) && rs.next ())
            {
                totalRows++;

                String name = rs.getString(1);
                String productCategory = rs.getString(2);
                String manufacturer = rs.getString(3);
                BigDecimal msrp = rs.getBigDecimal(4);
                BigDecimal ourPrice = rs.getBigDecimal(5);
                BigDecimal salePrice = rs.getBigDecimal(6);
                Timestamp saleStart = rs.getTimestamp(7);
                Timestamp saleEnd = rs.getTimestamp(8);
                Long sku = rs.getLong(9);
```

```
                    BigDecimal upc = rs.getBigDecimal(10);
                    int quantity = rs.getInt(11);
                    String description = rs.getString(12);
                    Clob longDescription = rs.getClob(13);
                    Blob thumbnailPicture = rs.getBlob(14);
                    Blob picture = rs.getBlob(15);
                    String otherOffers = rs.getString(16);
                    String rebateInfo = rs.getString(17);
                    BigDecimal userRating = rs.getBigDecimal(18);
                }
                rs.close ();
                rs = null;

            }
            try
            {
                stmt.close ();
            }
            finally
            {
            stmt = null;
            }

            // Stop the timer and calculate/record the
            // actual time elapsed and current CPU time
            end = System.currentTimeMillis();
            cpuEnd = tb.getCurrentThreadCpuTime();
            ThreadInfo.actualTime = (end - start) / 1000.;

        }
        catch (SQLException e)
        {
            e.printStackTrace();
            System.out.println ("Thread " + threadNumber +
                " failed with " + e);
        }
```

```
        finally
        {

            // Clean everything up
            if (rs != null) {
                try
                {
                    rs.close ();
                }
                catch (SQLException e)
                {
                    System.out.println (e);
                }
            }
            if (stmt != null) {
                try
                {
                    stmt.close ();
                }
                catch (SQLException e)
                {
                    System.out.println (e);
                }
            }
        }

        // Finish calculating and storing values for this thread
        ThreadInfo.cpuTime = (cpuEnd - cpuStart);
        ThreadInfo.numExecutes = totalExecutes;
        ThreadInfo.numRows = totalRows;
        ThreadInfo.done = true;
    }
```

Summary

Benchmarks are an essential tool to measure and predict performance. Some factors that affect performance are outside of your control. In this chapter, we focused on factors that you can influence, such as how efficiently your application is coded to access data and how efficiently your database middleware operates. When developing any benchmark, consider the following guidelines:

- Define benchmark goals to align with your business needs.
- Measuring CPU and memory use can be a good predictor of scalability, but make sure that you do it appropriately so your results are useful.
- Reproduce the essential characteristics of both your production environment and your production workload.
- Isolate your test environment from outside environmental influences.
- Measure the right tasks over a sufficient duration of time.
- Prepare your database before measuring by running the benchmark at least once, and introduce only one change at a time into the benchmark.

CHAPTER TEN

Troubleshooting Performance Issues

Perhaps you didn't get the opportunity to design the database applications that are in production; you just get the "opportunity" to maintain them and make sure that the performance is acceptable. And you just found out that the performance is unacceptable.

Or perhaps you did design the application, but after benchmarking it, you aren't satisfied with the performance. Whatever the scenario, this chapter walks you through how to troubleshoot your performance issues and provides some case studies that are similar to scenarios that we have encountered in our years of helping people troubleshoot their performance issues.

We recommend that you never deploy a critical application without first running benchmarks to determine whether performance is acceptable. Read Chapter 9, "Developing Good Benchmarks."

In this chapter, we assume that your database is not the issue, that it is tuned properly.

Where to Start

Before you begin troubleshooting, you must define the performance issue. Is the issue related to unacceptable response time, throughput, scalability, or a combination?

After defining the issue, think about what can cause the performance effects you are seeing. Table 10-1 lists some possible causes.

Table 10-1   Performance Issues and Possible Causes

Issues	Possible Causes
Response time	Database application causes: • Nonoptimal coding techniques, such as unnecessary data retrieved for the application • Large result sets returned from a streaming protocol database • Use of scrollable cursors • Excessive data conversion • Memory leak Database driver causes: • Poorly configured database driver • Memory leak Environment causes: • Network packet fragmentation • Excessive number of network hops • Insufficient bandwidth • Insufficient physical memory • Insufficient CPU capacity • Virtualization • Poorly configured connection pools • Poorly configured statement pools
Throughput	Database application causes: • Use of data encryption • Too many active transactions • Unnecessary data retrieved for the application • Memory leak

Table 10-1   Continued

Issues	Possible Causes
Throughput (continued)	Database driver causes: • Nonoptimal database driver architecture • Memory leak Environment causes: • High packet overhead • Runtime environment • Insufficient bandwidth • Insufficient physical memory • Insufficient CPU capacity • Virtualization
Scalability	Database application causes: • Use of data encryption • Memory leak Database driver causes: • Nonoptimal database driver architecture • Memory leak Environment causes: • Runtime environment • Insufficient bandwidth • Insufficient physical memory • Insufficient CPU capacity • Poorly configured connection pools • Poorly configured statement pools

To narrow the possible causes, you might find it helpful to troubleshoot in the following order:

1. Look at the complete picture and ask yourself the following important question: Has anything changed in any of the components of the database application deployment? If the answer is yes, start by looking at what changed. See "Changes in Your Database Application Deployment," page 268.

2. If nothing has changed, look at the database application. See "The Database Application," page 269.

3. If your database application does not seem to be the issue, look at your database driver. Are the runtime performance tuning options configured to match your application and environment? Is it time to benchmark another driver? See "The Database Driver," page 270.

4. If you are not satisfied with the performance after looking at the application and the database driver, look at the environment where your application is deployed. See "The Environment," page 272.

One important fact to note is that if the database server machine is resource bound, no amount of tuning of your applications or the database middleware results in acceptable performance.

Changes in Your Database Application Deployment

If you see a performance issue after something in the application or environment has changed, start by looking at that change. Here are some examples of the types of changes that could cause a performance issue:

- The database application has changed, for example, it now fetches more columns in a result set.
- The network has been reconfigured so that more network hops separate the client and database server.
- The client or database server has been moved to a different operating system.
- The number of users accessing the application has increased.
- Patches have been applied to one or more components in your environment, such as the database system, application server, operating system, or database driver.
- The database system has changed to a different version.
- New applications have been installed on the application server.
- Database tuning parameters have changed.

If an application's environment must change, the best advice we can give is to make sure that changes are made one at a time. That way, you can more easily determine the change that made the difference in performance.

The Database Application

Earlier in this book, we presented good coding practices that improve database application performance. Let's recap some of the general guidelines for good coding practices:

- **Reduce network round trips, which increases response time**—Coding practices that reduce network round trips include using connection pools and statements pools, avoiding auto-commit mode in favor of manual commits, using local transactions instead of distributed transactions where appropriate, and using batches or arrays of parameters for bulk inserts.
- **Don't keep more connections and prepared statements open than needed, which increases response time and scalability**—Make sure that your application closes connections immediately after it's finished with them. Make sure that connection pools and statement pools are configured correctly.
- **Don't leave transactions active too long, which increases throughput**—If your application uses transactions that update large amounts of data without committing modifications at regular intervals, a substantial amount of memory can be consumed on the database server.
- **Avoid using auto-commit mode for transactions, which increases throughput**—You can minimize disk I/O by using manual commits.
- **Avoid returning large amounts of data from the database server, which increases response time**—Always write your SQL queries to return only the data you need. If your application executes queries that return millions of rows, memory can be used up quickly. Returning long data can also consume a substantial amount of memory.
- **Avoid using scrollable cursors unless the database fully supports them, which increases response time**—Large scrollable result sets can quickly consume memory.
- **Maximize query plan reuse, which increases response time**—Each time the database creates a new query plan, it uses CPU cycles. To maximize query plan reuse, consider using statement pooling.
- **Minimize data conversions, which increases response time**—Choose data types that process efficiently.

These coding practices can affect one or more of your hardware resources. Table 10-2 lists good coding practices and the resources that they can impact. Not following these coding practices can contribute to hardware bottlenecks.

Typically, you notice a negative impact in the scalability of your application when a bottleneck is present. If only one or two users access an application, you may not see a negative effect on throughput and response time.

Table 10-2   Good Coding Practices and the Hardware Resources They Impact

Good Coding Practice	Memory/Disk	CPU	Network Adapter
Reduce network round trips	✓	✓	✓
Don't keep more connections and prepared statements open than needed	✓		
Don't leave transactions active too long	✓		
Avoid using auto-commit mode for transactions	✓		
Avoid returning large amounts of data from the database server	✓		✓
Avoid using scrollable cursors unless the database fully supports them	✓		✓
Maximize query plan reuse		✓	
Minimize data conversions		✓	

The Database Driver

Earlier in this book, we provided detailed information about database drivers and how they can impact performance. To recap, a database driver can degrade the performance of your database application for the following two reasons:

- The driver is not tunable. It does not have runtime performance tuning options that allow you to configure the driver for optimal performance.
- The architecture of the driver is not optimal.

In general, even when two database drivers implement all the same functionality, their performance may be quite different when used with your database applications. If you are experiencing less than optimal performance with the database driver you are using, consider evaluating another database driver.

Runtime Performance Tuning Options

Make sure you have configured your driver to work optimally with your application and environment. Here are some examples of runtime performance tuning options that can help performance:

- If memory is a limiting factor on your database server, application server, or client, use a database driver that allows you to choose how and where some memory-intensive operations are performed. For example, if your client excessively pages to disk because of a large result set, you may want to decrease the size of the fetch buffer (the amount of memory used by the driver to store results returned from the database server). Decreasing the size of the fetch buffer reduces memory consumption but results in more network round trips. You need to be aware of the trade-off.
- If CPU is a limiting factor on your database server, application server, or client, use a database driver that allows you to choose how and where some CPU-intensive operations are performed. For example, Sybase creates stored procedures for prepared statements (a CPU-intensive operation to create the stored procedure, but not to execute it). Choosing a driver that allows you to tune whether Sybase creates stored procedures for a prepared statement could improve performance significantly by conserving CPU.
- To reduce network round trips, which increases response time, use a database driver that allows you to change the size of database protocol packets.

Architecture

In general, make sure that the driver's architecture meets the requirements of your application. Here are some examples of good driver architecture:

- To minimize data conversions, use a database driver that converts data efficiently. For example, some database drivers don't support Unicode. If your database driver doesn't support Unicode, more data conversion is required to work with Unicode data, resulting in higher CPU use.
- To decrease latency by eliminating the processing required in the client software and from the extra network traffic caused by the client software, use a database driver that is implemented with a database wire protocol architecture.

- To optimize network traffic by reducing network bandwidth requirements from extra transmissions, use a database driver that is implemented with a database wire protocol architecture. Database wire protocol drivers can optimize network traffic by controlling interaction with TCP.

The Environment

We provided detailed information about the environment and how it can impact performance earlier in this book. In this section, we recap some of the most common environmental causes of poor performance of your database application. Chapter 4, "The Environment: Tuning for Performance," provides more detail.

Table 10-3 lists some tools that can help you troubleshoot poor system performance. Because these tools use system resources, you may want to use them only when necessary to troubleshoot or measure system performance.

Table 10-3   Performance Tools

Operating System and Category	Tool	Description
CPU and Memory Usage		
All UNIX/Linux AIX only HP-UX only Solaris only	vmstat, time, ps topas and tprof monitor and glance prstat	Provides data about CPU and memory utilization.
Windows	Microsoft Performance Monitor (PerfMon)	Provides data about CPU and memory utilization. PerfMon also has other counters you can set to monitor such functionality as connection pooling.
Network Activity		
UNIX/Linux/ Windows	netstat	Handles TCP/IP traffic.
AIX only	netpmon	Reports low-level network statistics, including TCP/IP and SNA statistics such as the number of network packets or frames received per second.

Using tools such as the ones listed in Table 10-3 can tell you where processing time is being spent and help you make educated guesses about where your efforts can improve performance.

Runtime Environment (Java and .NET)

Runtime environments can significantly impact the performance of your database applications. For Java applications, the runtime environment is a Java Virtual Machine (JVM). For ADO.NET applications, the runtime environment is the .NET Common Language Runtime (CLR).

JVMs

For Java, you have JVM choices. IBM, Sun Microsystems, and BEA (Oracle) develop JVMs. Differences exist in the way these JVMs are implemented, which can affect performance. The configuration of your JVM can also affect performance. See "Runtime Environment (Java and .NET)," page 77, for examples of how JVMs affect performance.

If you are running a Java application and you have exhausted other options for improving performance, consider benchmarking your application with a different JVM.

.NET CLR

Unlike JVMs, you do not have a choice when it comes to the vendor for the .NET CLR. Microsoft is the sole vendor. For important tips when running an ADO.NET application, see "Runtime Environment (Java and .NET)," page 77.

Operating System

If you are seeing a decrease in performance after changing either the client or server to a different operating system, you may have to live with it. We are not saying that one operating system is better than another; we are saying that you need to be aware that any operating system change can increase or decrease performance. See "Operating System," page 83, for a discussion of why.

Network

We have said many times that database application performance improves when communication between the database driver and the database is optimized. Here are key techniques for ensuring the best performance over the network:

- Reducing network round trips, which increases response time
- Tuning the size of database protocol packets, which increases response time and throughput

- Reducing the number of network hops between network destinations, which increases response time
- Avoiding network packet fragmentation, which increases response time

See "Network," page 86, for detailed information about the network.
Here are some causes of and associated solutions for network bottlenecks.

- **Insufficient bandwidth**—Look at these possible solutions.
  - Add more network adapters or upgrade your network adapter.
  - Distribute client connections across multiple network adapters.
- **Poorly optimized application code**—Develop or tune your application to reduce network round trips. See, "The Database Application," page 269.
- **Poorly configured database drivers**—Understand the runtime performance tuning options for the database driver you are using, and configure the driver to use the appropriate options to optimize network traffic (to reduce network round trips). See, "The Database Driver," page 270.

To detect a network bottleneck, gather information about your system to answer the following question:

- **What is the rate at which network packets are sent and received using the network adapter?** Comparing this rate to the total bandwidth of your network adapter can tell you if the network traffic load is too much for your network adapter. To allow room for spikes in traffic, you should use no more than 50% of capacity.

Hardware

Hardware constraints can cause poor performance. In this section, we discuss the symptoms and causes of bottlenecks caused by memory, disk, CPU, and network adapter.

Memory

The primary symptom of a memory bottleneck is a sustained, high rate of page faults. A page fault occurs when an application requests a page but the system can't find the page at the requested location in RAM. For detailed information about memory, see "Memory," page 107.

Here are some causes of and associated solutions for memory bottlenecks:

- **Memory leaks**—Memory leaks are often created when applications use resources and don't release them when they are no longer required. Database drivers have also been known to have memory leaks.
- **Insufficient physical memory (RAM)**—Install more RAM to your system.
- **Poorly optimized application code**—Develop or tune your application to minimize memory use. See "The Database Application," page 269.
- **Poorly configured database drivers**—Understand the runtime performance tuning options for the database driver you are using and configure the driver to use the appropriate options to minimize memory use. See "The Database Driver," page 270.

To detect a memory bottleneck, gather information about your system to answer the following questions:

- **How often are requested pages triggering a page fault?** This information gives you an idea of the number of total page faults, both soft and hard page faults, that occur over a period.
- **How many pages are retrieved from disk to satisfy page faults?** Compare this information to the preceding information to determine how many hard page faults occur out of the total number of page faults.
- **Does the memory use of any individual application or process climb steadily and never level off?** If so, that application or process is probably leaking memory. In pooled environments, detecting memory leaks is more difficult because pooled connections and prepared statements hold onto memory and can make it appear as if your application is leaking memory even when it isn't. If you run into memory issues when using connection pooling, try tuning the connection pool to reduce the number of connections in the pool. Similarly, try tuning the statement pool to reduce the number of prepared statements in the pool.

Disk

When an operation reads or writes to disk, performance suffers because disk access is extremely slow. If you suspect that disk access occurs more often than it should, first rule out a memory bottleneck. For detailed information about disk, see "Disk," page 110.

Here are some causes of and associated solutions for disk bottlenecks:

- **Stretching memory to its limit**—When memory is low, paging to disk occurs more frequently. Resolve the memory issue.
- **Poorly optimized application code**—Develop or tune your application to avoid unnecessary disk reads or writes. See "The Database Application," page 269.

To detect a disk bottleneck, gather information about your system to answer the following questions:

- **Is excessive paging occurring?** A memory bottleneck can resemble a disk bottleneck, so it's important to rule out a memory problem before you make disk improvements. See "Memory," page 107.
- **How often is the disk busy?** If your disk has a sustained rate of disk activity of 85% or more for a sustained period and a persistent disk queue, you may have a disk bottleneck.

CPU

The primary symptom of a CPU bottleneck is that the application is slow when multiple users are using it. A CPU bottleneck negatively affects scalability. For detailed information about CPU, see "CPU (Processor)," page 112.

Here are some causes of and associated solutions for CPU bottlenecks:

- **Insufficient CPU capacity**—Install additional processors or upgrade to a more powerful processor.
- **Poorly optimized application code**—Develop or tune your application to minimize CPU use. See "The Database Application," page 269.
- **Poorly configured database drivers**—Understand the runtime performance tuning options for the database driver you are using, and configure the driver to use the appropriate options to minimize CPU use. See "The Database Driver," page 270.

To detect a CPU bottleneck, gather information about your system to answer the following questions:

- **How much time does the CPU spend executing work?** If the processor is busy 80% or higher for sustained periods, the CPU can be a source of trouble. If you detect high CPU use, drill down to individual processes to determine if any one application is using more than its fair share of CPU cycles. If so, look more closely at how that application is designed and coded, as described in "The Database Application," page 269.

- **How many processes or threads are waiting to be serviced in the CPU's run queue?** A single queue is used for CPU requests, even on computers with multiple processors. If all processors are busy, threads must wait until CPU cycles are free to perform work. Processes waiting in the queue for sustained periods indicate a CPU bottleneck.
- **What is the rate that the operating system switches processes or threads to perform work for other waiting threads?** A **context switch** is the process of storing and restoring the state (context) of a CPU so that multiple processes can share a single CPU resource. Every time the CPU stops running one process and starts running another, a context switch occurs. For example, if your application is waiting for a row lock to release so that it can update data, the operating system may switch the context so that the CPU can perform work on behalf of another application while your application is waiting for the lock to release. Context switching requires significant processor time, so excessive context switches and high CPU use tend to go hand in hand.

Network Adapter

Computers that are connected to a network have at least one network adapter that is used to send and receive network packets across the network. See "Network," page 86, for more information.

Case Studies

This section provides several troubleshooting case studies to help you think through some varied performance issues and how to resolve them. All the information that you need to solve these issues has been presented in this book.

Case Study 1

The database application in this case study supports the FBI. The application is GUI based and displays one record at a time. The application allows FBI agents from around the country to retrieve information about at-large criminals by state. Each record contains first name, last name, crimes, previous convictions, last known address, and a photo of the person. Each query can return as many as

50,000 records. The JDBC application executes the SQL Select statement in the following code:

```
PreparedStatement pstmt = con.prepareStatement(
"SELECT fname, lname, crimes, convictions, laddress, photo " +
    "FROM FBI_most_wanted WHERE state=?");
    pstmt.setString(1, "NC");
ResultSet rs = pstmt.executeQuery ();

// Display all rows
while (rs.next()) {
// Retrieve information and display the contents
}
rs.close();
```

Environment Details

The environment details are as follows:

- The application is JDBC and is running on an application server.
- The database is Microsoft SQL Server running on Windows XP.
- The client machines are running a variety of Windows operating systems, such as Windows XP and Windows Vista.
- The application is deployed in a distributed WAN environment.
- The application server is running J2SE 5.
- The application is using a connection pool for connection management.

The Issue

Occasionally when a user exits the application, it closes very slowly (almost appears to hang). What could be the cause?

Here are some questions to ask:

- Why does this happen only upon closing the application, and why only occasionally?
- Which components in the environment affect the closing of the application?
- What tasks must be performed when the application is closed?
- What type of data is being returned?

- Are there any connection option settings in the driver that could be changed to improve performance?

Thinking Through the Issue

Let's think about what we know:

- The photo is long data, and long data can slow performance. However, the issue is not about the performance of displaying the records.
- A connection pool is being used. It might affect the opening of the application, but not the closing.
- CPU and memory are plentiful, so that isn't the issue.
- Microsoft SQL Server is a streaming protocol database.

What could be causing the issue?

- The driver is not configured for optimal performance. For example, the driver's packet size is configured smaller than the server's packet size, which results in more network round trips.
- The application is accessing a streaming protocol database. When a query is executed on a streaming protocol database, all records are returned. This means that even if the user doesn't look at all the records when he closes the application, all the records must be processed off the network before the application actually closes.
- The application design is not optimal, especially when accessing a streaming protocol database. The application is written to return long data with each record.

The Resolution

The performance issue revolves around the fact that the application is accessing a streaming protocol database and that long data is retrieved for each record. Do you know why this issue happens only occasionally? Let's say a user queries on the state of North Carolina and 15,000 records are returned. The user finds what he is looking for after displaying 21 records and closes the application. Before the application can close, all the other 14,979 records must be processed off the network. In this case, the application could take a few seconds to close. On the other hand, if the user displayed 10,000 records before closing the application, fewer records would need to be processed before the application closed, which would make the application close more quickly.

Let's assume that using a different database is not an option. We know that the SQL Select statement retrieves a photo for each criminal record. Can that be changed? Yes, the application can be changed to execute a query that retrieves all the data except for the photo and then execute another query to retrieve the photo. In this case, the photo can be retrieved only if the user actually displays the associated criminal record. Here is the application rewrite:

```
PreparedStatement getPhotoStmt = con.prepareStatement(
    "SELECT photo FROM FBI_most_wanted " +
    "WHERE state=? AND fname=? AND lname=? AND crimes=? " +
    "AND convictions=? AND laddress=?");

PreparedStatement pstmt = con.prepareStatement(
    "SELECT fname, lname, crimes, convictions, laddress " +
    "FROM FBI_most_wanted WHERE state=?");

pstmt.setString(1, "NC");
ResultSet rs = pstmt.executeQuery ();

// Display all rows
while (rs.next()) {
    String fname = rs.getString(1);
    String lname = rs.getString(2);
    String crimes = rs.getString(3);
    String convictions = rs.getString(4);
    String laddress = rs.getString(5);

    if (isPersonOfInterest(fname, lname, crimes, convictions,
      laddress)) {
        getPhotoStmt.setString(1, "NC");
        getPhotoStmt.setString(2, fname);
        getPhotoStmt.setString(3, lname);
        getPhotoStmt.setString(4, crimes);
        getPhotoStmt.setString(5, convictions);
        getPhotoStmt.setString(6, laddress);
        ResultSet rs2 = getPhotoStmt.executeQuery();
```

```
                 if (rs2.next()) {
                     Object photo = rs2.getObject(1);
                     displayPhoto(photo);
                 }
                 rs2.close();
            }
        }
        rs.close();
```

With this application rewrite, less data must be processed off the network when the user closes the application, which results in the application closing more quickly.

Case Study 2

The application in this case study allows users to refill their drug prescriptions over the Web and check the status of their orders. It is an interactive Web-server application.

Environment Details

The environment details are as follows:

- Active Server Pages (ASP) is used to create the application.
- The application makes ADO calls.
- The database is Oracle running on Windows.
- The database driver is an OLE/DB to ODBC bridge.
- The client machines are running a variety of Windows operating systems, such as Windows XP and Windows Vista.
- The application is using connection pooling of Microsoft's Driver Manager for connection management.

The Issue

The server is running out of memory, which causes poor overall performance. What consumes memory on the server? The most likely culprits are defects in the database driver, LOB data, scrollable cursors, statement pools, and connection pools.

Thinking Through the Issue

Let's think about what we know:

- The application does not retrieve or update LOB data.
- Statement pooling is not being used.
- Let's assume that the database driver is not causing the problem.
- The application does not retrieve large amounts of data, so scrollable cursors are not being used.
- We know the application is using connection pooling. Let's look into this more closely.

As discussed earlier in this book, ODBC connection pooling as implemented in Microsoft's Driver Manager does not provide a way to define a maximum pool size. Therefore, the pool size grows dynamically as the application uses the pool to get a connection. This can result in memory issues because the connection, even when not in use, holds on to resources. How can you determine if this is the issue?

One tool on Windows that you can use to monitor the pool is Performance Monitor (PerfMon). The following URL contains a Microsoft document[1] that explains how to use PerfMon to monitor connection pools:

http://msdn.microsoft.com/en-us/library/ms810829.aspx

Let's assume that after monitoring the ODBC connection pool, we did not see an issue with it. What next? We also know that we are using ADO. With ADO, resource pooling is turned on by default. Is the application using both ODBC connection pooling and resource pooling? Yes.

Using two implementations of pooling would definitely use more memory on the database server.

The Resolution

To limit the memory use on the database server associated with connections, turn off ODBC connection pooling. Microsoft's documentation recommends that you do not use these two types of pooling together—that you choose which implementation you want to use and use it exclusively within a given application.[1]

Case Study 3

The database application in this case study serves a large insurance company with many users. The company has many applications. This particular applica-

---

[1] Ahlbeck, Leland, Don Willits, and Acey J. Bunch. "Pooling in the Microsoft Data Access Components." May 1999 (updated August 2004). Microsoft Corporation. 2 February 2009 <http://msdn.microsoft.com/en-us/library/ms810829.aspx>.

tion allows customer service representatives to update the personal information of clients, including bank account information if the client pays his monthly bill with automatic draft. All the applications within the company must adhere to strict privacy and security requirements.

Environment Details

The environment details are as follows:

- The application is ODBC.
- The database server is Sybase Adaptive Server Enterprise 11.5 running on Windows.
- The client machines are running on HP-UX PA-RISC.
- The application is deployed in a WAN environment.
- The application is using distributed transactions to make sure that different databases stay consistent with one another.
- CPU and memory are plentiful on the database server.

Following is the connection string for the DataDirect Technologies ODBC driver in the production environment:

```
DataSourceName=MySybaseTables;NetworkAddress=123.456.78.90,
 5000;DataBase=SYBACCT;LogonID=JOHN;Password=XYZ3Y;
ApplicationUsingThreads=1;EncryptionMethod=1;
HostNameInCertificate=#SERVERNAME#;TrustStorePassword=xxx2Z;
TrustStore=C:\trustfile.pfx;ValidateServerCertificate=1;
SelectMethod=0
```

Before deploying the application, the IT department ran performance benchmarks on the application. The performance met the requirements, and the application was deployed.

The Issue

After deploying the application, performance degraded by twofold. Why?

Here are some questions to ask:

- Are there any differences between the test environment and the production environment? For example, was the data in the test environment modeled after the data in the production environment? Did the benchmark test the same number of users as is seen in the production environment? Was the same version of the database driver used in both environments? Were the drivers configured the same in both environments? Did the test environment use all the same operating systems for clients and database servers as the production environment?

• Are there any connection option settings in the driver that could be changed to improve performance?

Thinking Through the Issue

Let's think about what we know:

• The application was benchmarked in a test environment before being deployed, and performance was acceptable.
• The application is using distributed transactions, which can slow down performance because of the logging and network round trips needed to communicate between all the components involved in the distributed transaction.
• The connection string used in the benchmark does not show that the application is using data encryption, which is a requirement for all of this company's applications.

To solve this issue, we need to look at the test and production environments and see if there are any differences. The main question in this case study is why the test environment shows better performance. The performance issue is caused by data encryption. We discussed the effect that data encryption has on performance in Chapter 2, "Designing for Performance: What's Your Strategy." To summarize, encryption is performed on each byte of data being transferred, which means slower network throughput.

Another issue to point out in this case study is that the benchmark did not duplicate the production environment. See "Reproduce the Production Environment," page 246, to read about how important it is to do this when benchmarking.

The Resolution

As we discussed in "Data Encryption across the Network," page 86, performance penalties go along with using data encryption, and often there is little you can do about it. If your database system allows one connection that uses data encryption and another that does not, you may be able to decrease the performance penalty. For example, you could establish a connection that uses encryption for accessing sensitive data such as an individual's tax ID number, and another connection that does not use encryption for accessing data that is less sensitive, such as an individual's department and title. Oracle and Microsoft SQL Server are examples of database systems that allow this. Sybase is an example where either all connections to the database use encryption or none of them do.

Case Study 4

The small company in this case study was concerned about "machine creep"; too many machines resided in its lab, and some of the machines were outdated. The company decided to consolidate five of the machines into one 8-CPU virtualized machine. Each of the existing machines hosts at least one database application. The company's IT department started deploying the machine's images on the one virtualized machine. After deploying two of the images on the virtualized machine, IT ran performance checks. Performance was great. IT continued deploying machine images one at a time and testing the performance after each addition.

Environment Details

The environment details are as follows:

- The database applications on the virtualized machine vary greatly. Some are used only by one user a few times a week. Others are used by many users several times each day.
- Machine 1 has two applications that are used by the Accounting department. Only two employees use these applications, and the applications are used a few times a week.
- Machine 2 has a timesheet application that is used by all employees once a month.
- Machine 3 has an HR application that is used by one or two employees throughout the day.
- Machine 4 has one application that is used by the Sales department. Four or five people use this application many times a day.
- Machine 5 has one application that supports the Technical Support department. This application is used by seven or eight employees who are creating and updating support cases throughout the day.

- The virtualized machine is running a Linux operating system, Red Hat Linux Enterprise 5.0.
- The virtualized machine has four network ports/network adapters, eight CPUs, and plenty of memory.
- The operating systems running on the virtualized machine are Windows XP, Windows Server 2003, and Solaris x86.
- The database drivers used for all applications support virtualized environments.
- The virtualization software built into the Red Hat Linux operating system was used to virtualize the machine.

The Issue

After the final machine image was deployed to the virtualized machine, performance of applications on machine 4 slowed to an unacceptable response time. Why?

Here are some questions to ask:

- What applications are on machine 5 (the last machine image deployed)? Are the applications on machine 5 the cause of the performance degradation of the application on machine 4?
- Was the virtualized machine configured correctly for these five machine images?
- Does the virtualized machine still have ample CPU and memory?

Thinking Through the Issue

Let's think about what we know:

- The machines on the virtualized machine have different operating systems. This is probably not the cause.
- The virtualized machine has eight CPUs, which is adequate for the load associated with the five machine images on the virtualized machine. Therefore, that shouldn't be the issue.
- There are five machine images and only four network ports/network adapters. Which machine images share a network port and which applications are on those machines? Machines 4 and 5 are the ones that share a port. That means that the two machines that run the most-used applications share a port.

The Resolution

The performance issue revolves around the fact that machines 4 and 5 share a network port. When machine 5 was added to the virtualized machine, performance degraded because of more network activity. In this case study, machines 4 and 5 need a dedicated network port. The virtualized machine needs to be reconfigured. For example, a better configuration is to have machines 1 and 2 share a network port because the applications on those machines are used less frequently. Alternatively, an additional network adapter could be added to the virtualized machine so that each machine could have its own network adapter. In this case, that solution may be overkill.

Case Study 5

The database application in this case study is a bulk load application. The company uses this application to synchronize changes made to a DB2 for AS/400 database to an Oracle database at the end of each day. The ODBC application does the bulk load using parameter arrays, 1,000 rows at a time. The data is 120 numeric columns about geological maps. The code that does this operation is as follows:

```
// Assume at this point that a SELECT * FROM tabletoinsert
// WHERE 0 = 1 has been prepared to get information to do
// bindings

for (counter = 1; counter <= NumColumns; counter++) {
   rc = SQLColAttributes (hstmt, counter, SQL_COLUMN_TYPE,
            NULL, 0, &rgblen, &ptype);
   rc = SQLColAttributes (hstmt, counter, SQL_COLUMN_PRECISION,
            NULL, 0, &rgblen2, &prec);
   rc = SQLColAttributes (hstmt, counter, SQL_COLUMN_SCALE,
            NULL, 0, &rgblen3, &scale);
   switch(counter){
   case 1: rc = SQLBindParameter (hstmt, counter,
            SQL_PARAM_INPUT, SQL_C_CHAR, (SWORD) ptype,
            (UDWORD) prec, (SWORD) scale,
            pa_col1, sizeof(pa_col1[0]), cbValue);
```

```
         // pa_col1 is an array of character strings
         break;
case 2: rc = SQLBindParameter (hstmt, counter,
            SQL_PARAM_INPUT, SQL_C_CHAR, (SWORD) ptype,
            (UDWORD) prec, (SWORD) scale,
            pa_col2, sizeof(pa_col2[0]), cbValue2);
         // pa_col2 is an array of character strings
         break;
case 3: rc = SQLBindParameter (hstmt, counter,
            SQL_PARAM_INPUT, SQL_C_CHAR, (SWORD) ptype,
            (UDWORD) prec, (SWORD) scale,
            pa_col3, sizeof(pa_col3[0]), cbValue3);
         // pa_col3 is an array of character strings
         break;
...
default: break;
}
```

Environment Details

The environment details are as follows:

- Order management is done using a legacy AS/400 application. Every night, a batch job exports the AS/400 data into an XML document that is then transferred to a Linux machine using FTP. As part of a nightly consolidation process, an ODBC application reads in the contents of the XML document and bulk loads the data into an Oracle database.
- Auto-commit is turned off in the application.
- The application is reading the data in as character strings and binding the data on the server as the appropriate numeric type, such as int or floating point.
- The bulk load application is on a Linux machine.
- The Oracle database is on a Windows machine.

The Issue

The performance (response time) of the bulk load operation is too slow. Is there any way to speed up the bulk load operation?

Here are some questions to ask:

- Is the driver configured with optimal database protocol packet sizes? This is key when transferring this much data.
- Is the application optimized for bulk load? Does the application use an array of parameters? Does the application use prepared statements?

Thinking Through the Issue

Let's think about what we know:

- Auto-commit is turned off in the application, which is the correct configuration for this case. Because of the significant amount of disk I/O required to commit every operation on the database server and because of the extra network round trips that occur between the driver and the database, in most cases you will want to turn off auto-commit mode in your application. By doing this, your application can control when the database work is committed, which provides dramatically better response time.
- The application uses an array of parameters, which is optimal. When using an array of parameters, it's a good idea to experiment with the size of the arrays to find the maximum value that provides the best performance. In this case, the parameter array value of 1,000 rows per execute gets the best performance.
- The application efficiently uses prepared statements.
- The data being loaded is numeric, and the application is reading all the data into memory as character strings.
- A poorly configured database driver could cause performance issues. For example, the packet's size could be configured to a small value such as 16KB. For this case, let's assume the database driver is configured correctly.

The Resolution

The performance issue revolves around the fact that the application reads in the numeric data as character strings. Depending on the implementation of the database driver, either the driver must convert the character data to the appropriate format to be inserted into the database, or the driver must send the character data to the database and the database system must do the conversions. Either way, this involves a fairly expensive process of determining the appropriate types, converting the data to the right format, and then sending the correct information to the database.

When examining the application code, you should think, "What does my database driver have to do to make this bulk load work?" In this particular case, the driver/database must perform data conversions, which translates to CPU cycles. For every execution, 120,000 pieces of data must be translated (120 columns × 1,000 rows). Although the conversion is not the most time-consuming operation during the insert of the data, it does become significant for large executions.

In this case, the application can easily be rewritten to optimize the reading of the XML file to process the data as ints, floats, and so on. This application change ultimately saves CPU cycles, which improves performance. Here is the rewritten code:

```
// We know the columns being loaded are numeric in nature—
// bind them using the correct native types

// Assume at this point a SELECT * FROM tabletoinsert
// WHERE 0 = 1 has been prepared to get information
// to do bindings

for (counter = 1; counter <= NumColumns; counter++) {
    rc = SQLColAttributes (hstmt, counter, SQL_COLUMN_TYPE,
            NULL, 0, &rgblen, &ptype);
    rc = SQLColAttributes (hstmt, counter, SQL_COLUMN_PRECISION,
            NULL, 0, &rgblen2, &prec);
    rc = SQLColAttributes (hstmt, counter, SQL_COLUMN_SCALE,
            NULL, 0, &rgblen3, &scale);
    switch(counter){
    case 1: rc = SQLBindParameter (hstmt, counter,
            SQL_PARAM_INPUT, SQL_C_LONG, (SWORD) ptype,
            (UDWORD) prec, (SWORD) scale,
            pa_col1, sizeof(pa_col1[0]), cbValue);
        // pa_col1 is an array of integers
        break;
```

```
case 2: rc = SQLBindParameter (hstmt, counter,
           SQL_PARAM_INPUT, SQL_C_LONG, (SWORD) ptype,
           (UDWORD) prec, (SWORD) scale,
           pa_col2, sizeof(pa_col2[0]), cbValue2);
    // pa_col2 is an array of integers
    break;
case 3: rc = SQLBindParameter (hstmt, counter,
           SQL_PARAM_INPUT, SQL_C_BIGINT, (SWORD) ptype,
           (UDWORD) prec, (SWORD) scale,
           pa_col3, sizeof(pa_col3[0]), cbValue3);
    // pa_col3 is an array of 64 bit integers
    break;
...
default: break;
}
```

Case Study 6

The application in this case study is an executive dashboard, which allows the company's executive team to have a view into the sales system. The IT team responsible for deploying the application developed an extensive set of performance tests designed to measure response time while the system was under load.

Environment Details

The environment details are as follows:

- The dashboard is a browser-based application that connects to both systems inside and outside of the corporate firewall using JDBC.
- The application accesses data in Microsoft SQL Server and three DB2 databases.
- Outside the firewall, the application also accesses data from www.salesforce.com.
- During the performance testing of the application, the IT department used a third-party tool to emulate five to ten concurrent users on the system.
- The application is deployed in an IBM WebSphere environment.

The Issue

The IT team did not get consistent performance results from the benchmark. The process for running the benchmark was to fresh-start the application server, the database server, and the load test server before every run. The test environment was on an isolated network, so that ruled out interference from other applications as the cause of the inconsistent results.

The IT team ran the benchmark the first time, and the response time was unacceptable for many of the tests in the benchmark suite. When they manually reran the tests that had the performance issues, response time seemed acceptable. What is causing these inconsistent results?

Thinking Through the Issue

Let's think through what we know:

- Because manual testing indicated acceptable performance, was there a problem with the test environment? Was the third-party tool used to emulate concurrent users configured accurately? In this case, there was no issue with the tool.
- Perhaps the benchmark was not run long enough or measured short response times. Benchmarks that are run over short durations make it difficult to reproduce meaningful and reliable results. See "Measure over a Sufficient Duration of Time," page 254, for details. In this case, this was not the issue.
- Was the application coded correctly? Was the database driver tuned correctly? In both cases, IT checked, and the answer was yes.
- Does connection pooling or statement pooling come into play? Yes, both should be used; however, neither was the culprit.
- The database was not prepared. The first time the application accesses a table row in a database, the database places a copy of the row onto a page on disk. If the database can find the requested data on a page in memory when subsequent data requests are processed, the database optimizes its operation by avoiding disk I/O. See "Prepare the Database," page 257.

The Resolution

After carefully examining the benchmark results, the IT team saw that the worst performance occurred when each of the database systems was accessing data that had not been accessed previously. In a database system, the most recently accessed data is always kept in memory so that subsequent accesses are fast (no disk access is required to return the data). In this performance test scenario, the systems were all restarted to measure a "fresh" system.

The benchmark should have included some time to prepare the database systems by running the benchmarks once without measuring performance. Once the highly accessed data is in memory, it remains there for the most efficient access during runtime.

Case Study 7

The database application in this case study supports a distributed sales team. The application is GUI based and has multiple options with regard to the type of sales information that can be queried, such as sales leads by territory, sales leads by product, existing customers by product purchased, and revenue by territory. The application will be used by a maximum of ten concurrent users.

Environment Details

The environment details are as follows:

- The application is ADO.NET and is running on an application server.
- The database server is an Oracle 11g shared server running on AIX 5.3.
- The client machines are running the .NET Framework 2.x and a variety of Windows operating systems, such as Windows XP and Windows Vista.
- The application is deployed in a WAN environment.
- The application is using connection pooling and statement caching.
- CPU and memory are plentiful on both the middle tier and database server.
- The database provider is DataDirect Technologies ADO.NET data provider for Oracle. Here's the connection string:

```
"Host=Accounting;Port=1433;User ID=Scott;Password=Tiger;
Server Type=Shared;Load Balance Timeout=0;Wire Protocol Mode=2;
Enlist=False;Batch Update Behavior=ArrayBindOnlyInserts;
Pooling=True;Cursor Description Cache=True;Max Pool Size=10;
Connection Reset=False;Fetch Array Size=128000;
Session Data Unit=8192"
```

Before deploying the application, the IT department benchmarked the application with ten concurrent users in a LAN environment. The performance was great, and the application was deployed in the Chicago, San Francisco, and Atlanta offices.

The Issue

After deploying the application, performance dropped by 50%. Why?

Here are some questions to ask:

- Does it hold true that a maximum of ten concurrent users are using the application?
- Is there anything different about the environment in which the benchmark was run versus the actual deployed environment?
- Are there any connection option settings in the driver that could be changed to improve performance?

Thinking Through the Issue

Let's think about what we know:

- Let's assume that it does hold true that a maximum of ten concurrent users are using the application.
- The benchmark was run in a LAN environment, and the application was deployed in a WAN environment.
- The same connection string was used in the benchmark environment as in the deployed environment. Are there connection options that would provide better performance in a WAN environment?

The Resolution

The performance issue revolves around the setting for the Session Data Unit connection option. An Oracle Session Data Unit (SDU) is a buffer that the DataDirect Connect for ADO.NET Oracle provider uses to place data before transmitting it across the network.

Here is some information about SDUs from Oracle's documentation.[2]

---

[2] "Oracle® Database Net Services Administrator's Guide," 10g Release 1 (10.1), Part Number B10775-01. January, 2004.

The SDU size can range from 512 bytes to 32767 bytes; the default size is 8192 bytes for a dedicated server and 32767 bytes for a shared server. The actual SDU size used is negotiated between the client (provider) and the server at connect time and will be the smaller of the client and server values. As such, configuring an SDU size different from the default requires configuring the SDU on both the client and server computers, unless you are using shared servers, in which case only the client needs to be changed because the shared server defaults to the maximum value.

For example, if the majority of the messages sent and received by the application are smaller than 8K in size, taking into account about 70 bytes for overhead, setting the SDU to 8K will likely produce good results. If sufficient memory is available, using the maximum value for the SDU will minimize the number of system calls and overhead.

After reading this description of SDUs, we know that the default value for SDU size for a shared server is 32767 and the application is accessing a shared server. However, the setting for the SDU size in the provider is 8192. Therefore, to improve performance, the value for the Session Data Unit connection option should be increased to 32767.

Case Study 8

The database application in this case study executes OLTP-type transactions (returns small result sets). The application is Web based and allows users to query on the current trading value of financial stocks. Quick response time is key for this application.

Environment Details

The environment details are as follows:

- The application is JDBC and is running on an application server.
- The database server is Sybase ASE 15 running on HP-UX PA-RISC 11i Version 2.0.
- The application is deployed in a WAN environment.
- The client machines are running a Linux operating system.

The Issue

Response time has become unacceptable. Why?

Here are some questions to ask:

- Has the volume of users increased?
- Has the network configuration changed?
- Has anything changed on the database server, such as another database system was installed on the server?
- Is the configuration of the driver correct for this type of application?
- Is the application using connection pooling and statement pooling?
- Is the application returning only the data it needs, and is it returning the data in the most efficient way?

Thinking Through the Issue

Let's think about what we know:

- Many environment issues can cause slow response time, such as insufficient bandwidth, physical memory, or CPU. For this scenario, let's assume that more memory or CPU cannot be added.
- Many, many users access the application, but the application is not configured to use connection pooling.
- The use of large database protocol packets is not a good idea in this type of application. Check the database protocol packet's size configured in the driver. Often the default size is not the size that you should use for OLTP-type applications.
- One of the easiest ways to improve performance is to limit the amount of network traffic between the database driver and the database server—one way is to write SQL queries that instruct the driver to retrieve from the database and return to the application only the data that the application requires. Let's assume that the application is coded with optimal SQL queries.

The Resolution

Because more memory cannot be added to the database server, this issue must be resolved in the application and the database driver. The solution is twofold:

- You can optimize the application to use connection pooling. As we have stated several times throughout this book, connection pooling can provide significant performance gains because reusing a connection reduces the overhead associated with establishing a physical connection. In JDBC, the application must use a DataSource object (an object implementing the DataSource interface) to obtain a connection to use connection pooling. So, the application needs to be changed to use a DataSource object. See "Connection Pool Model for JDBC," page 223, for details.

- The driver was using a 32KB database protocol packet size. In this case, a smaller size would provide a better response time because small result sets are being returned to the application. In this case, a 32KB packet size has too much capacity for the amount of data being returned, which causes more memory use than when using a smaller packet size.

Summary

When the performance of a database application is unacceptable, the first step is to define the issue. Is the issue related to throughput, response time, scalability, or a combination? The second step is to think through the possible causes. For example, if response time is the issue, does your application have a memory leak or does it perform excessive data conversions? The third step is to narrow down the possible causes of the performance issue. You might find it helpful to troubleshoot in the following order:

1. Look at the complete picture and ask yourself the following important question: Has anything changed in any of the components of the database application deployment? If the answer is yes, start by looking at what changed.

2. If nothing has changed, look at the database application.

3. If your database application does not seem to be the issue, look at your database driver.

4. If you are not satisfied with the performance after looking at the application and the database driver, look at the environment where your application is deployed.

One important fact to note is that if the database server machine is resource bound, no amount of tuning of your applications or the database middleware results in acceptable performance.

CHAPTER ELEVEN

Data Access in Service-Oriented Architecture (SOA) Environments

In today's business environment, your application infrastructure must keep pace with shifting business requirements and be able to absorb new business partners and products. Over the years, companies have adopted different computing architectures designed to allow for distributed processing, programming languages designed to run on any platform, and a range of products designed to provide better and faster integration of applications. In many cases, these steps are no longer enough to provide businesses with the agility they require.

In response, companies are adopting **Service-Oriented Architecture (SOA)**, a design methodology for software that promises agility to quickly adapt their applications to the changing needs of the business through reusable services. SOA has been around for a long time, but it has been used in production only in the past two to three years. Today, nearly every sizable organization has either implemented some form of SOA or has plans to in the near future.

Although SOA is different from traditional architectures, applications in SOA environments still need to access and use data. In our experience, it's often SOA experts, and not data experts, that design these applications. As a result, performance issues often appear when applications are deployed. Although the guidelines discussed in previous chapters of this book also apply to SOA in one way or another, some differences specific to data access in SOA environments are worth a separate discussion. In this chapter, we'll share the main ways you can ensure that your data applications perform well in SOA environments.

What Is Service-Oriented Architecture (SOA)?

Before we discuss guidelines for data access in SOA environments, let's define what we mean by SOA. First, let's clear up some common misconceptions about SOA:

- SOA isn't a product that you can purchase. It's a design methodology that defines how applications should be built.
- SOA isn't the same as Web Services (although 90% of the time, companies implement SOA using Web Services).

SOA is a way of building software applications that allows you to design loosely coupled software components called **services**. What **loosely coupled** means depends on who you talk to, but generally, the term implies the following:

- Services are designed modularly based on business logic.
- Built-in knowledge of other services is minimized so that changes to one service don't ripple to others.

Services communicate using messages. When you create a service, you define what messages it can receive and send. A service can be used by any consumer (application or another service) as long as the consumer offers the service the information it expects and, if a response is generated, the response is useful to the consumer. For example, suppose you need to design a simple banking application that performs two common tasks: making a withdrawal and making a deposit. As shown in Figure 11-1, services are designed based on the task they perform in the business workflow. The Deposit service can be used by both the Teller application and the Wire Transfer application because the applications interact with the service using standard messages.

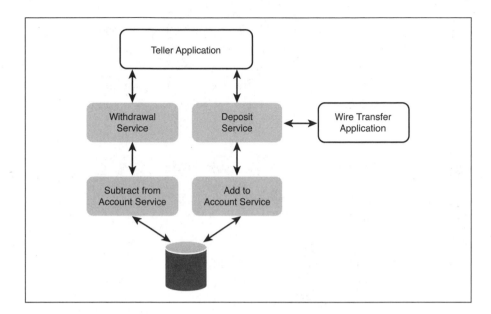

Figure 11-1   SOA environment

Services can be simple or complex. They can call other services, acting like building blocks to form composite services. For example, the Deposit service shown in Figure 11-1 calls the Add to Account service.

How do developers know what services are available for reuse? Typically, services publish details about themselves in a SOA registry/repository. For example, a service may publish the following characteristics:

• Operations the service performs
• Other services it uses
• Policies that must be followed when using the service, such as security methods
• Communication protocols the service supports

Which language the service was written in and which operating system the service runs on is irrelevant. As long as the consumer and service both support the same communication protocol, they can interact, regardless of their implementation.

SOA is commonly implemented using **Web Services**, which defines how services interact using the following standards: Extensible Markup Language (XML), Simple Object Access Protocol (SOAP), Web Services Description

Language (WSDL), and Universal Description, Discovery and Integration (UDDI). For example, if the scenario shown in Figure 11-1 was implemented using Web Services, the Teller application would request the Withdrawal or Deposit service using a SOAP message, and data passed between services would be exchanged in XML. Each service in this scenario would publish its details in a SOA registry using WSDL/UDDI.

Data Access Guidelines for SOA Environments

Do the following to ensure your database applications perform well in SOA environments:

- Involve data experts in addition to SOA experts.
- Decouple data access from business logic.
- Design and tune for performance.
- Consider data integration.

Involve Data Experts in Addition to SOA Experts

SOA guidelines are defined by SOA architects, who do a good job of creating and managing reusable services that represent business logic. But SOA architects aren't experts at databases or data access. As explained earlier, SOA is about business agility. SOA helps achieve agility by allowing you to build services that multiple applications can reuse.

For example, suppose you design a service to be used in an application that typically has no more than 50 users. When the application is deployed, the performance of the service remains good until other applications are deployed that start to use that same service. Quickly, there are 500% more users than the service was designed for, and performance takes a nosedive.

This is a problem we've seen over and over in real-world SOA service design—the performance of a service that performed well when it was first deployed breaks down as other applications begin to use that service. Designing a service that performs well for 500 users is different than designing one that performs well for 50 users. The performance guidelines discussed in previous chapters of this book will help you reach your scalability goals.

Performance Tip

To achieve the full promise of SOA, you need data access experts, not just SOA experts, involved in the design of services that access data.

Decouple Data Access from Business Logic

In both traditional architectures (such as object-oriented architectures) and SOA architectures, applications depend on technologies such as ODBC, JDBC, and ADO.NET for access to data stored in databases. In traditional architectures, data access code is contained within the application. Even when using an object-relational mapping tool such as Hibernate to abstract the data layer, data access code remains within the application. This **tightly coupled** method works because the applications aren't designed to share components with other applications (although code is routinely copied and propagated to other applications). When changes occur that affect data access, the code must be updated everywhere it appears.

In SOA environments, services are designed to be reusable, but we often find that data access has been implemented in the same way it always has, using the familiar, tightly coupled method shown in Figure 11-2. Data access code is built into each service that requires access to the database.

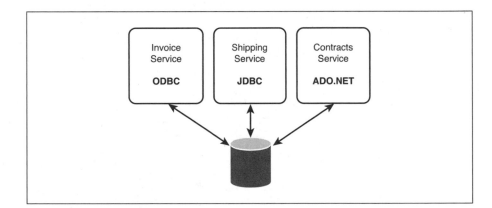

Figure 11-2   Tightly coupled: data access built into SOA services

Building data access dependencies into services produces the following bad side effects:

- It forces your business logic experts to become data access experts.
- It results in complicated deployment scenarios that are hard to maintain.
- It reduces scalability and performance.

Suppose that, as you read this book, you discover a tip that will speed up the performance of a service you've been developing. The next day, you go into work and implement that change in your service. With careful testing, you realize that the change has improved the response time of your service by 100% and allowed it to scale to many more users. This is a great benefit for your service, but can you implement the same tip in the thousands of other services that are deployed in your company? Achieving business agility, the real value of SOA, becomes more difficult when you have to modify many services to achieve the same goal across the board.

Performance Tip

The best way to provide data access in SOA environments is to follow the same principle that SOA advocates: Provide a loosely coupled **Data Services Layer (DSL)** that centralizes data access code as a service.

Figure 11-3 shows a DSL that can be called by any service that requires data access. Database drivers only need to be installed on the machine local to the DSL. Involve your data expert in designing this layer; his expertise will help you build best practices for data access into all your services. Any changes that affect data access code aren't made in the services but are centralized in the DSL.

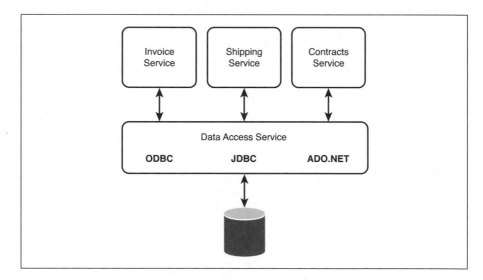

Figure 11-3   Loosely coupled: Data Services Layer (DSL)

One of the tenants of SOA is capturing best practices. If someone figures out the best way to implement a shipping service, all applications can use that "best in class" shipping service. Without SOA, that same code would have to be propagated to all the applications that need to perform the shipping function. Building a DSL allows you to capture best practices for data access within a data access service so everyone in your company can benefit from it.

Design and Tune for Performance

Although many of the tips provided in this book also apply to your data access code in SOA environments, here are a few that are particularly important for this type of architecture:

- Reusable services imply multiple users making many connections— the perfect scenario for connection pooling. Any service with many users that is called often will fail to perform adequately without connection pooling. See "Using Connection Pooling," page 12, for more information.
- Reusable services imply that the same statements are executed multiple times—the perfect scenario for using statement pooling. See "Statement Pooling," page 29, for more information.
- Be aware that each service that accesses the DSL may have different requirements. For example, one service may retrieve large objects and require tuning for this use, whereas another may load bulk data into tables and require a different tuning approach. Therefore, it's important for your database driver to be tunable. See "Runtime Performance Tuning Options," page 62, for more information about what runtime performance tuning options to look for in a database driver.

Consider Data Integration

Most companies start implementing SOA slowly, designing simple services that do simple things. For example, the scope of a first effort may be to design a service that looks up an order using an order ID. As developers become more comfortable with SOA, they design services that are more complex. For example, a service that handles the following workflow requires access to different data sources:

1. Retrieves an incoming Electronic Data Interchange (EDI) order

2. Validates client information stored in an Oracle database

3. Retrieves the customer number from the Oracle database

4. Submits an order to a DB2 database using the customer number

5. Sends a receipt to the client using EDI

Sequentially processing all the data involved in these steps can involve tremendous overhead. Comparisons of or conversions between data in different formats requires code to marshal the data from one format to another. Typically, this code changes the data from the XML data model to the relational data model and vice versa. Eventually, all data used by the service is marshaled to the XML format to create an XML response to a Web Service call. Retrieving all this data from disparate sources can require many network round trips and multiple transformation layers to marshal the data.

Let's think about this differently. Most SOA architectures use XML-based requests and responses. **XQuery** is a query language for XML. Some XQuery products allow you to query data from XML documents or any data source that can be viewed as XML such as relational databases. With this type of solution, you can query almost any data source as though it were XML, regardless of how the data is physically stored.

Just as SQL is a relational query language and Java is an object-oriented programming language, XQuery is often thought of as a native XML programming language. At the time of this writing, XQuery 1.0 is a recommended specification of the W3C that you can find at www.w3.org/TR/xquery/.[1]

The XQuery API for Java (XQJ) is designed to support the XQuery language, just as the ODBC, JDBC, and ADO.NET APIs support the SQL query language. The XQJ standard (JSR 225) is being developed under the Java Community Process that you can find at www.jcp.org/en/jsr/detail?id=225.[2]

Some databases, such as Oracle 11*g*, have already incorporated support for XQuery. There are also products on the market that provide an XQuery processor to optimize your access to both relational and XML data sources, as shown in Figure 11-4.

---

[1] "XQuery 1.0: An XML Query Language." W3C. 02/02/2009 (http://www.w3.org/TR/xquery/).

---

[2] "JSR 225: XQuery API for JavaTM (XQJ)." Java Community Process. 02/02/2009 (http://www.jcp.org/en/jsr/detail?id=225).

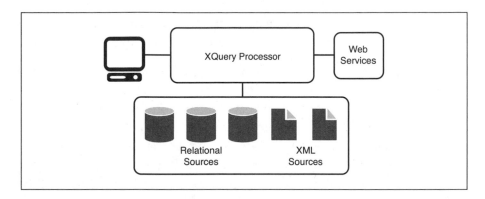

Figure 11-4   XQuery processor

XQuery simplifies data integration in the following ways:

- It provides native support for XML and for the operations most frequently needed when working with XML. Today, XML is at the heart of most data integration; this is certainly true for SOA environments where SOAP messages are expressed in XML. The XML produced by an XQuery query can be used directly in SOA applications. For example, a query result might be the payload of a SOAP message.
- It eliminates the need to work with different APIs and data models for each data source. The XQuery language is defined in terms of XML structures. Because most data can be mapped into an XML structure, you can use XQuery to query virtually any data source.
- It eliminates the need to write the code required to marshal data into different formats. With XQuery, the query result is XML.

We've seen a single XQuery query replace 100 lines of code because it can encapsulate all the business logic and integration logic into a single step. Because your service only has to execute a single XQuery query, network round trips are kept to a minimum.

Summary

Many companies are now adopting a SOA architecture to keep pace with shifting business requirements. SOA allows developers to design loosely coupled services that are reusable by other applications.

For the best performance in SOA environments, remember the following four guidelines when designing database applications for SOA environments:

- Involve data experts in addition to SOA experts to ensure that your services are designed for scalability and performance. Designing a service for 500 users is different than designing a service for 50 users.
- Decouple data access from business logic. Building data access dependencies into services can result in complicated deployment scenarios and reduce scalability and performance. A better approach is to build a loosely coupled data access service that can be called by other services to provide data access.
- Design and tune for performance. Because reusable services typically have many users and execute the same statements repeatedly, SOA services need to take advantage of connection pooling and statement pooling. In addition, some runtime performance tuning options offered by your database driver can improve performance.
- Consider data integration. Because most SOA architectures use XML-based requests and responses, the XQuery language is a good choice for data integration. XQuery allows you to query any data source that you can view as XML, including relational databases. It also provides query results as XML, which eliminates code that would be required to transform other data formats into XML.

A

active connections

In the context of connection pooling, connections that are currently in use by the application. *See also* idle connections

B

bandwidth

The amount of data that can be transferred from one point on the network to another in a specified period. Bandwidth is usually expressed in bits (of data) per second (bps).

benchmark

A test that measures the performance of an application or system on a well-defined task or set of tasks.

big endian

A byte order method used to store multibyte data, such as long integers, in memory. Big endian machines store data in memory big-end first. The first byte is the biggest. *See also* endianness and little endian.

boxing

A process that occurs in Java and .NET when a data type is wrapped in an object. When boxing occurs, memory is allocated from the heap on the database client to create the object, which can force a garbage collection to occur.

bridge
A database driver that bridges capabilities between an existing database connectivity standard and a new one. For example, for Java applications, a JDBC/ODBC bridge can provide access to all the data sources that the ODBC drivers support.

bytecode
A compiled format for Java application code. Once Java code is compiled into bytecode, the code can run through a JVM instead of the computer's processor. Using bytecode allows Java code to run on any platform.

C

CLR heap
A reserved pool of memory that the .NET Common Language Runtime (CLR) allocates memory from for new objects.

commit
An operation that causes all updates performed during a transaction to be written to the database.

connection pool
A cache of physical database connections that one or more applications can reuse.

Connection Pool Manager
In JDBC, a utility that manages the connections in the pool and defines attributes of the connection pool, such as the initial number of connections placed in the pool when an application server is started.

context switch
The process of storing and restoring the state (context) of a CPU so that multiple processes can share a single CPU resource. A context switch occurs when the CPU stops running one process and starts running another. For example, if your application is waiting for a row lock to release so that it can update data, the operating system may switch the context so that the CPU can perform work on behalf of another application while your application is waiting for the lock to release.

cursor-based protocol database system
A database system that assigns a database server-side "name" (cursor) to a SQL statement. The server operates on that cursor incrementally. The database driver tells the database server when to work and how much information to return. The network connection can be used by several cursors, each working in small slices of time. Oracle and DB2 are examples of cursor-based protocol databases.

D

data provider
A software component that an application uses on demand to gain access to a database using one of the following standards-defined APIs: ADO.NET, ADO, or OLE DB. Among many other things, a data provider processes the API function calls, submits SQL requests to the database, and returns results to the application.

Data Services Layer (DSL)
In a Service-Oriented Architecture (SOA) environment, data access logic and code designed as a loosely coupled SOA service.

database driver
A software component that an application uses on demand to gain access to a database using one of the following standards-defined APIs: ODBC or JDBC. Among many other things, a database driver processes API function calls, submits SQL requests to the database, and returns results to the application.

database protocol packets
A package that database drivers and database servers use to request and return information. Each packet uses a protocol for communication with the database defined by the database vendor. For example, Microsoft SQL Server uses communication encoded with the Tabular Data Stream (TDS) protocol, and IBM DB2 uses communication encoded with the Distributed Relational Database Architecture (DRDA) protocol.

disk contention
A situation that occurs when multiple processes or threads try to access the same disk simultaneously. The disk has a limit on how many processes/threads can access it and the amount of data that it can transfer. When these limits are reached, processes/threads must wait to access the disk.

distributed transaction
A transaction that accesses and updates data on two or more networked databases and therefore, must be coordinated among those databases. *See also* local transaction.

dynamic SQL
SQL statements that are constructed at runtime; for example, the application may allow users to enter their own queries. These types of SQL statements are not hard-coded into the application. *See also* static SQL.

E

embedded SQL
SQL statements written within an application programming language such as C. These statements are preprocessed by a SQL processor, which is database dependent, before the application is compiled.

endianness
The byte order used by an operating system as determined by the processor of the computer to store multibyte data, such as long integers, in memory. *See also* big endian and little endian.

environment
In the context of the Microsoft ODBC Driver Manager connection pooling model, a global context in which a database driver accesses data from an application. An environment owns the connections inside an application. Typically, there is only one environment within an application, which means that there is usually one connection pool for one application.

F–G

forward-only cursor
A type of cursor that database drivers use for sequential, nonscrollable access to rows in a result set.

garbage collector
A routine that a JVM runs to clean up dead Java objects and reclaim memory. *See also* generational garbage collection.

generational garbage collection
A method of garbage collection used by most later JVMs that separates objects into different memory pools within the Java heap based on the object's lifetime. *See also* garbage collector.

H–I

hard page fault
A type of page fault that is generated when an application requests a page in memory at its original address space, but the requested page is located in virtual memory. The operating system must swap the page out of virtual memory and place it back into RAM. *See also* soft page fault.

heap size
The overall size of the Java heap. *See also* Java heap.

idle connections

In the context of connection pooling, connections that are available for use in the connection pool. *See also* active connections.

insensitive cursor

A type of scrollable cursor that ignores any data modifications that could impact the result set of the cursor.

J–K

Java heap

A reserved pool of memory from which a JVM allocates memory for new Java objects. *See also* heap size.

Just-in-Time (JIT) compiler

A code generator provided by some JVMs and the .NET Common Language Runtime (CLR) that converts bytecode into native machine language instructions at runtime. Code compiled with a JIT compiler typically runs faster than code that hasn't been compiled.

Kerberos

A network authentication protocol that was originally developed at MIT as a solution to the security issues of open network computing environments. Kerberos is a trusted third-party authentication service that verifies users' identities.

L

latency

The time delay it takes for a network packet to travel from one destination to another.

lazy fetching

A method of returning data used by some database drivers. The database driver returns only as many result rows as necessary in as many network round trips to the database server as necessary and caches the result set on the driver machine. If the next request for a row is not in the cached result set, the driver makes the necessary number of round trips to return more rows.

little endian

A byte order method used to store multibyte data, such as long integers, in memory. Little endian machines store data in memory little-end first. The first byte is the smallest. *See also* endianness and big endian.

local transaction
A transaction that accesses and updates data on one database. *See also* distributed transaction.

loosely coupled
A resilient relationship between two or more systems with some kind of exchange relationship. In the context of a Service-Oriented Architecture (SOA) service, it means that services are designed modularly based on business logic, and built-in knowledge of other services is minimized so that changes to one service don't ripple to others. Contrast with tightly coupled.

M

managed code
In .NET, code that is executed by the Common Language Runtime (CLR). *See also* unmanaged code.

Maximum Transmission Unit (MTU)
The maximum packet size that can be sent across a network link. The MTU is a characteristic of the network type. For example, the MTU for Ethernet networks is 1500 bytes.

memory leak
Gradual and unintentional memory consumption that is caused when an application fails to release memory when it's no longer needed. The term can be confusing because memory is not physically lost from the computer. Rather, available memory, RAM, and then virtual memory is steadily used up.

N–O

network packet
A package that is used to transport communication across a network, such as TCP/IP. Database protocol packets are transformed into network packets for delivery over the network. Once the network packets reach their destination, they are reassembled with other network packets into a database protocol packet.

P–Q

packet fragmentation
The process of breaking up an oversized network packet into smaller sized packets to accommodate the MTU of a network link.

page
A fixed-length block of memory in RAM.

page fault
An error that the hardware generates when an application tries to access a page of memory that can no longer be found in RAM at its previous address space. *See also* hard page fault and soft page fault.

page file
A reserved part of the hard disk that is used to store pages of RAM in virtual memory.

paging
The process of transferring pages out of RAM into virtual memory.

path MTU
The lowest MTU of any network node along a particular network path.

path MTU discovery
A technique for determining the lowest MTU of any network node along a particular network path.

prepared statement
A SQL statement that has been compiled, or prepared, into an access or query plan for efficiency. A prepared statement can be reused by an application without the overhead in the database of re-creating the query plan.

private data network
A communications network that only one organization or group uses. A private data network may be implemented using a network switch to a dedicated network adapter, a leased T1 connection, or some other type of dedicated connection.

pseudo-column
A hidden column that represents a unique key associated with each row in a table. Typically, using pseudo-columns in a SQL statement is the fastest way to access a row because they usually point to the exact location of the physical record.

R

Random Access Memory (RAM)
The physical memory where code and data in current use are kept so that the computer's processor can quickly reach them.

reauthentication
A process that allows a database driver to switch the user associated with a connection to another user. Reauthentication can be used to minimize the number of connections required in a connection pool. Different databases refer to this functionality using different terminology. For example, Oracle refers to it as proxy authentication and Microsoft SQL Server refers to as impersonation.

response time
The elapsed time between a data request and when the data is returned. From users' points of view, it is the time between when they ask for data and when they receive it.

rollback
An operation that returns the database to a previous state. The transaction can be rolled back completely, canceling a pending transaction, or to a specified point. Rollbacks allow the database to be restored to a valid state if invalid operations are performed or after the database server fails.

S

scalability
The ability of an application to maintain acceptable response time and throughput when the number of simultaneous users increases.

scrollable cursor
A type of cursor that database drivers use to allow the driver to go both forward and backward through rows in a result set. *See also* insensitive cursor and sensitive cursor.

Secure Sockets Layer (SSL)
An industry-standard protocol for sending encrypted data over database connections. SSL secures the integrity of your data by encrypting information and providing client/server authentication.

sensitive cursor
A type of scrollable cursor that picks up any data modifications that could impact the result set of the cursor.

service
In a Service-Oriented Architecture (SOA) environment, a loosely coupled software component designed to perform a unit of work on behalf of an application or another service. Services are designed modularly based on business logic, and built-in knowledge of other services is minimized so that changes to one service don't ripple to others.

Service-Oriented Architecture (SOA)
A way of designing software applications for reusability and flexibility. It involves designing loosely coupled software components called services. *See also* service.

soft page fault
A type of page fault that is generated when an application requests a page in memory at its original address space but is eventually located elsewhere in RAM. *See also* hard page fault.

statement
A request sent to the database (including the result of the request).

statement pool
A set of prepared statements that an application can reuse.

static SQL
SQL statements in an application that do not change at runtime and, therefore, can be hard-coded into the application. *See also* dynamic SQL.

stored procedure
A set of SQL statements (subroutine) available to applications accessing a relational database system. Stored procedures are physically stored in the database.

streaming protocol database system
A database system that processes a query and sends results until there are no more results to send; the database is uninterruptable. Sybase, Microsoft SQL Server, and MySQL are examples of streaming protocol databases.

T

throughput
The amount of data that is transferred from sender to receiver over time.

tightly coupled
A dependent relationship between two or more systems or organizations with some kind of exchange relationship. In the context of Service-Oriented Architecture (SOA) services, data access is often inadvisably designed to be tightly coupled, or built into the service. *See also* loosely coupled.

transaction
One or more SQL statements that make up a unit of work performed against the database. Either all the statements in a transaction are committed as a unit or all the statements are rolled back as a unit.

U

Unicode
A standard encoding that is used to support multilingual character sets.

unmanaged code
In .NET, code that is not executed by the Common Language Runtime (CLR). *See also* managed code.

V

virtual memory
The capability to transfer data that is not immediately needed from RAM to a page file on the hard disk. This process known as paging typically occurs when RAM is used up. If the transferred data is needed again, it's copied back into RAM.

virtual private network (VPN)
A network that uses a public telecommunication infrastructure, such as the Internet, to provide remote offices or individual users with secure access to their organization's network.

virtualization
The process of partitioning a computer so that multiple operating system instances can run at the same time on a single physical computer.

W–Z

Web Services
As defined by the W3C, a Web service is a software system designed to support interoperable machine-to-machine interaction over a network. Web services are frequently just Web APIs that can be accessed over a network, such as the Internet, and executed on a remote system hosting the requested services. Service-Oriented Architecture (SOA) is most often implemented using Web services, which defines how SOA services interact using the following standards: Extensible Markup Language (XML), Simple Object Access Protocol (SOAP), Web Services Description Language (WSDL), and Universal Description, Discovery and Integration (UDDI).

XQuery
A query language for XML. XQuery allows you to query data from XML documents or any data source that can be viewed as XML, such as relational databases. With XQuery, you can query almost any data source as though it were XML, regardless of how the data is physically stored.

Index

K - L

M

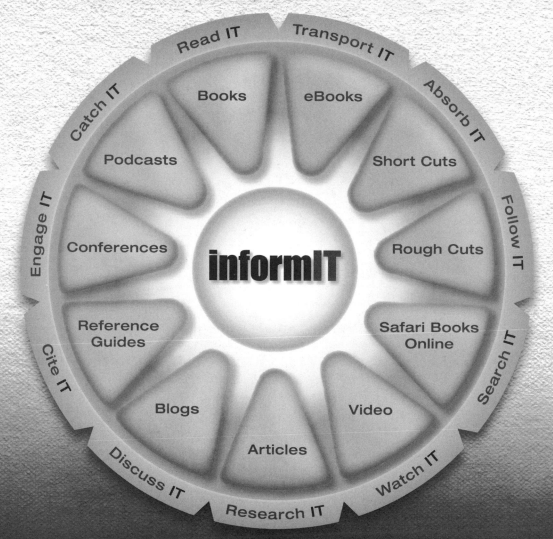

FREE Online Edition

Your purchase of **The Data Access Handbook** includes access to a free online edition for 45 days through the Safari Books Online subscription service. Nearly every Prentice Hall book is available online through Safari Books Online, along with more than 5,000 other technical books and videos from publishers such as Addison-Wesley Professional, Cisco Press, Exam Cram, IBM Press, O'Reilly, Que, and Sams.

SAFARI BOOKS ONLINE allows you to search for a specific answer, cut and paste code, download chapters, and stay current with emerging technologies.

Activate your FREE Online Edition at www.informit.com/safarifree

> **STEP 1:** Enter the coupon code: QPSFZCB.

> **STEP 2:** New Safari users, complete the brief registration form. Safari subscribers, just log in.

If you have difficulty registering on Safari or accessing the online edition, please e-mail customer-service@safaribooksonline.com